The End of Europe?

The End of Europe?

The Five Dilemmas of the European Union

Andreas Staab

LEXINGTON BOOKS
Lanham • Boulder • New York • London

Published by Lexington Books
An imprint of The Rowman & Littlefield Publishing Group, Inc.
4501 Forbes Boulevard, Suite 200, Lanham, Maryland 20706
www.rowman.com

6 Tinworth Street, London SE11 5AL, United Kingdom

British Library Cataloguing in Publication Information Available

Library of Congress Cataloging-in-Publication Data

Names: Staab, Andreas, 1965- author.
Title: The end of Europe? : the five dilemmas of European integration / Andreas Staab.
Description: Lanham, Maryland : Lexington Books, 2020. | Includes bibliographical references and index. | Summary: "The author argues that the European Union is under threat of collapse and that new international policy must tackle migration, the Euro, Brexit, and enlargement in order to avoid dissolution"—Provided by publisher.
Identifiers: LCCN 2020032667 (print) | LCCN 2020032668 (ebook) | ISBN 9781793634238 (cloth) | ISBN 9781793634245 (epub)
Subjects: LCSH: European Union—Membership. | Populism—European Union countries. | European Union countries—Politics and government—21st century. | European Union countries—Economic integration. | European Union countries—Emigration and immigration.
Classification: LCC JN30 .S699 2020 (print) | LCC JN30 (ebook) | DDC 341.242/2—dc23
LC record available at https://lccn.loc.gov/2020032667
LC ebook record available at https://lccn.loc.gov/2020032668

∞™ The paper used in this publication meets the minimum requirements of American National Standard for Information Sciences—Permanence of Paper for Printed Library Materials, ANSI/NISO Z39.48-1992.

To my family

In the twentieth century, members of my family lived in places, which after the occasional historical upheaval, now belong to the states of Brazil, Germany, Israel, Italy, Libya, Poland, Russia, South Africa, Switzerland, the United Kingdom, and the United States. Going back to the nineteenth century, the Czech Republic, Lithuania, and Sweden also feature on this list.

The notion of the "Citizen of Nowhere" does not exist, as the research of Norbert and Sergio has demonstrated.

Contents

List of Tables

Acknowledgments

This book came to life in the spring of 2017 and was, to a considerable extent, shaped by personal experiences. Like other EU nationals living in the UK, the months since the EU referendum of June 2016 were filled with uncertainty, and anger at the casualness and occasional ignorance with which the political establishment approached such a momentous development. How might my future and that of my family look like in a country that I had called my home for a quarter of a century. The first sections of chapter 4 on Brexit were written during that time. I am involved in the running of a German Saturday school in North London, and for the past four years, parents have been sharing their experiences on how the referendum had started to impact their lives. There were those who had packed their bags swiftly and had moved back to Austria, Germany, Switzerland, or South Tyrol in Italy. There were those who decided to embark on the cumbersome process of applying for British citizenship, assuming that their right to work and live in the UK might be jeopardized. But the majority merely hoped that their adopted country might just come to its senses and that—even if Brexit does happen at some stage—a close relationship with European neighbors will be established. Many went through a process of deep soul searching. What makes us European, and how will living in a future non-EU country affect our multilayered identities? The referendum campaign made frequent references to cultural coherence, to immigration being out of control, to foreigners sponging off the UK's welfare state. But many EU citizens had ended up in Britain without much proactive planning. It just happened: a job opportunity, a student exchange program, romance. But now that very essence of life in the EU—the free movement and the easy interaction between people from different countries—was questioned by Brexit.

My sister has been working for the administration of my hometown for her whole professional life. In the summer of 2015, the city's authorities were frantically trying to accommodate thousands upon thousands of refugees, mainly from the civil war in Syria. My mother's side of the family were refugees themselves fleeing from the advancing Red Army that was about to roll over East Prussia at the close of World War II. Like them, many Germans were reminded of their tormented past and welcomed the new arrivals with open arms. My hometown was fortunate. The US Army had just vacated enormous premises, which could now be used for much-needed shelter. But with the American soldiers went the shops, and in order to buy daily essentials, refugees were forced to cross a six-lane highway, which consequently prompted the town administration to reduce the speed limit from sixty miles per hour to twenty miles per hour; a decision that subsequently caused massive traffic jams during rush hour. Very soon, people began to complain about overcrowded parks and recreation areas, about rubbish, about migrants loitering in the city center. The public mood started to turn, and the initial optimism quickly gave way to resentment over Chancellor Merkel's open-door policy. My hometown had always been a leftish kind of place that had integrated migrants for sixty years: first from Italy, then from Greece, Turkey, and the former Yugoslavia. But now, populist, anti-multiculturalist sentiments as expressed by the *Alternative für Deutschland* were becoming ever more popular.

For the past twenty years, my work as a consultant often took me to Cyprus—an island defined by the deep divisions between the Greek Cypriot and the Turkish Cypriot communities. Every now and then, political developments offered a glimpse of hope, in particular during the 2004 referendum on the UN-brokered Annan Plan or in 2012, when both sides engaged in concrete talks on how a federation ought to be organized. After an absence of four years, I returned to the island in 2018 to find that the North had undergone a dramatic transformation. Most of my former Turkish Cypriot friends and colleagues had left, with the majority of them settling in London. In their place, mainland Turks but also increasingly Syrian refugees had moved in. Casinos had sprung up everywhere. Hotels, shopping malls, and holiday homes were being constructed on a breath-taking scale. It felt as if the population had doubled. The island was still divided, however, not between Greek Cypriots and Turkish Cypriots, but between Greek Cypriots and Turks. The EU's enlargement process had not worked for the island, and I had the strong impression that the Cyprus problem had been settled in a way that was unintended by both communities.

In 1999, I set up a small consultancy called EPIC—the European Policy Information Centre. We secured the first of several contracts in the western Balkan region with the Government of Croatia, which had asked us to train some of their junior diplomats. The seminar took place in a deserted

Dubrovnik to which tourists still had not returned to, four years after the end of the war. How times have changed. Before the Covid pandemic, Croatia had established itself as a tourist magnet, and Dubrovnik was overrun by cruise ship passengers. The country joined the EU in 2013 and offers much-needed expertise to other governments in the region that are trying to meet the targets of the EU accession process. Serbia and Montenegro have made significant progress and might join the EU within the foreseeable future. But other states, including Bosnia and Herzegovina, Albania, Kosovo, or North Macedonia, are still a great distance away from joining. For these countries as well, European integration, as practiced by Brussels, has been painstakingly slow.

Once a year, I meet up with some "expat" Londoners, who had been fortunate to have worked in the world's biggest center of finance during the heydays of investment banking. "Better lucky than smart" is their not entirely inaccurate assessment of our diverging career paths. We usually go for hikes in the mountains, and during one of those increasingly arduous treks, a scenario was discussed of what would have been had the Iron Curtain not come down. "No Euro then" was the emerging consensus since France would not have been in a position to force the Kohl administration into agreeing to a start date for Economic and Monetary Union in return for consenting to German unification. The financial minds of my friends were on fire, assessing the continued strength of a romanticized *Deutschmark* that would have guaranteed stunning prosperity levels to West Germans. We were standing on a mountain top in the middle of one of the most affluent countries in the world, yet the group's conclusion was that the euro was the worst thing the EU had ever done. And we were not even talking about Greece or Italy.

The structure of this book reflects these experiences of mine over the past two decades or so. I feel fortunate to have met and worked with a great many people who have tried (hopefully not in vain) to deepen my understanding of European issues. Of course, some of them might not share my views on recent developments, but I am grateful for the insight that they have provided. I tried to listen as close as I could and hope that this book will—at least to a certain extent—do justice to their efforts. I am therefore indebted to Munir Altuner, Ian Baker, Tony Bass, Dilek Behcetogullari, Daniel Cangemi, Damian Chalmers, Tatjana Čorlija, Jaksa Damjanić, Charles Dannreuther, Michael Dettmer, Alex von Frankenberg, Jean-Pierre Fauvre, Karan Green, Andrew Hadley, Bob Hancké, Sanela Klarić, Martin Lodge, Luka Majić, Tido Meyerhoff, Willem Noë, Helena Polomik, Bruce Ross, Karen Smith, Dubravka Smolić, Toni Steurer, Monica Tantele, Chris Vogelgesang, Stephen Woolcock, and Sencan Yesilada.

Special praise and my deep gratitude are reserved for Susie Thomas. A wonderful scholar on English literature, she took on the Sisyphean task of going over this manuscript. I will forever aspire to reach her command of the English language. I am also indebted to Susan Rupp and Joe Cook. They took a young student, who had just arrived in New England, under their generous wings and taught him a thing or two about life. Sue's highly developed artistic skills have come in very handy: she kindly agreed to design the book cover. My apologies go to all my American students who spent a semester in London as part of their academic education, and whom I asked to read my book *The European Union Explained*, while also encouraging them to make sense of some draft chapters of this publication. I would like to thank, in particular, Conner Donohoe, Christopher Emmett, Connor Farmer, and Danielle Miller for pointing me in the right direction. This is my first book published by Rowman & Littlefield. Many thanks to my editors Joseph Parry and Alison Keefner, who offered patient support and guidance, when the pandemic started to affect all of our lives. Thanks also to Arun Rajakumar for his invaluable assistance in finalizing the manuscript.

Introduction

The year was 2012. The European Union (EU) had just been awarded the Nobel Peace Prize for the contribution to "the advancement of peace and reconciliation, democracy and human rights in Europe."[1] The union was basking in the glory of seventy years of remarkable achievements. The deep antagonism between France and Germany, which had resulted in nine major military conflicts over the preceding 250 years, had been consigned to the annals of history. The former arch enemies—for centuries the fault line of European politics—had become affirmative pillars on which the latest project of European integration rested. Former fascist dictatorships in Germany, Italy, Spain, Portugal, and Greece had transitioned into stable democracies. A Single European Market brought impressive levels of prosperity to many citizens. An environmental agenda that gradually impacted all other EU policies had begun to make its mark and turned the EU into a vanguard of environmental protection in the battle against climate change, while former communist countries in central and eastern Europe joined the EU in the "Big Bang" enlargement of 2004, which finally put to rest the Cold War division of the continent.

These remarkable success stories were far from being foregone conclusions. In the 1960s, with EU membership comprising the six founding members of Belgium, the Netherlands, Luxembourg, France, Italy, and West Germany, several other blocs had their own distinctive versions of how European countries could collaborate with one another. There was the involuntary dictatorship of the Warsaw Pact, which tied the fortunes of Poland, Hungary, East Germany, Czechoslovakia, Romania, and Bulgaria to that of the Soviet Union. In 1960, the European Free Trade Association (EFTA) was founded as an explicit antidote to the EU as it focused predominantly on the free movement of goods, without embarking on its counterpart's more ambitious manifestation of the free movement of goods, capital, services, and people. EFTA's membership was bigger than that of the EU and included Austria, Denmark, Norway, Portugal, Sweden, Switzerland, and the UK.[2] By the turn of the century, however, the EU was transformed from one of several alternatives to organize Europe, into the only show in town. Apart from Switzerland, Iceland, Norway, and the microstates of Andorra, Liechtenstein, San Marino, and the Vatican, Europe had become synonymous with the EU: many more countries, in particular some of the successor states to the former Yugoslavia but also Ukraine and Turkey, were lined up for eventual integration.

But the first dark clouds had already appeared on the horizon by the time of the Nobel award. In 2002, EU member states established the Convention for Europe under the leadership of former French president Valerie Giscard d'Estaing, which was tasked with drafting a new Constitution for Europe that would unify previous EU treaties into one single document. Although the treaty was approved by eighteen member states, it was rejected in referendums in the Netherlands and in France. Its successor document the Lisbon Treaty of 2009 dropped the overly ambitious title of "constitution" but still took on board much of the proposed changes, including a Charter of Fundamental Rights, as well as the extension of majority voting to areas that had previously been agreed by unanimous consent from all member states. Once again, getting Lisbon approved resulted in much acrimony. In a referendum, Ireland rejected the treaty, prompting a second referendum, which passed in October 2008, but only after a government-led information campaign and the guarantee that the country would not lose its political representative in the European Commission. The controversial ratification processes of the Constitution and of Lisbon left a distinct sour aftertaste. Although the treaty greatly enhanced the powers of the European Parliament, many European citizens were flabbergasted by the term European Constitution as it implied that the power of national governments and parliaments would be severely compromised. Copying most of the Constitution's wording into the Lisbon Treaty also gave the justifiable impression that the concerns of many European voters were largely ignored. Three negative referendums in France, the Netherlands, and Ireland represented a powerful manifestation of a sentiment that viewed European integration as an elitist project, driven by the Brussels bureaucracy and waved through by national governments without much democratic interaction with citizens.

In 2009, many new member states in central and eastern Europe experienced the harshest economic crisis since the transition to free market economies in the early 1990s. The drop in the gross domestic product (GDP) in Latvia (−18 percent), Lithuania (−15 percent), and Estonia (−14 percent) was horrific.[3] The financial meltdown in the aftermath of the collapse of Lehman Brothers was often cited as the main reason. Yet, EU law stipulates that all new members must at some stage in their economic development adopt the EU's single currency. Consequently, consumers and businesses took out loans and mortgages in euro because of better interest rates and administrative ease. After all, why take out a mortgage in a national currency, which was about to be abandoned within the next years. When national currencies started to drop in relation to the Euro, the now higher loan repayments put a severe dent in the finances of businesses and private citizens. A general decline in global demand further pushed the region toward an economic collapse. Although the countries rebounded impressively in 2010 and 2011, this was the first manifestation that the introduction of a single currency might come with unintended consequences in some member states.

With the financial and economic crises, the political landscape started to shift, and many Eurosceptic parties began to attract ever-growing support. In the elections to the European Parliament in 2009, the United Kingdom Independence Party (UKIP) under the charismatic Nigel Farage came second, behind the leading opposition Conservative Party, by gaining 16 percent of the votes of the British electorate. A year later, the Dutch populist Geert Wilders achieved an electoral breakthrough when his "Party for Freedom" became the third-strongest political force with 15.5 percent in the election to the national parliament. In France, in the first round of the presidential elections of 2012, Marine le Pen's *Front National* achieved the party's highest ever vote share of 18 percent. At the same time as populism started to make its mark, many European economies began to struggle. Across the EU, GDP rose by only 0.1 percent in 2011. Unemployment across the bloc rose to 10.2 percent a year later.[4] But in some countries, the figures were much more depressing, particularly in the so-called PIGS of Portugal, Ireland, Greece, and Spain. In Greece, for instance, the economy contracted by a staggering 6.2 percent with one in five people without a job. Unemployment was even more severe in Spain, where one in four could not find work.

But crises are not new to the EU. Instead, it could even be argued that crises and the management of them are often the springboards for enhanced activity at the European level. The very start of the European project serves as an illustrative example. Political leaders came to the realization that without a transnational, European approach, and without a permanent peaceful settlement with erstwhile enemies, the process of rebuilding devastated economies might be severely jeopardized. A combination of powerful factors—the emerging Cold War, destroyed infrastructure, and waves of refugees from the advancing Soviet Empire—necessitated a novel approach that moved beyond merely national solutions. The same rationale also came to the surface in the 1980s. Just a decade earlier, the EU experienced an extended period of *Eurosclerosis* when member states preferred to seek national solutions to widespread economic challenges such as inflation or unemployment. At the same time, Japan and the United States emerged as the powerful leaders of the global economy, with European countries still stifled by divergent national regulations that prevented a true European Single Market and trade across borders. The ambitious Single European Act of 1986, which eradicated national economic borders, however, completely changed the parameters within which businesses now operate and catapulted the EU onto an entirely different economic platform. A set of powerful factors that politicians found hard to ignore also kicked the EU into action at the beginning of the 1990s. The fall of the Iron Curtain and the Berlin Wall resulted in severe challenges—not only for individual member states but also for European integration as a whole. How can former communist dictatorships succeed in transitioning to democracy? At the start of that decade, there was barely a person alive in central and eastern Europe who had affirmative experiences of such notions as pluralism, majority rule, or an electoral competition over how best to organize societies. Moving from communism to democracy simply had never been attempted before. The same conundrum also applied to the transition from a state-owned, socialist economy to capitalism. Concepts such as supply and demand, choice, quality, or price competition were merely empty phrases across the region. Lastly, adding sixteen million East German citizens to the already most powerful and economically strongest player in the EU caused much anxiety among many member states. But the EU responded with remarkable pro-activism. Two treaties in the 1990s (Maastricht in 1992 and Amsterdam in 1997), as well as two more in the new millennium (Nice in 2001 and Lisbon in 2007), placed European integration on a distinctly different institutional and policy footing. Powerful factors, which are potentially too devastating for political leaders to ignore, have always driven political action. And European integration has so far been no exception to this rule.

WHAT KIND OF EUROPE? MINIMALISM VERSUS MAXIMALISM

The need for European integration was much more straightforward at the end of World War II. The continent was on the verge of collapse with millions of casualties, bombed out cities, destroyed infrastructure, food shortages, and waves of refugees fleeing to West from the advancing Soviet Empire. The year 1945 was Europe's zero hour. But how could peace—vital for rebuilding destroyed countries—be established on a continent that had been ravaged by war throughout many centuries? It was Winston Churchill, just voted out of office by the UK electorate, who in 1946 proposed the establishment of a "United States of Europe."[5] The term was misleading since Churchill did not envisage the creation of a European version of the United States of America, but instead called for the establishment of a loose union, which allowed for increased trade across borders. Borrowing from the German philosopher

Immanuel Kant's dictum that trading nations do not go to war with one another,[6] Churchill rightly assumed that such a form of European integration would set the successful parameters within which a postwar recovery could take place. Given the limited emphasis on trade and economics, his vision is often cited as a minimalist Europe.

In contrast, scholars such as the Italian philosopher Altiero Spinelli argued that a trading union could not safeguard Europe from the rise of madmen and dictators of the ilk of Stalin, Hitler, or Mussolini. For peace to be long-standing, a proper, federalist United States of Europe that encompasses not only economic but also political integration needed to be established. This was the maximalist understanding of European integration. The question about the true nature of the EU—a loose union of states that interact with one another chiefly through trade, or an ambitious state union with common institutions and policies— is still with us today. It would have been highly unlikely for a Brexit referendum ever to have been called in the UK if the EU had followed the path of minimalist integration, as national sovereignty, and the power of national institutions would not have been deemed to be greatly compromised by Brussels. Likewise, given the depth of political integration that the EU has been undergoing, in particular, since the signing of the Single European Act in 1986, any candidate wishing to join the bloc now has to implement sweeping reforms, which safeguard democracy, human rights, and the protection of minorities. It is for this reason that the integration of Turkey seems many years away. On the other hand, the EU is far from being a super state. It does not have an army but instead relies on NATO and on national contingents in defense of the continent. Engagement in foreign affairs is subject to a cumbersome process whereby all member states must agree unanimously on any course of action. Neither has there ever been a European police force or an intelligence service. It is once again through collaboration among national agencies that threats such as terrorism are countered. Welfare provisions also remain the exclusive domain of the member states, and to this today, the EU does not have its own tax-raising powers and relies on minuscule budget contributions of only around 1 percent of each member's GDP. Yes, the EU is an economic giant, based on its Single Market and its common external trade policy with non-EU entities. But in many areas of government activity, it remains a dwarf when compared with the likes of the United States or China.

HOW: SUPRANATIONALISM VERSUS INTERGOVERNMENTALISM

Identifying the true character of European integration is one matter; how to organize it raises further controversy. Supranationalism refers to the creation of a level of government and a set of policies, which rise above the power of national governments. As such, authority over agricultural matters, for instance, lies with the supranational European Commission and not with national governments. Likewise, verdicts reached by the European Court of Justice (ECJ) trump any judgments passed by national courts. A supranational organization of the EU is therefore comparable to the federal set up of the United States, in which foreign policy falls under the authority of the state department in Washington, D.C., while monetary matters are handled by the Federal Reserve. The individual states have no input in these areas.

On the other hand, intergovernmentalism relies on the collaboration between national governments, which mirrors the usual set up of international bodies such as the Organisation for Economic Co-operation and Development (OECD). In this scenario, EU member states have not relinquished any national sovereignty but are instead the drivers for any EU activity. The EU's foreign policy is an illustrative example. Any engagement in international affairs is not coordinated by a supranational entity such as the Commission. Instead, member states have to agree with one another on the precise course of action.

Over the past seventy years, there has been much supranational activity. The Single Market, the Euro, agriculture, cohesion, external trade, or the environment now fall under the authority of supranational institutions. Yet, there are still crucial areas where member states have resisted any encroachment by Brussels. Apart from foreign policy, this also applies to asylum, immigration, as well as intelligence and security services, arguably policies that affect most closely the national sovereignty of a member state. The EU is, therefore, a hybrid. It is much more than an international organization such as the United Nations (UN). But it also remains much less than a super state such as the United States of America.

FIVE DILEMMAS

European integration never followed a master plan. The EU developed in a piecemeal fashion, unlike the United States, where from the outset, a constitution manifested the relationship between a government and its citizens, and between federal authorities and the constituent states. Three treaties in the 1950s laid the foundation,[7] but a further five treaties responded to often ground-shifting developments within and outside of Europe. The Single European Act of 1986 was a direct response to Europe's lack of competitiveness with the United States and Japan. The Maastricht Treaty of 1992 came shortly after the fall of the Iron Curtain and German unification. In 1997, the Amsterdam Treaty attempted, yet fell short, to offer a more transparent and internationally pro-active EU in the light of growing Euroscepticism. Nice (2001) and Lisbon (2007) were designed to update institutions and policies against the backdrop of the "Big Bang" enlargement to central and eastern Europe in 2004. As should be the case for any political system, the EU has a long record of responding to major economic, political, and social developments: sometimes successfully (as with the case with the Single European Act), sometimes insufficiently (such as with the Treaty of Amsterdam), sometimes with overwhelming support from the member states (for instance when the Treaty of Rome in 1957 established the four free movements), but also sometimes amid much controversy (as was evidenced in the Maastricht Treaty, which introduced the euro as the bloc's single currency, but only after opt-outs were granted to Denmark, the UK, and Sweden).

Lacking a masterplan and missing a clear direction, however, provides room for different interpretations on Europe's future path. Over recent years, we have witnessed a multitude of developments, which are tearing at the seams of the European project. The European ship seems rudderless, with one EU actor stepping up with a new vision, only for another group of actors to dismiss and reject any such proposals. Disagreements are, of course, normal in politics. But unfortunately, the challenges that the EU is facing at the moment are monumental, and if unaddressed are here to stay. The existing EU setup fell short in providing decisive solutions to grave contemporary problems. Continuing with the same modus operandi will not address these challenges and might thus provide critics of the European project with much ammunition, with a chorus of Eurosceptic voices growing ever louder that the integrationist project ought to come to an end. A failure to respond coherently might, therefore, threaten the very existence of the European project. It has been over a decade since the signing of the Lisbon Treaty. Since then, the institutional and policy design of the EU has been severely tested, with the bloc moving from one short-term crisis management to another. As a consequence, the perception of a union, which might no longer be fit for purpose, is gaining traction. What we are witnessing is a Europe that is at a highly critical juncture. Continuing in a similar vein as before might not offer any cogent remedies. But agreeing on new institutional or policy designs might not be forthcoming either, because of conflicting notions among member states of what a future EU ought to look like.

A dilemma can be defined as a situation in which a difficult choice must be made between two or more alternatives that might be equally undesirable. And indeed, since the signing of Lisbon in 2007, the EU has been caught between a rock and a hard place: embark on a new course of direction, which might offer better solutions to existing challenges but which, in turn, has the potential to antagonize some member states that might disagree with the bloc's new direction; or stick with the existing and agreed policy and institutional design, which might no longer be effective to tackle existing challenges. This book addresses five such dilemmas that each in their own way underline this conundrum.

First, the rise of populist parties has fundamentally changed the EU's political landscape. In 2019, four countries (the Czech Republic, Hungary, Italy, and Poland) were at some stage governed by politicians who are highly critical of Brussels and who, in some cases, make little effort to hide their contempt for the European project. At the elections to the European Parliament in May 2019, around one-fifth of the electorate supported populist parties. For a growing number of voters, the EU is no longer regarded merely as a bureaucratic inconvenience, which from time to time coerces and streamlines national politics. It is now judged to represent a counterproductive vehicle to democracy that distances voters ever further from the political process without much accountability. In addition, the free movement of people—a much-heralded achievement, which allows citizens of any EU country to travel, work, study, and retire in another EU member state—resulted in migration hot spots, in particular in western European cities, where the EU is now often viewed as a pro-active agent that undermines a country's cultural coherence. The ease to conduct one's life in other countries was once regarded as a progressive achievement. Now some citizens see it as the beginning of the end of the nation-state.

Second, the introduction of the euro as Europe's single currency in 1999 was heralded as the much-needed completion of the Single Market. It was also judged to provide a cogent vehicle to integrate an economically powerful and unified Germany. And as long as European economies boomed, the EU basked in the glory of achieving something that previously had never been attempted before on this scale: the switch from national currencies to a supranational one. Then came Lehman Brothers in 2008 and the collapse of global demand. What has been obvious for many years, but what was conveniently cast aside by the political and financial establishment, was the fact that the EU is not an optimal currency area. Levels of productivity and prosperity were simply too diverse between northern economies like Finland, the Netherlands, Germany, Luxembourg, or Austria, and southern ones like Greece, Portugal, or Italy. Regulators at the national and European levels were also very casual in the supervision of the banking sector with drastic consequences for the economies of Ireland, Spain, and Cyprus. The EU had established a single European currency but without a single European economic governance. The results were rising poverty levels and growing unemployment in many member states, most notably in Greece. At the outset, the EU was determined to improve the lives of its citizens; to make them safer and more prosperous. With the Eurozone crises, it failed spectacularly on this account.

Third, the high numbers of migrants and refugees that have been fleeing to Europe in large numbers in recent years changed not only the complexion of some cities but also the political discourse, occasionally beyond recognition. German chancellor Angela Merkel's generous offer to house Syrian refugees resulted in a stampede in the summer of 2015, with refugees trying to reach Germany by crossing countries whose policy stances were much less welcoming. Geography also meant that a disproportionate burden was placed on such "entry" states as Italy and Greece. Politicians discovered a fertile hunting ground of disenchanted voters, who either saw their former way of life being compromised in an unacceptable fashion or who, at the very least, shuddered at the prospect of it. The EU by and large "outsourced" the problem, especially when striking a deal with Turkey, which now accommodates a substantial number of refugees from Syria. Yet a coherent EU approach on how to handle migrants who have arrived on European shores, and those many millions who will continue to attempt to do so, has been lacking.

Fourth, the EU has often witnessed manifestations of discontent about the European project. In a referendum in France, the Maastricht Treaty only passed with the narrowest of margins. In Denmark, the same treaty was rejected outright and only a revised version, which granted the country a euro opt-out passed the electoral test. France and the Netherlands voted down the Constitution of Europe, and Ireland needed two referendums to approve the Lisbon Treaty. But no referendum was as earth-shattering as the decision by the UK electorate in June 2016 to leave the EU altogether, albeit by a small majority of 52 percent to 48 percent. But what was widely regarded as the first nail in the coffin of the EU, with many states about to follow Britain's lead, turned into an existentialist soul-searching of the type of country that the UK ought to become in the post-Brexit years. It seemed easy to identify what voters were freeing themselves from: much harder though to establish what they were freeing themselves for, with the government of Prime Minister David Cameron making no preparations for a potential "leave" vote. It left a country bitterly divided and politically paralyzed, yet continental Europeans showed a surprising level of unity and determination to safeguard the EU's integrity. The process of establishing a close and mutually beneficial partnership between the union and the world's fifth biggest economy has only just started. It will take many years and will most likely be subject to the fluctuating fortunes of politics, with different UK governments interpreting the character of the partnership in different fashions. Brexit might not turn out to be a finite process but instead could represent a constant undercurrent that dominates political headlines for a very long time.

Fifth, in 2003, the EU drafted a list of countries, which could potentially join the bloc. Israel and Russia were not on that list. But Turkey was, and so were the successor states of the former Yugoslavia. It is conceivable that the EU could host close to forty member states with its population increasing from the current 500 million to over 600 million citizens. Including countries, which are at different stages in their political, social, and economic developments, might severely challenge the EU and could result in an institutional deadlock and even a policy breakdown. Moreover, some of the current candidates have a distinctly different political culture, with corruption and nepotism all too common. If the EU embarks on this massive south-eastern extension, the character of the European project will change drastically. Yet, while negotiations with the likes of Serbia and Montenegro are at an advanced stage, discussions on the changes that the EU must undertake to absorb such a "Big Bang 2.0 enlargement" have been rudimentary at best.

MORE DILEMMAS

Outside of these five predicaments, other challenges to European integration show a comparable level of urgency, which merit an inclusion in a future—and thus expanded—edition of this book. For many years now, multinational companies have been in the news for all the wrong reasons. Big companies like Google or Apple managed to keep their tax liabilities at an often astonishingly low level.[8] While perfectly legal, yet morally questionable, tax avoidance is surprisingly simple in the EU. Taking advantage of the Single Market's free movement, a multinational company merely has to negotiate a preferential tax rate with an EU member state, in return for establishing its European headquarters there. Once a company operates in another EU country, it "buys" the product or service from headquarters at retail (or near retail) prices. In the end, the vast majority of the company's profits are accounted for at headquarters, where a substantially reduced tax base applies. The tiny duchy of Luxembourg is the unquestionable leader in enticing big multinationals to its shores. The country's economy was previously dominated by steel—an industry which ever since the 1960s was in a state of perennial decline. Under the stewardship of former Prime Minister Jean Claude Juncker (1995 to 2013), who incidentally became president of the European Commission (2014–2019), the country diversified its economy and pursued an aggressive tax policy with spectacular success. In 2003, Amazon created a European hub, followed a year later by AOL and Microsoft. Others like Ikea, FedEx, GlaxoSmithKline, Accenture, Disney, and Pepsi soon followed.[9] Luxembourg is not alone. Other EU members, including the Netherlands and Ireland, established tax havens. The UK—through its off-shore Channel Islands, which in a bizarre fashion are non-EU territories—has also been a magnet for a global financial elite for many decades.

Tax avoidance across the globe is now rampant, due in large parts to the indifference displayed by the EU and the US administration under George W. Bush in the run-up to the financial crash of 2008. The G20 summit in 2009 promised action, but secrecy on behalf of tax haven governments and clever accounting practices continue to this day. The solution is obvious for the EU: a European tax harmonization complemented by an international agreement. Alas, the political climate of the past years, which was dominated by the debt crises in the eurozone and the Brexit negotiations, pushed tax reform to the back of the agenda.[10]

The ramifications for the European project, however, are not pretty. Luxembourg and other tax havens turned themselves into honey pots for multinationals. Low relative tax revenues but high absolute tax income made Luxembourg the richest EU country by far with GDP per capita averaging 110,000 US dollars—nearly three times as much as the UK. This successful, yet aggressive and secretive approach simply means that the country lives at the expense of others given the loss of tax revenues encountered by its EU partners. Ultimately, member states like Luxembourg contribute to the erosion of politics, when public services and the welfare state are faced with dwindling financial resources. We have already witnessed a regulatory race to the bottom, whereby EU countries are trying to outperform each other in order to attract big business. This is a highly questionable consequence of free movement. Former Commissioner Pierre Moscovici (2014–2019), responsible for economic and financial affairs, had for many years proposed the establishment of a Common Consolidated Tax Base (CCTB), which would disallow the consolidation of profits in just one member state. First proposed in 2011 and subject to unanimity voting, the proposal was vetoed by the UK in 2015. With Britain on its way out, the Commission might relaunch the initiative and, if successful, would offer an encouraging sign that the EU could become a higher-minded political entity without its former partner. In any case, it would indeed be timely for the Commission to tackle a major irregularity of the Single Market, which is unfair to European citizens, who, in a time of economic stagnation, have witnessed big corporations contributing less to society than their fair and presumed share. Moreover, the fact that member states are competing over multinationals by means of lower rates and lighter regulations can hardly be described as acting in the spirit of European solidarity.

Terrorism—the unlawful use of violence and intimidation, especially against civilians in the pursuit of political aims—is not new to Europe. In the 1970s, the Irish Republican Army (IRA) in Northern Ireland, the Baader-Meinhof Gang in West Germany and the Red Brigades in Italy terrified citizens and shocked the political establishment. Religious terrorism arrived in 2004 when Al-Qaeda operatives detonated several bombs on commuter trains in Madrid. A year later, a group of four radical British Muslims killed fifty-two innocent people and brought London to a standstill with a series of bombs, which targeted the public transport system. Despite these incidents, EU member states continue to insist that antiterrorist capacities should be organized in an intergovernmental fashion. There are coordinating bodies at EU level, but the actual fight against terrorism continues to be under the domain of national agencies. An American-style Federal Bureau of Investigation (FBI) or Central Intelligence Agency (CIA) still does not exist on the European continent.

In the aftermath of the US invasion of Iraq, and with the raging civil war in Syria, terrorist incidents have increased sharply in recent years. Already in 2005 and as a first response to Madrid, the member states agreed on an EU "Counter-Terrorism Strategy," which has since been updated on a regular basis. Summarized under the heading "Prevent, Protect, Pursue, Respond," the EU offers assistance to member states, ranging from the tracking of terrorist financing to monitoring and potentially hindering access to explosives, chemicals, and biological substances. Member states have also agreed on a common definition of terrorism, thus facilitating the arrest and extradition of suspected criminals.[11] There is now a network of agencies designed to elevate the fight against terrorism onto a European platform, including Frontex (the European Boarder and Coast Guard Agency), Eurojust (the EU agency dealing with judicial cooperation in criminal matters), CEPOL (the EU Agency for Law Enforcement Training), as well as EMCDDA (the European Monitoring Centre for Drugs and Drugs Addiction). The most prominent of those has arguably been Europol, which was founded as early as 1998. But it is important to realize that this agency has no authority to arrest potential criminals. It merely offers intelligence, although its powers with regard to antiterrorist measures and investigations have been greatly increased ever since the 2004 Madrid bombings.

But this broad network of actions and programs proved to be unable to slow down the tide of terrorism. The British terrorists who targeted London's trains and buses argued that they were soldiers who were at war, and who intended to take revenge on what they perceived as unjust killings of Muslim brothers and sisters in the Iraq war. The civil war in Syria only heightened this tension. According to estimates, around 3,000 foreign and mainly European fighters were active in Syria in 2017. If only 1 out of every 15 to 20 fighters have terrorist potential, this will result in 150 to 200 individuals willing to take their battle to EU countries. Unfortunately, political action at the European level has not been able to alleviate this threat. The policies and programs did not create any new competences, supranational, or otherwise. Instead, EU authorities such as the Commission are merely issuing guidelines and general objectives but are not operationally involved in tackling the problem.[12] A lack of financial resources adds to this dilemma, as does the lack of any involvement of the European Parliament. In addition, different member states have very different capacities to tackle terrorist threats. France and Germany devote significant financial and human resources to this cause and therefore do not necessarily need an EU umbrella to combat threats. This is certainly not the case for Belgium, as evidenced by the bombings in Paris in November 2015 when terrorists were able to go into hiding in the Belgian capital Brussels. Member states also do not necessarily share security information with their European partners. In the aftermath of the Paris bombings, Germany's former interior minister Thomas de Maizière admitted that the EU and its member states have different data pools that are not always linked. Coordination leaves much to be desired. The Belgian suicide bomber who targeted Brussels airport in March 2016 had initially been arrested in Turkey and was then deported to the Netherlands where he was released. Even more astonishing, the EU and its member states still have not agreed on one system that transliterates Arabic names.

This reluctance to imbue the EU with more powers has many reasons. Setting up new capacities would bring about institutional rivalries between the Commission and the EU Counter-Terrorism Coordination unit within the Council of Ministers (an institution that represents member state governments). Furthermore, some member states, such as France, Italy, and Germany, are very collaborative when dealing with Europol. Others, most prominently countries in central and eastern Europe, are not as forthcoming. This can partially be explained by different risk scenarios since not all member states are equally affected by the recent terrorist attacks. While threat levels in the UK, Belgium, France, and Germany are very high, the same cannot be said for a country like Poland. In a similar vein, while western European countries might face the threat of foreign fighters, newer member states are much more worried about organized crime. Hence, the security landscape in the EU is highly diverse, and a "security union" might not be able to address such a diverse range of threats.

After any terrorist attack, calls for greater collaboration are always expressed, predominantly by France, Germany, Italy, and the Commission. But words are not followed up with concrete actions. Member states continue to be highly reluctant to give up national control over sensitive areas. This not only is true for tax issues and budget contributions but also applies to security information. Furthermore, enhancing powers for EU institutions in the field of justice and home affairs would require a new treaty. With the almost all-consuming task of organizing Brexit and the current, more nationalistic political climate in Italy, Austria, Hungary, Poland, the Czech Republic, and Slovakia, it seems very likely that notions of national sovereignty and interest will prevail. Given a widespread reluctance to promote EU solutions, we might witness a recourse to tighter national standards with the potential emergence of tighter border controls and restrictions to the free movement of people, and even capital.

Any climate change skeptic might want to visit the European Alps. Its glaciers are shrinking at a rapid rate with scientific studies stating that 90 percent of glaciers in the area will have disappeared by 2100.[13] In contrast to other industrial powerhouses of the global economy, the EU has a much less devastating environmental record. As the worst European culprit, Germany is ranked sixth among worldwide polluters with a share of 2.2 percent of global emissions of greenhouse gases, significantly behind China (27.2 percent), the United States (14.6), and India (6.9 percent), respectively.[14] Within the EU, Germany accounts for 21 percent of emissions, with the UK (11 percent) as well as France and Italy (10 percent each) trailing at a significant distance. On a promising note, the emission of greenhouse gases in the EU dropped by 22 percent between 1990 and 2017,[15] thanks in large part to an ever-increasing environmental agenda. I have argued previously[16] that the EU has a mixed environmental record. On the one hand, the bloc has developed a range of new initiatives and principles. With the help of so-called Environmental Action Plans, the EU established an environmental angle to its entire EU policy-making process and has dragged up the performance of some previously laggard member states. On the other hand, the EU continues to produce very significant emissions, not helped by the well-established car, transport, and energy lobbies, or the rise of dynamic sectors, such as pharmaceuticals or biotechnology that are potential creators of biohazards. At the international level, the EU was instrumental in the signing of the Paris Climate Accord in 2015, which attempts to limit global temperature rises to less than two-degree Celsius above preindustrial levels. Although, as of 2019, 195 states have signed the agreement, President Trump withdrew the support of the United States. While pressing and existentialist, the inclusion of a chapter on climate change would not do justice to the grave threat to human existence (and that of other animal and plant species). Instead, it warrants an analysis that goes far beyond the scope of this book. Global warming is not merely a technological challenge of inventing measures to limit pollution or foster biodiversity. It is instead a lifestyle challenge where citizens, businesses, and governments across the globe must depart from well-established patterns of consumption and production. There are much more qualified and knowledgeable writers than I who will make more cogent contributions to this endeavor.

NOTES

1. See: https://www.nobelprize.org/prizes/peace/2012/summary.
2. There was also a sizeable number of European countries that opted for military neutrality and did not seek integration into NATO, or indeed any other military alliance. To this day, these countries include Ireland, Austria, Malta, Sweden, and

Finland. Spain remained a neutral country until it joined NATO in 1982, while Serbia is the only country of the former Yugoslavia that does not seek NATO membership.

3. See: Andreas Staab. *The European Union Explained* (Bloomington: Indiana University Press, 2013), pp. 134–7.

4. Source: Eurostat.

5. See: https://winstonchurchill.org/resources/speeches/1946-1963-elder-statesman/united-states-of-europe.

6. Immanuel Kant wrote his seminal work "Perpetual Peace" in 1805.

7. The treaties were the European Coal and Steel Community (ECSC, signed in Paris in 1950), as well as the European Economic Community (EEC) and Euroatom; both of which signed in Rome in 1957.

8. For example, in 2014, Amazon reported sales of 9.1 billion euros in the UK. But the company paid corporation tax only on 20 million euros of profits (which amounts to 0.2 percent of its annual turnover).

9. But the country's creativity was not confined to big multinationals. For years, shoppers from the neighboring EU members Belgium, France, and Germany enjoyed low duties on alcohol, cigarettes, and petrol. A recently built "Freeport" located right next to the country's international airport invites global investors to store gold, diamonds, wine, or art in a discretely anonymous and tax-free fashion. Foundations and those eager to reduce inheritance duties also have long appreciated Luxembourg's ultra-low tax rates and light regulation.

10. As of late, the Commission's attempt to create a level playing field across the EU has taken on a much different dimension. In September 2016, the then Competition Commissioner Margrethe Vestager ordered Apple to pay back thirteen billion euros in unpaid taxes, arguing that the saved tax money amounted to illegal state aid. In 2014, Apple paid the astonishing rate of 0.005 percent tax on its profits. In a deal dating back to 1991, the US giant had never paid more than 1 percent in corporation taxes, whereas the usual tax rate for other businesses in Ireland is 12.5 percent. But successive Irish governments were quite happy with the arrangement, given the infrastructure boost and the establishment of over 5,000 high-paying jobs at the company's headquarters in Cork. It therefore came as little surprise that the Irish government does not want the money back for fear of antagonizing its most high-profile economic player. Apple's chief executive officer (CEO) Tim Cook branded the Commission's ruling as "maddening," and indeed it might seem questionable whether Vestager acted within her authority to impose such a large fee for an arrangement that dates back so many years. Not surprisingly, both the Irish government and Apple decided to appeal, with a final verdict, however, not expected for many years to come.

11. There is now a host of programs and initiatives in place: a crisis coordination mechanism called ARGUS represents a rapid alert system, which involves as many Commission services as feasible in pursuit of potential terrorist perpetrators. Since 2011, the EU also established the "Radicalization Awareness Network," which intends to connect social workers to younger people (who are often the most vulnerable to inflammatory radical rhetoric), as well as religious leaders. With regard to terrorists funding, the EU has since 2001 issued several money laundering directives.

In addition, any money transfers above 10,000 euros will automatically alert the security departments of all banks, while an EU wide terrorist list offers the potential to freeze a perpetrator's assets. There is an EU Action Plan on "Enhancing the Security of Explosives" (2008), the CBRN Action Plan (2006) designed to monitor chemical, biological, radiological, and nuclear substances, as well as the EPCIP; the European Program for Critical Infrastructure Protection (2006). Since 2011, the Terrorist Finance Tracking Program (TFTP) offers for collaboration with the United States.

12. See: Martina Prpic. "*Towards a New European Agenda on Security*," January 24, 2015. http://www.europarl.europa.eu/thinktank/en/document.html?reference=EPRS_ATA(2015)545727.

13. https://www.dw.com/en/almost-all-glaciers-in-the-alps-could-disappear-by-2100-study/a-48266333.

14. https://www.statista.com/statistics/271748/the-largest-emitters-of-co2-in-the-world/.

15. https://ec.europa.eu/eurostat/statistics-explained/index.php/Greenhouse_gas_emission_statistics.

16. Andreas Staab. *The European Union Explained* (Bloomington: Indiana University Press, 2013), pp. 177–8.

Chapter 1

Populism

The year 2016 saw the manifestation of a markedly different political movement, which subsequently spread across many established democracies. In June, the UK had narrowly voted to leave the EU, backed up by a rallying call to "take back control" from Brussels. In November, Donald Trump confounded the political establishment in the Republican Party and opinion pollsters by winning the presidency and promising to "make America great again." A year later, in April 2017, Marine le Pen of the French Front National easily beat the candidates of established political parties to advance to the second round of the presidential elections. Although she subsequently lost handsomely to Emanuel Macron—another newcomer on the country's political scene—one in three voters supported le Pen, who for a long time represented the far-right fringe of French politics. In the same year, the party of Dutch politician Geert Wilders was widely predicted to become the strongest political force in the national elections. Only an appeal by Prime Minister Mark Rutte on the eve of the elections to take on board the growing concerns about migration and multiculturalism pushed Wilder's party into second place. A similar scenario had already unfolded in Austria. In 2016, Norbert Hofer, the candidate of the right-wing Freedom Party, won the first round of the presidential elections before losing the second run-off to the Greens' candidate Alexander van der Bellen (54–46 percent). In the general elections a year later, the party leader Heinz-Christian Strache was topping the polls. This galvanized the conservative politician Sebastian Kurz—Strache's rival to the chancellorship—to deliver a series of speeches in which he voiced sympathy over the growing concerns about migration. Kurz subsequently won the election and formed a government with the Freedom Party as his junior coalition partner.[1] In neighboring Germany, the Alternative für Deutschland (Alternative for Germany) had become the largest opposition party in national elections held in September 2017. By 2018, new political movements were governing Austria, the Czech Republic, Poland, Hungary, and Italy. Moreover, established political parties that had been part of the political mainstream since the end of World War II in western Europe, and since the collapse of communism in central and eastern Europe, now witnessed their electoral bases being eroded and upstaged by a new breed of politicians and new political platforms. Populism had truly arrived.

CAUSES

As with many political ideas, populism arose as an antidote to social, political, and economic upheavals. The financial crash of 2008 brought the golden age of capitalism to a shuddering end. Ever since the end of World War II, market economics complemented by social welfare state reforms had delivered an impressive degree of prosperity and stability to many citizens in western Europe. With the fall of the Iron Curtain, the same model also became the modus operandi in the former communist states of central and eastern Europe. It prompted Francis Fukuyama and other academics to proclaim the "end of history" where a widespread societal consensus had now been reached on how countries ought to be governed. But in subsequent years, the welfare society began to be compromised by the looser regulation of the financial sector, as well as by ever more business-friendly tax regimes with countries trying to undercut one another in order to lure multinational businesses to invest on their shores. Consequently, the gap between top and bottom earners, between rich and poor continued to widen. The collapse of the US investment bank Lehman Brothers and the subsequent nationalization (at taxpayers' expense) of entire financial sectors in countries like Ireland, Spain, and the UK represented the bleak termination of a decades-long equilibrium that had allowed businesses to reap profits, as long as wages, social standards, and welfare support were maintained and gradually expanded. Now, large sections of society felt that they were on the losing side of capitalism, that market economics had lost its social dimension, and thus might still work for a privileged few but no longer for ordinary citizens. History had not come to an end. It was getting uglier.

It comes as little surprise that populist movements target multinational corporations and big businesses with the EU being one of the focal points of their criticism. The Single Market—one of the world's largest trading blocs—enables businesses to freely produce and sell their goods and services across the entire continent aided by a uniform set of rules. Smaller businesses that were previously protected by national markets and national regulations stand with little chance against the big corporate beasts with their ambition to implement ever more profitable economies of scale. This growing inequality is exacerbated by harsher industrial relations and a threat to financial security. The gig economy of taxi services and food delivery might be good for employment statistics, but also turn significant sections of the workforce into an armada of self-employed, one-person companies with welfare benefits, such as sick leave or holiday pay, undermined by zero-hour contracts. It all added to a heightened sense of insecurity to which the political establishment did not react in an appropriate fashion. Amid these significant changes to working lives, the EU is often regarded as an agent for big business: A club that feeds fat cats and disregards the economic and financial concerns of middle to low-income earners. By extension, through furthering EU integration, national governments and national political elites were complicit in this process and were thus no longer on the side of ordinary people. In the end, the economic status quo of wages, wealth, working conditions, and income distribution was no longer acceptable for many citizens. This was particularly prevalent in the run-up to the Brexit referendum in the UK. Prime Minister Cameron tried in vain to shift the focus to such issues as financial stability and economic prosperity that EU membership guaranteed. For people on low wages and with growing job insecurity, his arguments merely added insult to injury, and notions of a better Britain, not purely driven by growth, profits, and dividends, but in charge of its own laws and rules, and thus outside the EU's Single Market became very attractive.

During the same period, the free movement of people—one of the cornerstones of the EU's Single Market—encouraged ever larger numbers of EU citizens to seek employment in more prosperous countries. When the former communist states of central and eastern Europe joined the EU in 2004, only three member states—the UK, Ireland, and Sweden—guaranteed the application of the free movement principle in their countries. All other established EU members, including the likes of France, Germany, Spain, and Italy imposed a seven-year moratorium, which greatly inhibited the chance to seek employment in those states. Not surprisingly, the UK, Ireland and Sweden saw their net migration figures increase rapidly.[2] The moratorium was lifted in 2011, which meant that citizens from Poland, Hungary, or Lithuania could now freely settle across the EU.[3] But it was still upheld until 2014 (this time also by Sweden, Ireland, and the UK) for new members Bulgaria and Romania who had joined the union in 2007. Given the vastly different wages, the economic pull of working in western EU countries was strong, in particular in Romania, where an astonishing fifth of the population now lives in other EU states.

Although large parts of Europe, in particular, in central and eastern Europe, remain highly homogenous, we witnessed the emergence of migration hotspots in many western European cities. Often caused by language barriers, these migrants entered low-skilled and low-wage jobs, thus competing directly with less prosperous locals. The effect on communities, on their norms, habits, and ways of live was on occasion vast and in many incidences came rapidly. It challenged their capacity to cope with change. Even in places where migration was not as pronounced, such as in more rural areas, there was a fear of migration, a projected concern that this might at some stage in the future threatens to undermine established cultural norms and practices. While economic worries over job security and wages were undoubtedly prominent, such a line of argumentation had very distinctive cultural undertones, which focused on the belief that the way of life of locals and natives might be incompatible with those of incoming migrants.

Moreover, a national discourse on the emergence of an increasingly multicultural society was largely absent. In Germany, for instance, the former President Christian Wulff declared in 2010 that the Muslim faith now belonged to Germany, thereby flabbergasting many traditional, socially conservative people. In the UK, a meaningful political dialogue had long been scarred by Enoch Powell's "River of Blood" speech in 1968, which called for the compulsory expatriation of immigrants. The subsequent widespread support among white, working-class citizens traumatized the political establishment for fear that dealing with migration issues might fan racism and xenophobia. Hence, when the Labour government of Tony Blair kept the UK borders open to central and eastern Europeans (which after all was a very useful tool for keeping inflation under control and for sustaining a prolonged economic boom), the country sleepwalked into an ever-growing contentious, yet unaddressed, issue.

Such a growing sense of alienation was further exacerbated by a traditional political party landscape that found it increasingly difficult to respond to an ever-growing diversity of norms and standards. The postwar era in western Europe, and the aftermath of the fall of communism in central and eastern Europe, saw the establishment of mass parties that embraced large tracts of society under broad ideological umbrellas. In the earlier postwar years, European integration was by and large an elitist concept with prime ministers shaping EU policies and institutions, with the wider public content with letting their politicians and bureaucrats make key decisions. This all changed with the ratification of the Maastricht Treaty in 1992. In France, the subsequent referendum on the treaty scraped through by the narrowest of margins. Denmark first rejected Maastricht and only came on board, once a euro opt-out had been granted. The process to ratify a European constitution in 2005 was rejected by the public in France, the Netherlands, and Ireland, and in 2015, Greek citizens voted by a margin of 2 to 1 against austerity measures imposed by the EU and the International Monetary Fund (IMF).[4] These were voices that argued that the path of European integration was at best controversial and at worst unwanted. But those voices were largely ignored, fueled by a consensus that elections to the European Parliament (the only time citizens have a direct vote to elect representatives to any of the EU's institutions) continuously brought to power a large majority of parties, which supported a deeper and wider integration. All these developments led to a growing divide between ruler and ruled, and between governments and their citizens.

Furthermore, in the post-material age, concerns of citizens often go beyond wages and social security (for workers) or tax regimes and regulation (for businesses). Now, an environmental agenda, quality of life, a more participatory democracy, multiculturalism, but also a longing for the good old days of cultural homogeneity have entered the political agenda in many countries. And the traditional party system struggled to take these new aspirations and ideas on board. Social democracy in particular has undergone a severe, if not yet terminal, decline. In years gone by, these left-of-center parties had to ensure that their constituents received decent wages and could enjoy gradually increasing standards of living and better conditions at work. Social democratic parties were the natural ally of working women and men, with a voter base, which was predominantly culturally traditional and socially conservative. Nowadays, however, those parties are also trying to satisfy a more progressive clientele that cares about climate change, gender equality, self-expression, LGBTQ rights, or work-life balance issues. Such voters, often living in urban areas with a distinct multicultural background, share a fundamentally different outlook on life than the traditional, social democratic voter base.

This schism is exemplified by the decline of the German Social Democratic Party (SPD), which saw its vote share plummet to only 20 percent in the national elections in 2017; the lowest ever in the postwar history of the Federal Republic. At the same election, the Green Party stabilized its electoral appeal by receiving 8.4 percent, and the party now governs the affluent southern state of Baden-Württemberg as well as its capital city Stuttgart.[5] The struggle to integrate increasingly divergent strands has also affected the British Labour party. During the Brexit referendum of 2016, many Labour supporters in struggling northern, former industrial towns voted in large numbers to leave the EU. Further south, in metropolitan areas such as London, or in university towns, such as Oxford, Canterbury, or Cambridge, its voter base were largely "Remainers." Unlike in Germany, however, where the SPD had seen voters moving to newer movements, such as the Greens or the more radical, and left-wing Die Linke, the UK's Labour party's share has not been compromised. But this is not necessarily down to Labour's programmatic vision or ideological flexibility. It is predominantly a by-product of the country's majoritarian electoral system, which prompts voters to support traditional parties, since a ballot cast for minor parties might represent a vote, which is being wasted. It is the preference for the most-likely and least-worst choice, instead of a vote in line with one's value system that saved Labour from further decline.

On the other side of the political spectrum, the voter base of established right-of-center political parties was also eroding. Conservative voters had always placed a high emphasis on law and order, on faith and religion, and were in general of a more socially conservative nature. An ever more liberal, diverse, internationalist, and progressive society was regarded as a direct challenge to long-established values. Owners of small businesses, self-employed people, and middle-to-lower-income brackets were also strongholds of conservative parties' support. Here, globalization, the growing reach of multinational companies, rising inequality, and declining social safety nets made such voters increasingly receptive to a different message that the established parties failed to provide. Traditional voters often complained about the "liberal" assault on traditional values, where notions such as law and order, family, tradition, and a national culture were sacrificed on the altar of multiculturalism and diversity.

At first, such changes in the perceived and experienced way of life were gradual but have now reached a tipping point that turned silent resentment into vocal political activism. The consensus of mainstream politics has been eroding and former mass parties are finding it impossible to offer a catch-all umbrella for voters with such diverse expectations. The political landscape continues to shift, presenting newcomers with opportunities to address unclaimed and previously not serviced electoral spaces.

There is growing public resentment against the direction of EU integration. In a survey commissioned by the European Parliament in the summer of 2018, 62 percent of respondents agreed that EU membership is by and large a good thing, which was the highest EU approval rate since the signing of the Maastricht Treaty in 1992.[6] But the survey also revealed that exactly 50 percent of respondents voiced concerns that the EU is moving in the wrong direction, which was a significant increase from the previous survey in the spring of 2018 when figures were only at 42 percent. There is a widespread perception that the EU is run by old men in Brussels: privileged, self-satisfied, and utterly detached from the life experiences of ordinary citizens. These accusations are not new, but the chorus of dissenting voices has grown louder recently and instead of attempting to find new solutions, the EU establishment (Brussels officials and national governments) defended the status quo, merely arguing that the EU continues to be the least bad alternative.

A perfect storm began to brew, with the established postwar consensus being subject to growing pressures: standards of living and prosperity levels were no longer safeguarded while a financial elite was enjoying a disproportionate and on occasion absurd degree of wealth. Traditional ways of life were subject to fast and vast cultural diversifications, which often went beyond a community's capacity to absorb change. Competition over jobs and housing only heightened the sense of disconnect from a metropolitan, more affluent elite that held the key jobs in government, finance, media, and politics. And all the while, a traditional party landscape was expanding its ideological umbrella to cater for an increasingly diverse voter base, thus often disregarding traditional, socially more conservative and less progressive voices. Multicultural change, growing inequality, and an overstretched traditional party system provided the perfect breeding ground for populism, for a new style of politics and a new political agenda.

WHAT IS POPULISM?

New political movements responded to these trends by taking on board widespread and entirely legitimate concerns and anxieties by appealing directly to "normal" citizens. Populism is targeting a political landscape that is detached from the wishes of ordinary people, and therefore can no longer represent them. It aims for a fairer distribution of income against the globalizing forces of multinational corporations, based on socially conservative and traditional values. In addition, it often focuses on mechanisms to make the voice of the people heard in a more coherent fashion—hence the appeal of more direct democracy and referendums, and the vociferous criticism of, and desire to replace a global, unchallenged elite that fails to aspire to a common good. Its ideological base lies in a focus on the national community, on a set of coherent norms and standards, which give rise to a deeply felt national identity (as opposed to a European or international identity) in the strong belief that nations across the globe are fundamentally different in character and that out of multiple identities (whether it be gender, profession, or local and regional affiliations), the emotional attachment to the nation supersedes all others.

A perceived national decline is often blamed on the political establishment, a liberal media and international corporations that are devoid of any national roots or sentiments. When assuming power, in 2016 UK prime minister Theresa May briefly followed the populist bandwagon by referring to the so-called JAMs—people who are just about managing—as opposed to the "citizens of nowhere" who have failed to put down roots in communities and revel in an internationalist, de-nationalized existence that technological advances and the forces of globalization have made increasingly possible. As a logical consequence, populist movements aim for a Europe without immigration; a Europe of nations, as opposed to a United States of Europe; a union of states as opposed to a super state union.

Issues such as more political participation, fairer income distribution, the creation of jobs or better working conditions are concerns that are usually associated with left-wing politics. Indeed, the manifestos of populist movements such as *Podemos* in Spain or the *Movimento 5 Stelle* (5Star Movement; M5S) in Italy would certainly fall into this category. It is for this reason, that populism cannot be categorized as purely far right. However, it is also fair to say that a version of populism, which integrates concerns about migration and a call for more cultural homogeneity—points that do not appear on the agenda of *Podemos*—tends to fare better in elections.

WHAT POPULISM IS NOT

One ought to be careful not to dismiss populist voters as undereducated, mainly male, old, Christian, and white individuals at the lower end of the income ladder. Such an impression would fail to grasp the widespread approval of the populists' agenda. In fact, significant parts of the established middle-income bourgeoisie have joined their cause. It is not the lack of educational proficiency that plays a large role here, but instead a lack of exposure to those experiences, which the metropolitan elite might take for granted: living in a multicultural environment as offered by bigger cities or pursuing a university education filled with cultural and personal exchanges with international students, or the opportunity to travel. Quite often populism appeals to people with more traditional values that emphasize stability, maintaining law and order, or social hierarchies. These legitimate values, however, do not correlate to the priorities of more outward looking, progressive, and internationalist metropolitans. Education therefore can on occasion play a limited role in explaining the populists' appeal. It is more productive to focus on prevalent and traditional value systems of a group of people who experience life in fundamentally different ways. The rise of populism is therefore often also the manifestation of a culture war between traditionalists and progressives. Although educational attainment often boosts the latter the lack of it does not necessarily identify the former.[7]

Populism is also often referred to as a protest movement against the established political elite, the liberal media, and big, multinational corporations. Such a portrayal is often accompanied by dismissive characterizations of a mythical longing for a past where life was simpler, more authentic, and more meaningful. Indeed, slogans such as Trump's "Make America Great Again," and Brexit's "Take Back Control" provide much support to such an explanation. But it fails to acknowledge that a desire for less migration, more democracy, and more power wrestled away from international institutions and corporations can represent legitimate political ambitions in their own rights. Populist supporters might not just protest against the status quo. They are also calling for a rethink. The fear of an erosion of established cultural norms and concerns over the changes that migration might bring to a national community can leave a profound mark; not just on some individuals whose lives are subject to sudden ruptures but on a country's national identity as a whole. And given the lack of political discourse, voicing those concerns goes well beyond a desire to hark back to past glory days. It can also represent an affirmative statement and a call for the establishment of a new social and economic contract.

Populism is also not necessarily anti-democratic. Many populist movements, whether the *Alternative für Deutschland* in Germany, *Rassemblement National* in France, the M5S in Italy, or Spain's *Podemos*, have called for an increase in participatory democracy. In fact, they are lamenting the loss of democracy and the lack of an involvement of citizens and are campaigning for a Swiss-style model of democracy with more referendums, so that the popular will of ordinary citizens is heard and acted upon. In fact, populism claims to be a guarantor of democracy as it defends people and gives them a voice against unelected bureaucrats, detached politicians, uninhibited journalists, and unregulated corporations. The same cannot be said of fascism, which ultimately desires the establishment of a new, fundamentally different, cultural and social order, and aims for the rise of an authoritarian regime and the mythical rebirth of the nation led by strong leaders. This certainly is not democratic, and is therefore fundamentally different from populism, which is more often about galvanizing the will of ordinary people against powerful elites. But it is not about bringing new authoritarian elites to power. The distinction between "radical right" and "far right"[8] is therefore far more compelling. Populism is part of the "radical right" that is critical of some key aspects of the prevalent established system of liberal market democracy. But it has no intention of abolishing it. The far right's aim, however, is precisely that.

Populism is also not racism, and anti-migration stances are not necessarily racist. On occasion they most certainly are, but treasuring one's traditional values and customs, and fearing that those norms might be challenged can also represent a legitimate and not automatically racist concern. It might, but this does not necessarily entail a sense that one's culture is superior to those of other people. While it is undoubtedly true that racists voted for Brexit, the reverse relationship is not necessarily true. Yes, for some, Brexit was about national and often racial purity, of turning back foreigners and migrants of a different religious, ethnic, and racial ilk, often tinged with the assumption of a superiority of Britain over other countries and their peoples. But for the vast majority, Brexit was about a desire for more cultural coherence, for being in control of borders, and for a stake in deciding the country's future: all of which were perceived to be undermined by the rule of Brussels and the EU's free movement of people. Controlling borders and controlling the influx of migrants were long regarded as political relics in the ever-advancing European age of integration. But the nation-state (or the four-nation-state as is the case for the UK) has not lost its political relevance to many voters, and citizens are not racists just because they are reluctant to abide by the Europeanization of politics. For them, it will never be the EU institutions, which have the responsibility to secure welfare standards or to maintain security. Proper legitimacy of a political system—that of a meaningful relationship between ruler and ruled—can only ever be achieved at national level. Such an understanding might be attractive to racists, but it is not by itself racism.

POPULISM IN ACTION

Right-wing populist parties have become a staple of national politics in many EU member states. In the summer of 2019, populist parties were involved in government in Austria, the Czech Republic, Hungary, Italy, and Poland (see table 1.1). In Germany, the *Alternative für Deutschland* (AfD; Alternative for Germany) was founded in 2013 by prominent economists, business leaders, and journalists who had arrived at the conclusion that the eurozone had proven to be financially unsustainable as a currency area and ought to be abolished. In its first election to the German Bundestag, the party came narrowly short of the 5 percent threshold, gaining 4.7 percent of the votes. However, at the next national elections in 2017, the AfD became the largest opposition party with 12.6 percent of votes. This electoral breakthrough came on the back of several successes at the regional state level, and in 2019, the AfD was represented in all sixteen state parliaments.[9] The party's ideological base was initially that of soft Euroscepticism. While the AfD largely supports EU membership, it is vehemently opposed to the existence of the single currency and to the bailout programs for such states as Greece or Portugal. Italy's financial struggles are often commented upon by leading AfD politicians with rhetorical swipes against reckless spending and unsustainable public finances. In addition, the party advocates classic populist policies, such as direct participatory democracy based on the Swiss model, as well as calls to end migration and the threat posed by Muslims on German culture. Its voter base tends to be among the traditionally minded, conservative middle class as exemplified by its very vocal criticism of Germany's 2017 legalization of same-sex marriage. The most controversial aspect of the AfD's political platform, however, is a markedly nationalistic rhetoric with frequent references to *Vaterland*, and *Volk* peppering the speeches of its leading politicians. Most notorious of all, is the party's call for the repudiation of a so-called national culture of shame that harks back to the atrocities committed by the Third Reich.

Table 1.1 Populist Parties in the EU: Share of Votes in National Elections

Country	*Name of Party*	*Election Year*	*Vote Share (%)*	*Role in National Legislature*
Austria	Freedom Party	2019	17.2	No government formed (as of December 2019)
Belgium	Vlaams Belang	2019	12.0	In opposition to caretaker government (as of December 2019)
Bulgaria	Volya	2017	4.2	In opposition
Czech Republic	Ano	2017	29.6	Largest party in coalition
Denmark	Danish People's Party	2019	8.7	In opposition
Estonia	Conservative People's Party	2019	17.8	Junior coalition partner
Finland	Finns	2019	17.5	In opposition
France	Rassemblement National	2017	13.0	In opposition
Germany	Alternative for Germany	2017	12.6	Largest opposition party
Greece	Golden Dawn	2015	7.0	In opposition
Hungary	Fidesz	2018	44.9	Sole Ruling party
Italy	Lega	2018	37.0	Largest party in coalition
	Five Star Movement	2018	32.7	Second largest party in coalition
Latvia	National Alliance	2018	11.0	In opposition
Lithuania	Order and Justice	2016	7.6	In opposition
Netherlands	Party for Freedom	2017	13.1	Largest opposition party
	Forum for Democracy	2017	1.8	In opposition
Poland	Law and Justice	2015	37.6	Ruling party
Slovakia	National Party	2016	8.6	In opposition
Slovenia	Slovenian National Party	2018	4.2	In opposition
Spain	Unidas Podemos	2019	12.8	Junior coalition partner
	VOX	2019	15.1	In opposition
Sweden	Sweden Democrats	2018	12.9	In opposition
UK	United Kingdom Independence Party	2019	0.1	Not represented in parliament
	Brexit Party	2019	2.0	Not represented in parliament

Elections refer to the lower house of parliament, thus excluding votes for upper houses such as the Italian Senate or the German *Bundesrat*. Fascist parties such as Jobbik in Hungary are not listed. *Front National* under the leadership of Marine le Pen renamed itself to *Rassemblement National* (National Rally) in June 2018.

In France, the *Rassemblement National* (National Rally, RN) is the successor party of the long-established *Front National* (FN) after a name change in 2018. Jean-Marie le Pen had founded the FN in 1972, and, while on the political margins at first, achieved a surprising breakthrough at the presidential elections in 2002 when he managed to make the shortlist of the final two candidates (although he lost the subsequent second run-off with a historically low 17.8 percent of the votes to incumbent President Jacques Chirac). Le Pen resigned in 2011 to make way for his daughter Marine. Since then, the movement garnered considerable support among French voters. At the elections to the European Parliament in May 2014, the *FN* achieved the highest share of votes of any party in France (24.9 percent), which was the first time ever that an outspoken anti-EU party had won a national poll. Although the elections to the national parliament in the same year were disappointing (13.0 percent), the party bounced back in 2015, when the FN once again topped the polls with 28 percent. At the presidential elections in 2017, Marine le Pen comfortably made the second round of voting although she was comprehensively defeated by Emanuel Macron by a margin of 2 to 1.

Comparable to the German *Alternative für Deutschland*, the party is vehemently opposed to the existence of the euro single currency, while also advocating cuts to legal migration (the target is 10,000 per year), and the deportation of illegal migrants, criminals, and even unemployed foreigners. In contrast to the AfD, *Rassemblement National* wants France to leave the EU altogether and has been arguing as such ever since the creation of the FN nearly fifty years ago. Opposition to NATO membership and of the Schengen passport-free travel area are also part of its programmatic base. The approach to law and order is also more pronounced. The call for the reintroduction of the death penalty (illegal under EU rules) was only dropped in the run-up to the presidential elections in 2017, although calls for harsher sentencing and increased prison capacities remain an ideological staple. In the sphere of economics, it is more difficult to locate RN on the political spectrum. Unlike the neoliberal approach of the AfD, le Pen argues for protectionism and more government intervention in the creation of jobs.

Marine le Pen tried to soften the image of her movement, away from the notorious nationalistic and xenophobic outbursts of her father, who together with other controversial party members was suspended and subsequently expelled from the party in 2015. While le Pen senior had a revisionist view on the Holocaust and the Nazi occupation of France, Marine regards the Jewish population of her country as integral to France's cultural community in the fight against the ongoing encroachment of traditions and values by Muslim migrants. She is also a supporter of Vladimir Putin, and in 2014 referred to the Russian leader as "the defender of the Christian heritage of European civilization,"[10] claiming that the continued sanctions against the country represent the start of a new America-led Cold War.

In Hungary, Victor Orbán—the poster boy of European populism—and his party *Fidesz* rose to power in the national elections of 2010. *Fidesz* was founded in 1988, one year before the fall of the Iron Curtain, as an underground student movement opposed to the ruling communist party. After disappointing election results in 1994, the party switched from a liberal ideology to conventional European conservatism. Orbán led *Fidesz* to power in 1998 in a coalition government, which subsequently lost to the SPD four years later and to an alliance of social and liberal democratic parties in 2006. *Fidesz*'s electoral record since 2010, however, has been nothing but spectacular. In that year, the party won by a landslide and established a strong majority in parliament by claiming 68 percent of seats. Although the two-thirds supermajority was lost by two seats in 2014, the 2018 elections saw the return of its previously unchallenged status. The grip that *Fidesz* has on the electoral landscape of Hungary is astonishing. It runs all the nineteen county legislatures, twenty out of twenty-three urban centers, as well as the city council in the capital Budapest. The supermajority in the national parliament provides *Fidesz* with the opportunity to change the country's constitution at will. Orbán took full advantage of this power, by aiming to establish what he openly refers to as "illiberal democracy": a one-party state, unchallenged by a suppressed opposition, with control of the media, and supported by a network of oligarchs who have grown prosperous on government contracts.

Like Marine le Pen in France, Orbán supports an interventionist economic style and the country embarked on a widespread public works program, raised the minimum wage, increased pensions, and set a price cap on utility bills. He also sings from the same hymn sheet as le Pen when it comes to the assessment of Russia. The country, together with Turkey, China, and Singapore is often referenced as a model democracy of strong and decisive leadership. It therefore comes as little surprise that Hungary was critical of EU sanctions against Russia and Orbán also vetoed financial support to Ukraine in its military struggle against Russian separatists. He rose to notoriety during the refugee crisis during the summer of 2015, when Hungary erected a barbed wire fence on its border with non-EU Serbia in order to stem the flow of Syrian refugees. His nationalist stance and disdain for migration and multiculturalism is best summed up by a speech given in 2018:

> We do not want to be diverse and do not want to be mixed. We do not want our own color, traditions and national culture to be mixed with those of others. . . . We do not want to be a diverse country.[11]

His domestic policies, which are aimed at supporting the elderly and struggling families, have made him very popular while a fragmented and disjointed opposition has so far failed miserably in mounting a credible challenge to his authority.

In Poland, the Law and Justice Party (*Prawo i Sprawiedliwość* in Polish or PiS) was founded in 2001 by the Kaczyński twins Jaroslaw and Lech. It first came to power between 2005 and 2007 with Lech serving as president and Jaroslaw as prime minister. The former as well as several members of PiS died in a plane crash in 2010. Eight years in opposition ended in 2015 when the party claimed the absolute majority in both the Lower House (51 percent of seats) as well as in the Senate (61 percent of seats). Lech rose to prime minister with his party colleague Andrzej Duda winning the presidency by a narrow majority of 51.5 percent of votes in the second round of that election contest.

The party's economic platform is modestly right of center with some minor cuts to taxes and welfare spending. Given the close geographic proximity and Poland's communist past, PiS is fiercely anti-Russian and a strong advocate of NATO and transatlantic relations. But it is with its strong social conservatism and ruthless attempts at curtailing opposition forces that the party started to make headlines. Since 2015, Poland became notorious for widespread human rights violations and an undermining of judicial independence.[12] In June 2017, emergency access to contraception was restricted, even in the case of rape. A month later, a law was passed, which gave the minister for justice full control over judicial appointments, a clear violation of the separation of powers between the executive and the judiciary. Furthermore, all sitting judges at the country's Supreme Court were subsequently removed and replaced by officials chosen by the government. After much international protest, Duda vetoed the law, but the justice ministry continues to appoint the presidents of lower courts and has the right to dismiss the president of any court—whether lower or supreme.

In September 2017, a new government body was created that began overseeing the distribution of public funds to nongovernmental organizations (NGOs). Subsequently, NGOs working on migration, asylum, and women's and LGBTQ rights reported difficulties in securing their former level of state support. In June 2018, the government passed another controversial law that made it a crime to ascribe any responsibility to Poland for Nazi-era atrocities committed on Polish soil. After much consternation from its EU partners over freedom of speech, the jail sentence for such an offence (a rather high maximum of three years) was removed, although the imposition of fines is still legal. In July 2018, another law reduced the retirement age of the Supreme Court judges, which meant that twenty-seven officials were immediately suspended. The government, however, was forced to back track, since the ECJ ordered Poland to suspend the application of the law.[13]

In Italy, M5S was founded in 2009 by comedian Beppe Grillo. The movement's origins reflect the wide-reaching economic and financial crises that have engulfed Italy for most of the twenty-first century. Grillo continues to be the president, although the so-called political head is Luigi Di Maio who assumed this post in 2017 at the tender age of thirty. Political success and a representation in national and regional legislatures came very soon. At the national elections in 2013, the movement received the highest share of votes for the lower house of any party (25.6 percent). It fared equally well in the Senate with 23.8 percent of votes. However, Grillo stayed in opposition and refused to join a coalition made up of established parties. The movement consolidated its electoral success with a 21.2 percent vote share in the European elections in 2014. Its rise to power came in the national elections of 2018. M5S increased its share of votes in the lower house (32.7 percent), as well as in the Senate (32.2 percent) and formed a coalition with the far-right *Lega* of Matteo Salvini under the ambitious title of "government of change." Led by Guiseppe Conti, a former law professor who is ideologically close to M5S, Di Maio assumed the role of deputy prime minister and minster for economics.

Locating the party on a left-right axis is difficult. The five stars in the movement's name stand for public water, sustainable transport, sustainable development, right to internet access, and environmentalism. The latter point raised many eyebrows among the political establishment as it called for "de-growth," the creation of green jobs with an emphasis on quality of life and social justice over the accumulation of wealth. An emphasis on direct democracy, basic income levels, the nationalization of some key industries, and a general anti-establishment aura ought to put M5S in the camp of left-wing populism. But the party also has a fierce, very much right-wing, anti-immigration rhetoric, calling for the expulsion of illegal immigrants and—most notoriously—criticizing NGOs that helped to rescue stranded migrants in the Mediterranean Sea, which was exemplified by Di Maio's outburst in March 2018 that the "sea-taxi service bringing migrants to Europe has to stop."[14] During the same year, the party also argued for Italy to leave the Eurozone, although once in power, Di Maio and his party colleagues very much softened their anti-EU rhetoric.

Italy has another populist strand: La *Lega* is the second largest party in a coalition government, which has been ruling the country since June 2018. Founded in 1991 by Umberto Bossi as a federation of regional, independence-minded parties in northern Italy, the party's full name is *Lega Nord per L'Indipendenza della Padani* (Northern League for the Independence of Padania), with the snappier rebranding of *la Lega* adopted just before the 2018 elections. In 2013, Bossi lost to the current incumbent leader Matteo Salvini who continues to keep faith in the party's roots by arguing for greater regional autonomy and fiscal federalism. Unlike Bossi, however, calls for the secession of the North have been muted under Salvini, who instead reached out to southern regions by forming a sister party ("Us with Salvini"), making *la Lega* not only the most popular party in the North but also garnering significant support across the whole of Italy. The change in direction paid off at the ballot box. In 2013, the party received only a fraction of votes in the national elections: 4.5 percent for the lower house, and 4.3 percent for the Senate. The European Parliament elections a year later were also disappointing with a vote share of 6.2 percent. But fortunes turned dramatically in 2018 when the party won 17.4 percent of votes in the lower house and 17.6 percent in the Senate, making *la Lega* the third biggest party in Italian Politics. A coalition with the M5S followed, with Salvini as deputy prime minister, as well as minister for the interior. At the regional level, *la Lega* now rules the northern regions of *Lombardi*, *Veneto*, *Trentino*, *Friuli-Venezia-Giulia*, as well as the central region of *Abruzzo*.

The party has embraced classic right-wing populism and thus is very much in the mold of other similar parties in Austria, in the Netherlands, and in Germany. Economically, it has called for tax deductions (most notably a flat tax rate of 15 percent) and cuts in government subsidies, while it maintains a socially conservative stance on issues such as same-sex marriage, family, or abortion. Frequent references to Italian nationalism also form part of this standard package. But it is crude actions, often accompanied by provocative rhetoric, which made Salvini notorious. He is ridiculed and lambasted by his opponents but very much cherished by his supporters. As interior minister, he closed Italian ports to NGO rescue ships and argued that the Italian coast guard and navy should ignore distress calls.[15] He also outsourced the coordination of rescue missions of migrants stranded in the Mediterranean Sea to the Libyan coast guard without questioning that country's organizational capacity or indeed its human rights record. Salvini was at loggerheads with Brussels over the processing of refugees and migrants,[16] which has been marked by a highly antagonistic discourse. Apart from being fiercely anti-immigrant, Salvini also caused jitters in the international money markets with threats of leaving the Eurozone and ignoring austerity measures as advocated by fellow member states and EU institutions to stabilize public finances. Here is a politician who revels in the chance to upset the Brussels status quo, although concrete reform actions designed to turn the Italian economic malaise around have been thin on the ground.

In Spain, a left-wing movement emerged amid the persistent economic and financial crisis in the aftermath of the collapse of Lehman Brothers. *Podemos* ("We Can") was founded in January 2014 out of a protest movement against inequality, financial mismanagement, and corruption, drawing inspiration from similar populists, such as Hugo Chavez in Venezuela or Evo Morales in Bolivia. The party had an almost instant electoral impact. At the elections to the European Parliament in May 2014, *Podemos* received a modest 8 percent of the votes, but at the national elections a year later, it emerged as the third strongest party with 21 percent; a result it repeated in the 2019 elections. It also has the second highest party membership in Spain after the Peoples Party. *Podemos* advocates a closer involvement of citizens in the democratic process through an increased use of referendums, most notably on constitutional reform. The party wants Spain's departure from NATO, but it is not isolationist, nor is it anti-European, although it voiced heavy criticism of some EU policies, in particular those that benefit large corporations and multinational businesses. Instead, and like le Pen, *Podemos* calls for a leftist reorganization of the economy, including nationalization, a basic income for everyone, a widespread reduction of poverty through government intervention, heavy fines for tax avoidance and the promotion of smaller businesses against the might of multinational corporations. Unlike le Pen, however, *Podemos* has a distinct environmental agenda, calling for a massive expansion of public transport and more use of renewable energies. As is common for a left-wing populist movement, references to nationalism, culture, and anti-immigration are largely absent from the party's rhetoric.

Spain also hosts a prominent movement on the right of the political spectrum: Vox was founded in 2013 as a splinter group from the conservative People's Party. Electoral success came in 2018, when the party entered the regional parliament in Andalusia as the fifth strongest force. At the national level, 2019 proved to be pivotal. In the first election of that year, which was held in April, Vox once again came fifth, gaining 10.3 percent of the votes. In the November election though, the vote share increased to 15.1 percent, making Vox the third most popular party. What worried the political establishment and many mainstream voters was the party's promise to repeal the 2007 "Law of Historical Memory," which had denounced General Franco's fascist regime and ordered the removal of many Franco-era symbols and statues. Other ideological tenets are the adherence to socially conservative principles, including an emphasis on family values, and the opposition to abortion, feminism, and same-sex marriage. Economically, the party is an advocate of free market principles, calling for less bureaucracy and more fiscal prudence, while referencing Donald Trump's slogan of "Making Spain Great Again." Just like its counterparts in many European countries, Vox had taken an anti-immigration stance, although it advocated what the party referred to as "good immigration" from Latin America to Spanish areas with a declining population. But these standard right-wing populist notions were only partial reasons for the rise to electoral prominence in recent years. It was the party's vocal defense of national unity and its call for re-centralization during a time when the separatist movement in Catalonia dominated much of the country's political discourse. Fearing a disintegration of Spain, Vox's promise to defend the country's political and territorial integrity was highly attractive to some voters.

In Britain, UKIP arguably had the biggest impact of any populist party on national politics. It was its appeal to conservative, old, and white voters on the right of center of the political spectrum, which contributed to Prime Minister David Cameron's decision to hold an in-out referendum on EU membership, as he feared that his electoral base was about to be compromised. Founded in 1993 by the historian Alan Sked, UKIP started to exert a wider impact on the electoral landscape of Britain when Nigel Farage became leader in 2006. At the national elections in 2010, the party only mustered 3.1 percent of votes, but electoral support rose to 12.6 percent in 2015. Because of the majoritarian nature of the British electoral system, the party only ever managed to get two candidates elected to the House of Commons, the UK's lower house of parliament. At the European level, the party fared much better, with its vote share rising steadily from 6.7 percent in 1999 to 16.1 percent in 2004, and to 16.6 percent in 2009. At the 2014 elections to the European Parliament, UKIP emerged as the strongest British party with a vote share of 27.5 percent.

The ideological base of the party is firmly on the right. Moving on from being a single-issue Euro-sceptic movement, Farage in particular expanded its policy range to advocate for classic liberalist, Thatcherite economic policies, complemented by a strong nationalistic agenda that opposes a so-called Islamification of Britain, migration, and any developments leading to the establishment of a multicultural society. UKIP also holds socially conservative values on such matters as LGBTQ rights, education, crime, and justice. With the Brexit referendum won and Nigel Farage stepping down as leader, the party lost much of its appeal. Since 2016, UKIP has adopted a much more extreme political agenda by turning from a typical populist party into a radical, far right, and fascist grouping. In the national elections of 2017, its voter support slumped to 1.8 percent and Farage left the party a year later. The party moved to the far-right under the leadership of Gerard Batten who controversially hired Tommy Robinson, the founder of the Neo Nazi English Defence League as an advisor. It is therefore safe to argue that UKIP is no longer an authentic, populist movement but is stretching its programmatic base to include anti-democratic, homophobic, and, thus, fascist strands. The party suffered a meltdown at the European elections of 2019 (when it only received 3.2 percent) and at the general elections in December of that year when its vote base collapsed to 0.2 percent.

UKIP's demise can largely be explained by the meteoric rise of the Brexit Party. Founded in January 2019, it was once again fronted by Nigel Farage who used his considerable charisma to charm voters into turning his party into the most popular political force (30.8 percent) at the European elections in May 2019. For many, Farage had become the face of Brexit, and widespread frustration over the UK government's inability to leave the EU allowed for rich and easy pickings at the ballot box. The spectacular success was even more astonishing given the party's refusal to publish a manifesto. Instead, Farage focused exclusively on the one issue that was at the forefront of its voters' mind. The Brexit Party was not only the name of a new political grouping, but it was also its sole programmatic base. At the general elections in December 2019, Farage decided to contest only those seats that the Conservative party had failed to secure in 2017. This paved the way for an electoral landslide for Boris Johnson[17] and only 2 percent of voters cast their ballot for the party. Its electoral future largely hinges on the progress—or lack thereof—of the Brexit negotiations. Once a departure from the EU is secured, it will seem rather pointless to cast a vote for Farage.

POPULISM AT EU LEVEL

In the run-up to the elections to the European Parliament in May 2019, many commentators anticipated a surge of the populist vote. As seen in table 1.2, the center-right European People's Party (EPP; which unified national Christian democratic parties) as well as the Socialists and Democrats (S&D; which was the umbrella organization for left-of-center social democratic parties) suffered substantial setbacks and lost their combined majority. EPP's number of seats was reduced by 39 (from 221 to 182). S&D also struggled and relinquished 38 seats (from 191 to 153), which confirmed the long-term trend

Table 1.2 Results of Elections to the European Parliament, 2019

Name of Party Grouping	*Political spectrum*	*Seat Numbers*	*Seats (%)*
EPP: European People's Party	Pro-EU Christian Democratic	182	24.2
S&D: Socialists & Democrats	Pro-EU Social Democratic	153	20.4
Renew Europe	Pro-EU Liberal Democratic	108	14.4
Greens/EFA: Greens & European Free Alliance	Pro-EU Green	75	10.0
ID: Identity and Democracy	EU-sceptic, right-wing populism	73	9.7
ECR: European Conservative and Reformists	EU-sceptic, conservative	63	8.4
EFDD: Europe of Freedom & Direct Democracy	Anti-EU, conservative	43	5.7
GUE/NGL: Confederal Group of United Left and Nordic Greens	EU-sceptic, hard left	41	5.5
Non-Attached members	n/a	7	0.9
Others	n/a	6	0.8
Total		751	100

of established mass parties facing difficulties in mobilizing their traditional voter bases. But other pro-EU parties made significant gains. The number of seats for Liberal democratic parties surged from 67 to 108. Green parties fared equally well, and their number of seats rose from fifty to seventy-five. By contrast, populist parties fared less well than predicted. The European Parliament of 2019 will host three Euro-sceptic and anti-EU groupings. The newly formed umbrella of "Europe of Nations and Freedom" integrates Salvini's *la Lega*, le Pen's *Rassemblement National*, and the *Alternative für Deutschland*. It became only the fifth biggest party bloc with seventy-three seats. The "European Conservative and Reformists Group," which is home to Poland's Law and Justice Party went from seventy to sixty-three seats. And "Europe for Freedom and Direct Democracy," which now provides a forum for Nigel Farage's newly founded Brexit Party, went from forty-eight to forty-three seats. Adding up all EU-sceptic and anti-EU seats results in a total of 179. This is a significant rise from the 118 seats that these party groupings received in 2014, but it still only represents 23.8 percent, and the large majority of members of the European Parliament belong to pro-EU parties.

The populist movement might also suffer from its fundamental inability to establish a firm common ground among different national parties, which is essential in influencing European politics through the EU parliament. The programmatic bases of populist parties can differ substantially from one another. For instance, one of the key electoral promises of *la Lega*'s Matteo Salvini was a fairer distribution of migrants and refugees across the whole of the EU. This, however, is strictly opposed by Poland's Law and Justice Party and by the Hungarian prime minister Victor Orbán. Poland's stance toward Russia is also much more antagonistic than those of the French *Rassemblement National*. It, therefore, came as little surprise that Poland's Justice and Democracy party and Hungary's *Fidesz* rejected Salvini's advances to join his EP umbrella group, with the latter preferring to be part of the EP largest bloc, the EPP. And the "Europe of Nations and Freedom" grouping is set for a rocky ride. The *Alternative für Deutschland* has frequently criticized Italy's finances arguing that Berlin should not pick up the tap for excessive public spending by Rome. Thus, while the anti-EU, anti-euro, and anti-globalism rhetoric can be found across much of the populist spectrum, it is ironic that the distinct national focus of those parties might undermine a coherent collaboration at European level.

But the political establishment in Brussels and Strasbourg has no reason for complacency. Table 1.3 lists populist parties across Europe and how they fared in the 2019 European elections. The results revealed that in six countries, populist parties are the most popular political force, in some cases such as Poland, the UK, or Hungary by a very substantial margin. As such, *la Lega* (34.3 percent), Law and Justice (45.4 percent), the Brexit Party (30.8

Table 1.3 Populist Parties in the EU: Share of Votes in Elections to European Parliament 2019

Country	Name of Party	Year and Share of Votes in Last National Election (%)		Share of Votes in EP Election 2019 (%)	National Ranking in EP Election 2019
Austria	Freedom Party	2019	17.2	17.2	3
Belgium	Vlaams Belang	2019	12.0	12.1	2
Bulgaria	Volya	2017	4.2	3.6	6
Czech Republic	Ano	2017	29.6	21.2	1
Denmark	Danish People's Party	2019	12.3	10.8	4
Estonia	Conservative People's Party	2019	17.8	12.7	4
Finland	Finns	2019	17.5	13.8	4
France	Rassemblement National**	2017	13.0	23.3	1
Germany	Alternative for Germany	2017	12.6	10.9	4
Greece	Golden Dawn	2015	7.0	4.9	5
Hungary	Fidesz	2018	44.9	52.6	1
Italy	Lega	2018	37.0	34.3	1
	Five Star Movement	2018	32.7	17.1	3
Latvia	National Alliance	2018	11.0	16.4	3
Lithuania	Order and Justice	2016	7.6	14.3	4
Netherlands	Party for Freedom	2017	13.1	3.5	10
	Forum for Democracy	2017	1.8	11.0	3
Poland	Law and Justice	2015	37.6	45.4	1
Slovakia	National Party	2016	8.6	4.1	8
Slovenia	Slovenian National Party	2018	4.2	4.0	8
Spain	Podemos	2019	12.8	10.1	4
	VOX	2019	10.3	6.2	5
Sweden	Sweden Democrats	2018	12.9	15.3	3
UK	Brexit Party	2019	2.0	30.8	1
	United Kingdom Independence Party	2019	Ax0.1	3.2	8

Elections refer to the lower house of parliament. *Front National* under the leadership of Marine le Pen renamed itself to *Rassemblement National* (National Rally) in June 2018.

percent), *Rassemblement National* (23.3 percent), and *Fidesz* (52.6 percent) are now major players on the EU scene. It is also noteworthy that in four of the six largest member states (France, Italy, Poland, and the UK), populist parties came out on top. Among those bigger countries, only in Germany and Spain did traditional parties manage to cling to the top spot. But it also became evident that the populist movement is far from surging across the political landscape. Out of the twenty-five listed parties, only ten managed to increase or maintain their share of votes when compared with the last national elections.

The new age of populism brought with it a much harsher discourse in the way member states and thus presumably partners are interacting with one another. In 2016, the Polish foreign ministry summoned the German ambassador to complain about "anti-Polish" rhetoric applied by some German politicians. Germany has also been accused by Orbán of "moral imperialism" in the wake of the country's generosity in accommodating Syrian refugees. And images of German chancellor Angela Merkel depicted in military uniform with a Hitler moustache were all too prominent in Greek newspapers during the country's bail out crisis. It seems that old, historic animosities, long forgotten during the successful postwar restoration of Europe were starting to find new leases of life at every turn. Beyond historical anti-German feelings, France and Italy—neighbors and two of the founding members of the EU—were also at loggerheads. In early 2019, Paris recalled its ambassador from Rome (the first time it did so since World War II) over the Italian governments support of the *gilets jaunes* (the yellow vests) protest movement against Emanuel Macron's government. Defying diplomatic conventions, Italy's Deputy Prime Minister Luigi Di Maio had met with a radical member of the movement who had previously asked for Macron's resignation and his replacement by a former army chief. When recalling his ambassador, Macron stated that "playtime is over" and that a "nationalist leprosy" was eating away at Europe.[18] This was an extraordinary diplomatic spat of controversial actions and strong unfettered language.

But despite some fierce anti-EU rhetoric, countries such as Poland or Hungary have benefited tremendously from EU funds. Ever since accession in 2004, Hungary—a small country with a population of ten million people—received a massive financial boost of forty billion euros from Brussels. The financial support for Poland—the biggest of the new member states with forty million people—is even more staggering. Since accession, the country received a total of 116 billion euros, which is twice the amount (in today's money) allocated to the Marshall Plan that brought US American aid to Europe after the end of World War II.[19] Without the EU's financial aid, the transformation from backward agrarian societies into economic and financial growth centers would not have been possible. It is therefore safe to assume that the country's political leaders will only push the EU so far, as a significant degree of financial prosperity is at stake.

Still, the populist march across Europe continues. With an ever-increasing number of right-wing populist parties in government in many member states, we might witness the end of consensual politics at EU level. In the European Commission—the EU's bureaucracy—the individual commissioners are appointed by national governments. Four of the twenty-seven commissioners (the representatives from Poland, Italy, Hungary, and the Czech Republic) have a populist background. It is safe to assume that the Commission's departments, which are run by those politicians, will be much less integrationist. The Commission is also the only EU institution that can propose legislation, which must be backed by a majority of commissioners (i.e., fourteen in an EU of twenty-seven member states). As such, the populist bloc might need the support of ten more countries to scupper EU legislation. In most cases, this should be a threshold, which is simply too high. But on occasion, during the drafting of controversial legislation, the populist agenda could certainly put a spanner in the works.

The Council of Ministers—the representative forum of the member states—is tasked with voting on the Commission's proposals (which it does so jointly with the European Parliament). For the vast majority of legislation (except for tax issues, foreign policy, and some justice and home affairs measures), the so-called system of qualified majority voting is applied, which states that at least 55 percent of member states, which, in turn, represent at least 65 percent of citizens, must approve an initiative. In an EU of twenty-seven member states, the populist four account for 14.8 percent of member states with just over a quarter of the EU's overall population. Again, this does not represent an outright blocking minority but could prove to be crucial when attempting to pass controversial legislation. As for the big decisions (including integrating new members, engaging in foreign policy activities, or signing new treaties), these require the unanimous support of the European Council, which brings together the twenty-seven heads of government. Here, a populist bloc of practically any size can severely damage any progress toward more European integration. As such, for many years to come, the populist voice will find much more reverberation in the corridors of Brussels.

POPULISM GONE WRONG

In the previous sections, the case was made for a populism that taps into legitimate sentiments. The liberal market capitalism of the past decades resulted in an ever-widening gap of wealth and income. The proverbial 1 percent seems to be raking in the benefits of an economic system that struggles to work for large sections of society. Traditional mass parties are finding it difficult to cater for all their membership caused by diverging value systems, which can no longer be accommodated under one programmatic umbrella. Many people feel a sense of disconnect where their voices are no longer heard, and their hopes and aspirations are ignored by a detached political process. And migration—whether through the EU's free movement of people, or through migrants coming from further shores—has brought vast and fast changes to many communities, with fiercer competition over low-paying jobs, housing, and public services, while also bringing with them new cultural norms and values that many people found difficult to accommodate. Such concerns are neither racist, nor are they anti-democratic, reactionary, or culturally illiterate.

But this authenticity does not mean that such sentiments can now claim to represent all of society. Consider my children, and with them many million people across Europe. They can choose among several passports and nationalities, and due to their parental roots and that of their grandparents are welcomed in three different houses of worship. Naturally, their horizon—whether it taps into notions of national identity, social norms, or cultural practices—differs from someone whose upbringing has been more homogenous. But it was not their choice. It simply happened. Yet, people of a more diverse background are precisely the people that former UK prime minister Theresa May had in mind when she tried to galvanize her traditional voters by what turned out to sound like a highly ignorant reference to the "citizens of nowhere." Of course, my daughters and others are from somewhere and like many people, their parents and grandparents ended up moving abroad for a variety of reasons, whether professional or romantic, or because they simply liked the place. Or compare the transformation, which cities like Berlin, London, Amsterdam, Dublin, or Paris have undergone during the past generation: a multicultural, multiethnic mix that wasn't planned or even advocated by politicians. It just happened, fostered by technology, the EU's Single Market and globalization, which made the switch from one country to another an easy and feasible prospect. And with these forces also came an appreciation of—and in some cases strong emotional attachment to—diversity. Such sentiments are, of course, also authentic and legitimate.

Populism therefore reaches the limits of acceptability once it claims to be the sole representative of a nation's political agenda. It is one thing to argue for national traditions and customs to be preserved. It is another to argue for the suffocation of other, divergent views of life. Naturally, the distinction between the two is a fluid one and is often hard to establish. Where do you draw the line in a small town, for instance, which has seen an influx of Muslims into a community that previously was exclusively Christian? When and how can diversity be respected, without compromising national customs and traditions? Yet most people are not aversive to change. We all have to adapt to, and keep up with new developments, may they be technological, economic, social, and yes, also cultural. It is what humans do. It is not change as such that people are frightened of. It is the scale and speed of change, which might be overwhelming for some. This, the political process must recognize. But it is also clear that the historical clock cannot be turned back, by romanticizing a presumably glorious past. Life is evolving constantly and at some stage that Muslim community needs to be given permission to build its mosque.

Populism also tends to provide simple answers to rather complex questions. Some citizens have neither the time nor the inclination to follow political deliberations in detail. It, therefore, is the responsibility of politicians and the media to add transparency to the political process and to provide as much background information as feasible. Of course, this is rarely the case, and misinformation on the scale that we have witnessed during the Brexit referendum (with both pro and anti-EU camps being culpable), as well as the scaremongering over migrants and refugees and the presumed threat to a country's national identity, is not conducive to the political process, to decision making, and above all to democracy. The use of derogatory, debasing language, the appeal to a heightened sense of anxiety, panders to irrational human instincts and a simplistic view of the world. It might also unleash darker political forces of political extremism and violence. Once again, populism is not intrinsically racist, but racists are attracted by a populist rhetoric.

We have seen that populism places a great emphasis on more democracy, on giving more power to the people. But as the examples of Hungary and Poland have shown, it can also metamorphose into a call for action for domestic oppression of opposition parties and the media, in a nationalistic, occasionally racist fight against multicultural, "anti-Christian" and outward-looking values, while simultaneously developing a capitalist autocracy based on oligarch networks, massive corruption, and the implosion of the rule of law. Such actions go against the populist grain of giving power to the people, but instead intend to concentrate that power in the hands of a ruling oligarchy. Power then simply shifts from one set of actors (multinational corporations, the liberal media, and established political elites) to another one. This is no longer populism but instead the onslaught of fascism.

COMBATING ANTI-DEMOCRATIC BEHAVIOR

The key to any action that the EU might want to take against a rogue member state is Article 7 of the Treaty of Nice (2000). It refers to a clear risk of a serious breach of the EU's values, including human dignity, freedom, democracy, equality, rule of law, or human rights. Once such a breach becomes apparent, the EU can agree on a so-called preventive action procedure, which can be initiated either by the European Parliament or by the European Council (the representative body of the member state governments). For the former, at least two-thirds of members of the European Parliament (MEPs) present at the vote can trigger this process. In the case of the Council, 80 percent of member states must agree. Once these majorities are established, it is then down to the Council to come up with recommendations for specific actions.

Article 7 also refers to a "sanctions procedure," which can only be called upon by the Council in a unanimous fashion, although the member states can take on board advice from the Commission. Just as is the case in the preventive action procedure, at least two-thirds of MEPs voting in the European Parliament must give their consent. Once agreement on the "sanctions procedure" has been reached, specific measures then require the approval of at least 72 percent of member states on a specific course of action (the further approval of the EP is not required), which could include the suspension of membership rights, such as voting. But the Nice Treaty is rather vague about the suspension of any other rights, and judicial clarification from the ECJ is desperately required. In any case, the EU has no provision for the expulsion of member states. Although the inclusion of such a provision was discussed in the run-up to the Lisbon Treaty of 2007, it failed to make the final version. As demonstrated by Brexit, getting out of the EU is not straightforward and requires a series of amendments to the existing treaty structure, which—as is common for treaties and treaty changes—requires unanimity. Hence, if a member states does not want to leave, there is little that the other member states can do.

Hungary and Poland are acutely aware of the limitations of the EU in trying to make a rogue member come to heel who has careered off the democratic path. In 2018, Orbán ran a publicly funded poster campaign, brandishing George Soros, the Hungarian born, Wall Street-based financier who had advocated a more humane treatment of refugees. The poster campaign, the threatened closure, and subsequent relocation of the Central European University (largely funded by Soros) to Vienna, and an aggressive anti-Soros rhetoric, which portrayed the billionaire as the embodiment of evil global capitalism inflamed anti-Semitism. After Soros came an equally vitriolic poster campaign against Commission President Jean-Claude Juncker, which accused him (and implicitly all EU institutions) of pro-migration policies that undermine the national integrity and cultural homogeneity of Hungary.

By September 2018, the European Parliament had seen enough. For the first and so far, only time, the EP triggered Article 7, citing a clear risk of a serious breach of EU values, citing threats to the freedom of expression, to academic freedom, and to judicial independence, while also referring to a rigged electoral system and the maltreatment of minorities, asylum seekers, and refugees. The EP's pro-active stance against Hungary lost much of its impetus in the subsequent months. The Romanian Presidency of the EU in the first half of 2019 failed to place Hungary's alleged democratic violations on the agenda of the European Council, which in any case was preoccupied by ongoing Brexit discussions. As of 2019, there has been no concrete response to the EP's initiative, and it is safe to assume that national governments are wary of the European Parliament taking control of a process, which could ultimately lead to sanctions against member states. This would radically shift the balance between a supranational entity like the EP and the national governments as embodied by the European Council. It is once again the ECJ to which EU actors are turning in a much-needed clarification on the next steps in addressing the Hungarian case.

Undermining the power of the judiciary, the strengthening of the executive, the takeover of the state media by government officials, corrupt and crony capitalism, and the suppression of civil society, all aimed at establishing a nationalistic, ethno-centric community that defies multiculturalism, diversity, and immigration (in particular from non-European countries) while proudly and shamelessly adopting a Christian, yet often xenophobic rhetoric are not only hallmarks of Hungary and Orbán's regime. Although lacking *Fidesz*'s supermajority, all these elements can also be found in Poland. As these examples demonstrate, there was clearly enough evidence for the European Commission to trigger Article 7, which it duly did in December 2017 by stating a clear breach of the separation of powers between the judiciary and the executive, while also proposing to reduce the amount of money that Poland would receive during the EU's next financial perspective running from 2021 to 2027. However, a sanctions procedure failed to materialize since—not surprisingly—Hungarian prime minister Victor Orbán vetoed the motion.

THE DILEMMA

The rise of populists such as Orbán, Salvini, or le Pen is often attributed to short-term factors such as the refugee crisis, which peaked in 2015, terrorist attacks by Islamist fundamentals, or the Great Recession in the aftermath of the collapse of Lehman. But populism might be here to stay as none of its underlying causes—multicultural change caused my migration, growing inequality, detached elites, and a party landscape that does not cater for all voices—are set to disappear or even soften their impact on countries any time soon. The undercurrents, which are shaping politics are long term: a political process that disregards many voices; a growing wealth gap and unfair income distribution where more and more people feel that liberal market democracy no longer works for them; the rise of multinational corporations, which have brushed aside smaller, local businesses; industrial relations that seem unable to reign in a business-friendly gig economy, which, in return, undermines social standards; the threat to traditional values and cultural homogeneity prompted by the powerful forces of globalization; these are not short-term trends that will disappear soon. They are long-term developments, which have not been addressed in a coherent fashion—whether at EU or at national level. It allowed populist movements to attract a large, but also diverse following: from the blatant racist intent on purifying the nation to the morally decent, yet social conservative who worries about her or his job. Populism filled the empty programmatic spaces left behind by traditional mass parties.

And even if the appeal of populist parties at the ballot box might start to wane, we have already seen many traditional parties that have absorbed the rhetoric and the political agenda of populism. Brexit is a perfect example. UKIP has become electorally irrelevant, but its key issue—that of leaving the EU—has been dominating the national political discourse for many years, which is exemplified by the astonishing performance of Nigel Farage's newly founded Brexit Party at the European elections in May 2019. We have also witnessed politicians—from chancellor Kurz in Austria to Prime Minister Rutte in the Netherlands and to Horst Seehofer (the chairman of the Christian Social Union, Angela Merkel's Bavarian sister party and coalition partner) who have adopted a more right-wing tone to respond directly to voters' concerns about migration and cultural change. In Britain, the post-referendum period saw a marked sharpening of the political rhetoric with rabble rousers like hard Brexiters Mark Francois or Jacob Rees Mogg fanning English nationalism to pander to their largely anti-EU constituency.[20] Populism has already gone mainstream.

Euro-sceptic voices argue that Brussels forms an integral part of a political and economic consensus, which has gone wrong, maintaining that the EU is one of the chief culprits of a system, which works for a privileged few with distant unelected bureaucrats being able to affect people's lives at will. Such an interpretation, however, only offers a limited perspective. The EU has been much criticized for a so-called democratic deficit. The Commission is run by appointed but not by elected officials. The European Council and the Council of Ministers offer a forum for national governments without much supervision from the European or national parliaments. And the legitimacy of the European Parliament as the only directly elected EU institution is undermined by a low voter turn outs (and thus a citizens' lack of interest in EU affairs) and the inability to propose and initiate legislation. While this is all true, one also must acknowledge the persistent rise in the powers of the EP. It now discharges the budget and jointly passes legislation with the Council of Ministers on practically all initiatives. Granted, the powers of the EP still do not match those of a democratic national parliament—most notably the lack of coherent powers on the foreign policy stage—but progress in this regard is steady and substantial. There is also now the so-called citizens' initiative, which requires the Commission to put forward legislative proposals based on a petition by at least one million people, which is a significant boost for direct, participatory citizenship. Democracy at EU level is not perfect, it might not even reach the standards of national democracies, but it is certainly much more advanced than those of other international organizations such as the UN or the OECD, and furthermore has been on an upward trajectory ever since the European Single Act of 1986.

The EU—despite early federalist attempts—is also not a super state, and looking at the political landscape across Europe, it is extremely unlikely that a federalist union will emerge at all. What the EU does is to offer a vehicle for interaction on a regulated and regular basis. The EU does not aspire to be a country. It does not have a coherent *demos*—a populace that interacts with political leaders at the European level. But the EU makes life easier when traveling, marrying an EU national, investing across borders, taking up a new job in another country, or buying foreign goods. The EU is therefore a gigantic regulation machine, which allows for a more streamlined interaction between governments, citizens, consumers, or businesses. It is not an entity, which inspires emotional attachments, loyalty, and support, and thus will never replace the role of the nation-state. The EU is also to a certain extent the product of national politics. National governments shape the Commission by appointing candidates to head the organization's individual departments. They have their representative institutions in the shape of the European Council and the Council of Ministers. And national political parties propose candidates for the European Parliament. Hence, a national discourse—whether populist or otherwise—can always feed into the EU's political agenda. Blaming the EU for all society's ills, as a lot of Brexit supporters did, is therefore misconstrued. It is often national politics that feeds the European beast and not the other way around.

Europe has been struggling under a so-called demographic deficit for a long time.[21] Countries including Poland or Germany will see their population dwindle over the next generation, which will severely threaten to undermine economic prosperity. Consequently, native populations will increasingly become aware that the size of their own ethnic group will shrink in relation to incoming migrants. Politics therefore faces a fickle challenge: to convince voters of the economic necessity of migration, while simultaneously responding to concerns over a cultural alienation. Out of this conundrum, populists will continue to gain political strength.

The party-political system will continue to be torn at the seams. Traditional mass parties will struggle to build winning coalitions, given the ever-diverging values and norms of their original voter bases. Party loyalty is on the wane with floating voters moving from one-party platform to another. The controversies and diametrically opposed opinions on EU integration, on multiculturalism, and on migration will further expose these schisms. Hence, an ever-growing number of voters are looking for a new political home. In the absence of a true political alternative, some might have temporarily withdrawn into political apathy. A charismatic leader, triggering the right emotive sensors, however, can easily take advantage of such dormant political capital. Established parties have been very slow to respond to these changes and might face the potentially unachievable challenge of returning to a broad electoral church, which galvanizes diverging value systems into voting coalitions. It therefore remains a distinct possibility that the political landscape continues to fracture. Should this be the case, populist movements will become a staple of politics. They have not forced that change; there are consequences of it.

A simple recipe on how to confine populism to a historical footnote is impossible to identify. Yet, if governments could manage to offer their citizens a broader stake in society, then the ground on which populism has thrived over the past years might begin to shift. The UK in the run-up to the EU referendum serves as an illustrating example. To a considerable extent, the Brexit vote was fueled by concerns about migration and the threat to established norms and practices. But it was also caused by economic austerity, by a political system that is utterly London-centric with limited representation of the periphery. Having a parliament where 45 percent of members of the ruling conservative party and 29 percent of all parliamentarians are now privately educated[22] also does not bode well for a representative democracy, nor does an unelected House of Lords. The vote to leave the EU was also a vote against the status quo of the country.

Populism will not go away, but its impact can be greatly diminished once an economic model and industrial relations are put in place that work for businesses, as well as for employees. Improving political representation and offering channels for a participatory political culture will give citizens a sense of their voices being heard once more. Greater social mobility might soften many citizens' impression of a disconnected elite that is out of reach. And once steps in those directions have been taken, the notion that a national culture and identity might be under threat by migration could soon lose much of its momentum. Populism thrives on fear, anxiety, insecurity, and a perceived loss of control. Addressing those concerns could soon deprive the movement of its oxygen. Failure to do so, however, will only heighten the populists' impact. The dilemma for European integration is that Brussels formed an integral part of the political and economic consensus of the past generation, which has fostered the creation of a dangerous animal that threatens to undermine its very existence. But the consensus is no more and if politics and economics remain unchanged, national governments and the EU will not be able to soften the animal's ever-louder roar.

NOTES

1. The coalition came to a spectacular end with the Ibiza affair of May 2019. In a video filmed with a hidden camera, Strache was seen in very casual dress, lounging on a sofa while consuming copious amounts of an Austrian energy drink mixed with

vodka and talking to a hoax niece of a Russian oligarch. During lengthy discussions, Strache was willing to offer influential positions at key Austrian media outlets and companies in return for cash. Upon the release of the footage, Strache was forced to resign, which also brought down the government of Chancellor Sebastian Kurz when the Austrian parliament passed a vote of no confidence.

2. Net migration is the difference between the number of people leaving, and the number of people entering a country. A more in-depth discussion on migration across the EU is offered in chapter 4.

3. The seven-year moratorium was also applied to the late EU entrants of Romania and Bulgaria (2007). On this occasion, the UK, Ireland, and Sweden joined their fellow EU partners in applying the restriction. Bulgarians and Romanians thus had to wait until 2014 before they could seek employment in other EU member states.

4. More information on the drama of the Greek bailout is provided in chapter 2.

5. The Greens rose to national power in the elections of 1998, when a coalition with the Social Democrats replaced Chancellor Helmut Kohl. The prominent Green politician Joschka Fischer remained as the government's foreign minister until 2005.

6. See: www.europarl.europa.eu/at-your-service/files/be-heard/eurobarometer/2018/parlemeter-2018/report/en-parlemeter-2018.pdf.

7. Roger Eatwell and Matthew Goodwin. *National Populism. The Revolt against Liberal Democracy* (London: Pelican Books, 2018), pp. 25–8.

The authors convincingly explain the rise of populism according to the four "Ds" of *distrust* (in the political system and the governing elites), *destruction* (of cultural norms and traditions brought about by migration), *deprivation* (i.e., a material insecurity and growing inequality caused by liberal market capitalism) as well as *de-alignment* (i.e., the demise of traditional mass parties that struggle to establish winning voter coalitions among an increasingly diverse electoral base).

8. See: Roger Eatwell and Matthew Goodwin. *National Populism. The Revolt Against Liberal Democracy* (Pelican Book, 2018), p. 69.

9. In 2014, the AfD entered the regional parliament of Thuringia in eastern Germany with a vote share of 10.6 percent. In the same year, the eastern state of Brandenburg also voted in similar numbers for the new party (12.2 percent). In 2016, entry into the regional parliament of two further eastern regions was achieved, namely in *Mecklenburg-Vorpommern* (20.85) and most notably in Saxony Anhalt (24.25). But support for the AfD is certainly not confined to the eastern states, as the 2016 result for the state elections in *Baden-Württemberg* (15.1 percent) and Rhineland-Palatinate (12.6 percent) have shown.

10. See: www.wsj.com/articles/marine-le-pens-pro-russia-far-right-politics-1401128335.

11. See: http://www.miniszterelnok.hu/prime-minister-viktor-orbans-speech-at-the-annual-general-meeting-of-the-association-of-cities-with-county-rights/.

12. For more information, please go to hrw.org/world-report/2019/country-chapters/Poland.

13. See: http://europa.eu/rapid/press-release_STATEMENT-19-3376_en.htm.

14. See: www.theguardian.com/world/2018/mar/05/five-star-leader-open-to-coalition-talks-despite-founders-warning.

15. See: www.maritime-executive.com/article/salvini-italian-coast-guard-should-ignore-migrants-distress-calls.

16. The refugee crisis in Italy is discussed in greater detail in chapter 4.

17. See chapter 4.

18. See: The Guardian, February 9, 2019, p. 27.

19. See: https://www.theguardian.com/commentisfree/2014/may/01/eu-poland-10-years-economic.

In 2017, the EU budget allocated twelve billion euros to Poland while the country's financial contribution only amounted to three billion euros; a net spent of nine billion euros, which represents 2 percent of Poland's gross national income.

See: https://europa.eu/european-union/about-eu/countries/member-countries/poland_en#budgets-and-funding.

In the same year, Hungary collected 4 billion euros of EU money. Based on a budget contribution of 0.8 billion euros, the net income from Brussels equates 2.7 percent of the country's gross national income.

See: https://europa.eu/european-union/about-eu/countries/member-countries/hungary#budgets-and-funding.

20. Mark Francois caused outrage in the aftermath of a letter written by the (German) chairman of Airbus, which stated that the company's operation will be greatly compromised by Brexit. Francois responded by stating: "My father, Reginald Francois, was a D-Day veteran. He never submitted to bullying by any German. Neither will his son." See: www.independent.co.uk/voices/brexit-mark-francois-history-jacob-rees-mogg-suez-second-world-war-a8758806.html.

21. For more information on the demographic deficit, please refer to chapter 2.

22. See: Parliamentary Privilege—the MPs 2017. Sutton Trust, June 10, 2017. www.suttontrust.com/research-paper/parliamentary-privilege-the-mps-2017-education-background/.

Chapter 2

Economic and Monetary Union

A mere ten years after its introduction in 1999, Economic and Monetary Union (EMU) was rattled to its core by the large public deficits and faltering economies of many of its members. The severity of the economic downturns prompted some commentators to predict the end of EMU and indeed of the entire European integration project, arguing that the union could no longer sustain the strains imposed by the working mechanisms of the single currency. While the EU might be able to avert such a doomsday scenario, it is without doubt that a policy, which was trumpeted as a bold achievement, went spectacularly wrong and caused hitherto inconceivable hardship to millions of European citizens.

Why did the union embark on such a perilous journey? There is a widely held belief that the single currency was a cunning German invention, which provided a formidable boost to the country's buoyant export sector. But EMU was predominantly a French initiative, which at the outset was rejected by Germany's financial institutions and by successive finance ministers.[1] Ever since 1979, trade and capital exchanges across borders were organized by the so-called European Monetary System (EMS), which required states to keep the value of their national currencies within a narrow band of 4.5 percent in relation to other participating currencies. The system was complemented by a reference currency, the European Currency Unit (ECU): a basket of all European currencies, which could be used for financial transactions across national borders. A currency hitting the floor (or the ceiling) of the band necessitated the intervention of central banks. But the system had one essential flaw. The powerful West German economy with its strong, export-driven manufacturing sector often prompted the value of the Deutschmark to hover along the top of the band, while economically less vibrant countries, such as France and Italy found themselves at the bottom end. On occasion, this necessitated a rearranging of the band with some currencies (e.g., the French Franc and the Italian Lira) being devalued. France's President François Mitterrand (1981 to 1995) did not like being at the mercy of Germany's mighty central bank the Bundesbank, and in 1983 toyed with the idea of leaving the EMS altogether. His cabinet convinced him otherwise and Mitterand instead changed tactics and managed to place his Finance Minister Jacques Delors in Brussels, as the president of the European Commission. Delors was instrumental in the ratification of the finer details of the Single European Act of 1986, which proposed EMU at some stage in the EU's future. The moment to cash in on this price came in 1989 with the fall of the Berlin Wall. Germany was not yet a sovereign country and needed the approval of the Soviet Union, the UK, the United States and France to embark on unification. Mitterand, however, insisted that his approval was conditional on Germany agreeing in return on a start date for EMU negotiations. The financial establishment in Germany—from the president of the Bundesbank Karl-Otto Poehl to a succession of finance ministers including Gerhard Stoltenberg and Theo Waigel—had for a long time resisted any moves toward monetary integration, which was unsurprising given that the EMS had served the country so well. But chancellor Kohl sensed that the small window of opportunity—the toppling of an unpopular regime in East Germany without much interference by the Soviet Union's leader Mikhail Gorbachev—could also just as easily close again with the appointment of a hard-line apparatchik in the Kremlin. Kohl convinced his cabinet that agreeing to EMU was a small price to pay for German unification, and ten years later, on January 4, 1999, bank accounts were switched over from national currencies to the Euro.

One of the key ingredients of EMU is that national central banks no longer possess the ability to set their own interest rates. This is now done by the European Central Bank (ECB), which sets one rate for all Eurozone countries. Quantitative easing[2] and thus the ability to inject cash into the economy now also falls under the exclusive domain of the ECB. The ability of member states to fine tune their economy is therefore greatly reduced, leaving the setting of wages and taxes as the only viable alternatives. From the outset, EMU was therefore criticized for establishing a monetary union (one currency, one ECB, and one interest rate) without having one economic government, since all member states of the Eurozone were still responsible for their own fiscal affairs. A further point of criticism was the absence of a so-called optimum currency area (OCA), with productivity and inflation levels of southern European countries, such as Italy, Spain, and Greece, very much different from their northern neighbors in the Netherlands or in Germany. The Maastricht Treaty of 1992 therefore included the so-called Stability Pact, which required participating Euro countries (Denmark, the UK, and at a later stage Sweden decided to maintain their national currencies) to keep their economic parameters in line with that of their partners. As such, inflation targets were set,[3] as were spending limits with two vital benchmarks: A country's annual deficit ought to be restricted to 3 percent of that country's GDP, while overall debt levels must not exceed 60 percent of GDP. Alas, Germany and France in particular merely regarded these treaty requirements as guidelines and continued to violate the Stability Pact on a frequent basis; in the case of Germany as late as 2009. This, at first, proved to be of little consequence given the buoyant economic upturn during the first years of the millennium. However, when matters turned sour in the aftermath of Lehman in 2008, the Commission shied away from imposing legally possible fines on these two anchors of the Eurozone, fearing a punishing response from the international money markets, that such actions would undoubtedly have prompted. The Stability Pact designed to keep Eurozone members on a tight leash was instead fundamentally eroded. It greatly nourished the argument that EMU was primarily a political project, which overrode financial and monetary concerns.

THE ECONOMIC DOWNTURN IN THE EUROZONE

The sovereign debt crisis that shook the Eurozone affected in particular the so-called *PIGS*—Portugal, Ireland, Greece, and Spain. The acronym became obsolete when Italy and Cyprus also suffered a massive contraction to their economies. By the end of 2011, the economic and financial situation in these countries indeed revealed a grim picture (see table 2.1). Greece's public debt was a staggeringly high 165.3 percent of GDP; nearly three times as high as the Stability Pact's ceiling of 60 percent, and all affected countries had annual account deficits that violated the Pact's 3 percent of GDP rule.[4] Turning to GDP growth, the figures were equally sobering. Greece's economy had

Table 2.1 Economic Downturn in the EU: Selected Member States

Country	*Debt 2011 (% of GDP)*	*Account Deficit 2011 (% of GDP)*	*Growth Q1 2012 (% of GDP) **	*Unemployment March 2012*
Greece	165.3	9.1	−6.2	21.7
Portugal	107.8	4.2	−2.2	15.3
Ireland	108.2	13.1	1.0**	14.5
Spain	68.5	8.5	−0.4	24.1
Italy	120.1	3.9	−1.3	9.8
EU 27	82.5	4.5	0.1	10.2

* Figures in comparison with the first quarter of 2011.
** Figures for fourth quarter of 2011.
Source: Eurostat.

contracted by 6.2 percent, having shrunk by 7.4 percent in the previous year. As to unemployment, the governments in Spain and Greece in particular had to confront the prospect of intensified social unrest, since a quarter of their populations (and up to half of their youth population) was out of work. These dramatic circumstances were exacerbated by international financial markets that were reluctant to lend money to these countries and only did so by charging punishing interest rates. While the governments of Germany and the UK had to pay a relatively modest 2 percent in order to finance their debts, the figures for Greece (31.0 percent) heavily undermined any chances of a coherent economic recovery.[5] The money markets' lack of confidence, however, affected the whole of the Eurozone. By May 2012, the credit rating agency Standard & Poors granted its triple A status to only four states: Finland, Germany, Luxembourg, and the Netherlands. Just a couple of years previously, this accolade had been granted to all members of the single currency.

GREECE: THE NEW SICK MAN OF EUROPE

The appellation of Europe's sick man had originally been given to the UK in the 1970s. Some forty years later, Greece proved to be a worthy successor to this title. Prior to the introduction of the euro, the country had become accustomed to high inflation (e.g., 11 percent in 1994) with a currency—the drachma—to which international investors hardly flocked. With the late introduction of the Euro in 2001, two years after the currency was originally launched, interest rates fell to below 2 percent, and Greeks for the first time had the benefit of a stable and solid currency. Unfortunately, the country used this newfound stability to fund wage growth rather than pay off existing debt. Salaries in the public sector skyrocketed and nearly doubled within ten years. During the same time, 75,000 additional civil service jobs were created, while pensions in the public sector rose to an incredibly generous 92 percent of preretirement salary rates. This spending spree could only be described as madness with an irresponsible political class using financial hand-outs to win over the electorate. These generous gifts stood in marked contrast to the performance of the Greek economy. The country was notorious for its rather reluctant taxpayers and successive governments lost about thirty billion euros each year because of uncollected tax receipts. Although the country had the second longest working hours among OECD countries (with 2,120 hours per year only trailing to South Korea), productivity was well below European standards. On top of this, Greeks enjoyed very early retirement levels, since it released its work force at an average age of 61.4 years.

Clearly, Greece had an unsustainable economic model. The country simply spent more than it earned, resulting in steadily growing public debt levels, which by 2009 had hit 127 percent; more than double the benchmarks of the Stability Pact. Add blatant corruption to the mix, for instance, in the assignment of lucrative EU funded projects, and the spiraling debt caused by staging the Athens Olympics in 2004, it became evident that Greece was heading for a disaster. It was down to the newly elected socialist government of George Papandreou to confront Greeks with the shocking yet unavoidable truth: only the combination of radical spending cuts and tax rises could save the country from financial collapse. In December 2009, two months after assuming office, Papandreou admitted that previous Greek governments had "cooked the books" and had presented falsified figures in order to gain entry into the Eurozone in the first place and to avoid potential fines from the EU in the subsequent years of Euro membership. It came as little surprise that Papandreou's disclosure was met with disbelief—both in Europe and in Greece itself, and his imposed tax rises and spending cuts resulted in widespread social unrest, often violent demonstrations and general strikes.

In March 2010, with the international financial markets becoming ever more concerned about the growing possibility that the country might not be able to meet its financial commitments, Papandreou announced an austerity package. Being a member of the Eurozone, his move started to have a severe effect on the reputation of the single currency. The pivotal figure was German chancellor Angela Merkel, who wanted to delay an EU response until the time after regional elections were held in the German state of North Rhine Westphalia. Merkel and other European leaders rightly calculated that any rescue package for Greece was hugely unpopular among their citizens, who with some justification claimed that they should not foot the bill for excessive Greek spending. International markets continued to be jittery and in April 2010—and just a week before the elections (which her party incidentally lost)—Merkel, under pressure from French president Nicolas Sarkozy, agreed to a thirty-billion-euro rescue package, accompanied by widespread tax increases and spending cuts.[6]

By spring 2011, Papandreou had failed to reduce the rapidly accumulating public debt. In a desperate attempt to reschedule some of its debt, Greece issued a two-year bond, which traded at an astonishing rate of 23.6 percent. But the government could do little about another design flaw of EMU. Membership of the Eurozone automatically eliminated the option to devaluate a country's currency. Hence, Greece did not have a short cut for dealing with its debt, or a path to regain, at least temporarily, competitiveness by offering its goods cheaper on the international markets. A devastating conclusion was starting to emerge: given the economic parameters that the country was finding itself in, where could growth (and consequently an economic recovery) come from?

Table 2.2 Timeline of the Debt Crisis in Greece

October 2009	Prime Minister Papandreou reveals extend of crisis. Budget deficit is 15.4 percent of GDP public debt is 126.8 percent of GDP
May 2010	EU and IMF organize rescue package of 30 billion euros in return for tax rises and spending cuts
July 2011	Bailout package increased from 30 to 109 billion euros
November 2011	Papandreou resigns Unelected caretaker government under Lucas Papademos
February 2012	Private creditors write off 100 billion euros 48 billion euros recapitalization package Second bailout package of 130 billion euros
June 2012	Centrist coalition government under Antonis Samaras
January 2015	Alexis Tsipras elected as new prime minister
July 2015	Referendum rejects bailout conditions Third bailout package of 86 billion euros
July 2017	Return to money markets selling five-year bonds
April 2018	Budget surplus 4.2 percent of GDP (excluding interest on debt)
June 2018	EU extends maturities on 100 billion euros by ten years Greece promises to keep budget surplus of 3.5 percent of GDP until 2022, then 2.2 percent of GDP until 2060
August 2018	Greece exists from bailout program

The EU responded to the deteriorating situation by making even more funds available. In July 2011, the initial 30-billion-euro rescue was enlarged to a staggering 109 billion euros (see table 2.2). Apart from this cash injection, private banks were asked to write off 21 percent of the credit they had given to Greece. A longer time frame and lower interest rates to pay off debt had already been agreed in March 2011. This deal, at least in the short run, prevented the country from defaulting on its 350 billion euros debt burden. On the other hand, analysts quickly pointed to a number of shortcomings. The so-called "hair cut" of 21 percent by private banks was only on a voluntary basis. While 90 percent of creditors signed up to the deal (including Deutsche Bank, HSBC, BNP Paribas, Allianz, and Axa) others, including Unicredit, Credit Agricole, and the Royal Bank of Scotland, did not. There was also uncertainty over hedge funds and their willingness to write off such substantial debts. In any case, the package did not address the underlying malaise of the Greek economy. The fundamental question remained: How could the country raise productivity levels and gain competitiveness?

The July agreement therefore only provided the EU with some momentary breathing space, and it was not long before another emergency summit had to be called to appease financial markets, which continued to charge unsustainably high interest rates on Greece's government bonds. In October 2011, EU leaders agreed on yet another Euro rescue, which consisted of a voluntary write down of 50 percent of the country's debt. In an attempt to add a popular mandate to his negotiations with the EU, Papandreou announced a referendum on the conditions of the bailout; a move, which was met with fury by Merkel and Sarkozy who threatened to stall the next tranche of rescue money.[7] In the end, and amid growing political unrest, the beleaguered prime minister resigned and a caretaker government of technocrats under Lukas Papademos (a former vice president of the ECB) was put in place in November 2011.

But despite the unprecedented financial support, there was no sign of Greece turning the corner. By the beginning of 2012, the country found itself in its fifth successive year of recession. It became ever more apparent that Greece needed yet another rescue and EU leaders agreed in February 2012 to the second bail out—this time even higher with 130 billion euros.[8] It was not until June, that a democratically elected government was put in place once more. The established political forces under new prime minister Antonis Samaras from the centrist New Democracy Party formed a coalition with the social-democratic PASOK party. But by June 2015, the widespread public resentment and outright despair over the severe austerity measures of the bailout packages brought to power the populist left-wing party *Syriza* under Alexis Tsipras.

In the meantime, a series of further rescue measures kept the country afloat. The numbers were staggering, turning Greece into the country that received the highest financial assistance in history. Throughout the crisis, a total of 300 billion euros was committed by international organizations, out of which 260 billion euros was taken up by successive Greek governments. It is worth noting, however, that most of the money was instantly handed back to creditors in the form of debt repayments and thus did not materialize as a liquidity injection into the Greek economy. The often-reckless lending by northern European banks, which poured speculative cash into Greece, was therefore left largely unpunished. In return, the so-called troika of International Monetary Fund (IMF), the ECB, and the European Commission took control of the country's public finances and imposed a harsh regime of ever-increasing tax rises and budget cuts while also attempting to privatize or sell off any remaining assets that the state might have had.

Greek citizens expressed their discontent with austerity through regular public demonstrations, but also most notably in a referendum on the terms of the third bailout package, which was called by Tsipras in July 2015. German chancellor Angela Merkel in particular was heavily criticized, even demonized by Greece for her single-minded adherence to the neoliberal principles of deficit reduction and balanced budgets, which ultimately could only be achieved through a widespread privatization of the country's economy and drastic reductions to the standards of living of Greek citizens. References to the war-time occupation by Nazi Germany became ubiquitous with the EU

Table 2.3 Terms of the Third Bailout Package for Greece, July 2015

Size	85 billion euros
Transfer of assets	Up to fifty billion euros of assets to be transferred to a privatization fund; assets include government-owned airports and other infrastructure, banks, as well as utilities
Pensions	Retirement age up to sixty-seven
Sales and other taxes	Sales tax discount of 30 percent given to Greek islands to be removed; sales tax bands to be streamlined to bring more goods onto the 23 percent band
Budget	Automatic spending cuts if annual budget is not balanced; instant payment of 7 billion euros by August 2015 before bailout cash can be handed out
Reforms	Ambitious market reforms, including Sunday trading laws, the opening-up of professions, the privatization of the energy sector, as well as a new tax system that demands higher contributions from the Greek oligarchy

bailout plan being widely regarded as a capitalist plot designed to exploit ordinary people. But Merkel and the EU did not budge one inch. Germany even threatened to suspend Greek membership from the euro on a temporary basis, if the country refused to accept the bailout's terms. A couple of weeks later, with the tail between its legs, the Greek parliament ratified the highly controversial package (see table 2.3). As a result, the country had to hand over fifty billion euros of public assets (e.g., ports, banks, or airports) to a privatization fund.[9] Half the fund was used to recapitalize Greek banks with the other half earmarked to repay public debt. In addition, tax rises and spending cuts were superimposed. Commentators referred to the establishment of an economic protectorate and a debt colony with all key financial and economic decisions now taken by the troika, and thus by unelected, foreign officials.[10]

But Greece was ill-equipped to steer the negotiations into a different direction. In the run-up to the finalization of the package, Tsipras could have drafted an alternative. With more fiscal flexibility from the troika, he could have raised wages in the public sector, could have slowed down the pace to job cuts, and could have raised pensions to boost consumer spending and thus economic growth. Roping in wealthy Greek oligarchs into a fairer tax system would also have been highly beneficial to such an economic recovery. The country could have pleaded with the EU over a different path on how to repay its debt. Instead of a flat-sum schedule, lowering public debt could have been achieved on a proportional basis, for instance, as a percentage of export revenues. Such an approach would have been in the interest of EU creditors: the more the country prospers, the more debt would be repaid.[11] In this way, Tsipras would have been able to implement Keynesian reforms, which were in line with the economic philosophy that had catapulted him into power half a year earlier.

It is speculative to argue whether a plan B would have broken fierce German resistance, but the absence of an alternative to austerity gave a glimpse of the power relations that underlined the negotiations at the European summit. In one corner was Tsipras, the new kid on the block, Greece's first ever far-left leader, representing a country whose reckless financial behavior brought EMU—the showpiece of European integration—to the brink of collapse. In the other corner was the EU establishment, led by the economic powerhouse of the continent, Germany and its long-serving chancellor Angela Merkel. It was no contest. A couple of weeks later and despite heavy opposition from within his own party, Tsipras agreed to the troika-imposed bitter medicine in order to receive further bailout money that safeguarded his country's liquidity. In the process, social-democratic economics, which had brought Tsipras to power, was cast aside, poignantly illustrated by his dismissal of the outspoken and radical finance minister Yanis Varoufakis. It was as if Keynesian economic philosophy—the belief that cutting spending and raising taxes during a recession are counterproductive since such measures reduce demand and thus dim the prospect of recovery—had never existed.

By 2017, Greece had turned a surprising corner (see table 2.4) and reported its first budget surplus since 2007. It prompted EMU Commissioner Pierre Moscovici to declare Greece as "a normal country in the Eurozone." But eight years of economic and financial drama left deep scars. Austerity pushed the country into a long-lasting recession and stifled economic growth.[12] Those with a chance to emigrate did precisely that, in particular the young and the most educated, resulting in a devastating brain drain. In 2010, the country was already bankrupt. But creditors pretended that Greece represented merely a cash flow problem, when what was required was a massive restructuring and partial write-off of its colossal public debt.[13] But such a move was simply never on the cards for fear of the potentially disastrous consequences for the balance sheets of creditors, most notably banks in France, Italy, and Germany.

Table 2.4 Economic and Financial Data for Greece 2011–2018

	GDP Growth (% Change from Previous Year)	*Unemployment (%)*	*Annual Deficit (% of GDP)*	*Government Debt (% of GDP)*
2011	−9.1	17.9	−9.1	172.1
2012	−7.3	24.5	−8.9	159.6
2013	−3.2	27.5	−13.2	177.4
2014	0.7	26.5	−3.6	178.9
2015	−0.4	24.9	−5.6	175.9
2016	−0.2	23.6	0.5	178.5
2017	1.5	21.5	0.8	176.1
2018	2.2	18.5	1.0	182.2

Source: Eurostat.

The result was the implosion of the Greek economy and a society that was left traumatized. Many countries have historical crack-up moments: the winter of discontent in the UK in 1978–1979; America's stock market crash of 1929; Germany's hyperinflations of 1923 and 1929. This was Greece's moment of national humiliation, which was imprinted on the public psyche.

The Greek crisis also had widespread ramifications for the European project. The treatment of Athens was unrelenting. In the attempt to discipline a fellow Eurozone member, the EU, led by Merkel and her Finance Minister Wolfgang Schäuble, dismissed the public will of Greek citizens as expressed in the referendum on the bailout conditions. It also dismissed the economic philosophy of the ruling *Syriza* party as a mere inconvenience. Instead, austerity became entrenched for many years. Casting aside democracy in such a fashion never bodes well for a union that is often criticized for being elitist and detached from its citizens. But the deal was not only about Greece. EU governments also had to pay reference to the will of their own voters. And any financial support for Greece was highly controversial, not only in Germany, but also in countries like Slovakia or the Baltic states, whose welfare systems were substantially less generous but whose taxpayers now had to foot the bill of perceived Greek decadence. Resentment, frustration, and anger were not only felt in the streets of Athens. It was felt across Europe, but for different reasons.

The governments and the media in northern Europe were very harsh in their assessment of Greece, its political class, and its people, and there was little sympathy that years of financial frivolity had come to a crushing end. There is some truth to this point of view. Greek voters had lapped up the lavish promises of their political leaders, which simply represented economic fantasy. But the sacrifices that the country had endured since 2010 deserve much recognition. Against the harsh social climate, growing poverty levels, mass unemployment, in particular among the young, it seems a miracle that the Greek state survived at all and that a democratic system prevailed and resisted any electoral temptations, for instance, by the fascist Golden Dawn movement. Moreover, throughout this time, thousands of refugees, mainly escaping the civil war in Syria, arrived on Greek shores; a humanitarian crisis, which EU countries further north were spared.

But austerity is not finished. The deal of July 2018 between the troika and Greece committed the country to budget surpluses of 3.5 percent of GDP until 2022, and 2.2 percent of GDP until 2060; nearly two generations from now. Further budget cuts worth 1.8 billion euros were implemented in January 2019. In an economy blighted by low productivity and innovation, one can safely assume that spending on welfare will be kept in check for a long time to come. Yes, an economic and financial Armageddon had been averted but at what price to social cohesion? Despite the positive developments of 2018, a potential return of the economic crisis and with it a recurrent threat to the livelihoods of normal people cannot be discounted.

ITALY: THE END OF DOLCE VITA

Massive public debt had been a fixture of Italy's public finances since the expansion of the welfare state from the 1970s onward. Unlike most of its partners, in the first years of the Euro, Italy was one of the few countries that did not experience a boom, and per capita income stayed flat during the past twenty years. Lack of reforms to a stifling economic structure were not implemented, which left the country utterly unprepared when the collapse of Lehmann Brothers in 2008 signaled the start of the global financial crisis. By 2011, the inability of Prime Minister Silvio Berlusconi to embark on a reform course to support Italy's competitiveness within the EU's Single Market resulted in a sudden loss of confidence by international financial markets. Some of the country's structural characteristics were indeed appalling: A vast black market accounting for around 20 percent of Italy's economic activity; endemic corruption with goods and services sold to the public sector being subject to "side payments" that were siphoned off by the political establishment; widespread tax evasion to which successive governments turned a blind eye; poor school and university systems with a substandard research output; a web of vested interest groups and closed professions, which severely undermined innovation. In the end, it was of considerable irony that the financial markets, which Berlusconi had claimed to be a master of, imposed ever higher interest rates on Italy. This ultimately led to his downfall. In the run-up to an EU summit in October 2011, Berlusconi received a firm demand from other Eurozone leaders to commit to firm spending cuts and other austerity measures. The Italian government responded with a "letter of intent." In a press conference, Merkel and Sarkozy were asked about the likelihood of Italy being able to stick to its promises. Both leaders involuntarily mustered an embarrassed smirk. In the following days, it became ever clearer that Berlusconi had lost the support of his coalition partners. Given his devastatingly poor record and economic policies, which benefited his personal business interests, it was with great relief among investors and EU leaders, that Berlusconi resigned in November 2011 (see table 2.5). He was replaced by yet another unelected government of technocrats, fronted by the highly respected former EU Commissioner Mario Monti.

Monti instantly introduced austerity measures to calm financial markets. Tax rises, modest reforms to the pension system, and the labor market were implemented, and the country, at least temporarily, returned to some degree

Table 2.5 Timeline of the Eurozone Crisis

June 2009	ECB's liquidity injection of 442 billion euros
April 2010	EU bailouts for Greece begin with initial 30 billion euros
May 2010	EU and IMF establish European Financial Stability Fund (EFSF) of 750 billion euros
November 2010	Bail out for Ireland: 85 billion euros
December 2010	European Stability Mechanism (ESM) established
March 2011	Intergovernmental Euro Plus Pact
May 2011	Bail out for Portugal: 78 billion euros
July 2011	Bail out for Greece raised from 30 to 109 billion euros
October 2011	Euro Rescue Deal
November 2011	Italian prime minister Silvio Berlusconi resigns
December 2011	ECB's offers three-year loans worth 489 billion euros
January 2012	Intergovernmental Fiscal Compact
February 2012	ECB's offers three-year loans worth 529 billion euros
February 2012	Second bail out for Greece: 130 billion euros
June 2012	Bailout to rescue Spanish banks: 100 billion euros
June 2012	EU leaders agree to set up a supervisory system for banks
March 2013	Cyprus starts bailout package of ten billion euros
December 2013	Ireland exits bailout program
January 2014	Spain exits bailout program
May 2014	Portugal exits bailout program
July 2015	Third bailout package for Greece of 86 billion euros
March 2016	Cyprus bailout program ends
June 2018	New government in Italy with Salvini as interior minister
August 2018	Greece exits bailout program
July 2019	Tsipras replaced by Kyriakos Mitsotakis
September 2019	Salvini ousted from government

of stability. Monti's center-right coalition contested the parliamentary elections in February 2013, only to be replaced by a grand coalition under Enrico Letta, who himself was succeeded barely a year later by the moderate left-winger Matteo Renzi in February 2014. For what seems an eternity in Italian politics, Renzi held on to office for thirty-four months backed by a coalition of centrist parties. His tenure as prime minister was cut short by losing a referendum on electoral reform,[14] which prompted him to resign. His Foreign Minister Paolo Gentiloni stepped in, but in June 2018, he too was swept aside by an electoral storm, which brought to power a coalition of the populist M5S under Prime Minister Giuseppe Conti and the right-wing *Lega* fronted by the interior minister Matteo Salvini.

Salvini shook the foundations of European integration. He regarded himself as a friend of Russia's autocratic president Vladimir Putin and his speeches were peppered with admiring references to Italy's fascist dictator Benito Mussolini. He blamed EMU and the German government under Angela Merkel for the country's economic malaise; attacks, which were often complemented by an inflammatory rhetoric against refugees and migrants.

Salvini's fierce anti-EU and anti-EMU rhetoric, however, never resulted in the promised spending spree and thus a violation of the Stability Pact. In fact, in 2018, Italy's annual deficit was 2.1 percent of GDP and therefore very much in line with Brussels's target of 3 percent, and less than the 2.4 percent figure of the previous year.[15] Salvini resigned from the coalition in August 2019, hoping for a snap election that would have given his party a working majority, catapulting him into the premiership. Conti and his M5S, however, were able to find a new coalition partner in the center left *Democratic Party* and Salvini was at least temporarily side-lined.

As troublesome as the case of Greece was for the EU, Italy assumes a different dimension altogether. The country is the world's eighth biggest economy (and number three among Eurozone countries after France and Germany). What if Salvini and Conti had kept their electoral promises, abandoned austerity, and increased public spending, thereby effectively reneging on the EMU's Stability Pact? The ECB would then have found it legally impossible to continue to buy up Italian bonds. Financial markets would have been ever more reluctant to lend the country money. Bond yields would have risen, making the government insolvent. The country then would have little choice but to ask to be bailed out by the European Stability Mechanism. The troika would then have taken over the finance ministry in Rome. Apart from public outrage and potential civic unrest, Italy's colossal public debt of 2.3 trillion euros would have pushed the troika to the edge of its financial capabilities, with the country simply being too big to be rescued. This horror scenario would have resulted in the ultimate nightmare of politics: a union where fiscal rules and legal commitments were thrown out the window by a member digging its own grave, eventually resulting in state failure. The financial collapse of Italy almost certainly would have led to the collapse of the euro itself. The volatility of Italian politics, with frequent government changes the norm, means that such a nightmare cannot be discounted. It is the Damocles sword, which continues to hang over EMU.

CYPRUS: BAILING IN BEFORE BEING BAILED OUT

The first signs of a financial crash emerged on the small eastern Mediterranean island in 2012. In January of that year, Russia had come to the country's temporary rescue with a loan facility of 2.5 billion euros. In November, the government announced that it would need up to seventeen billion euros to keep the country afloat, and negotiations with the troika over yet another bailout commenced. For a long time, Cyprus had been a tax haven, which allowed global investors, predominantly from Russia, to deposit money without too many questions being asked, and the island was a convenient entry point into the Eurozone for laundering money. At one stage, the banking system had assets equivalent to eight times the country's GDP. But Cyprus's banks had also offered sizeable loans to Greece. With the financial meltdown of that country, and with little revenue coming from its citizens who enjoyed ultra-low taxes, the economic model became fragile and ultimately unsustainable.

By March 2013 financial panic ensued. The Cyprus government was just weeks away from running out of money. In a radical departure from previous crises management, the troika demanded a "bail in," whereby the government had to come up with 5.8 billion euros before a bailout of 10 billion euros could be granted. This prompted President Nicos Anastasiades to propose a 6.75 percent tax on all bank deposits below 100,000 euros and a 9.9 percent levy on investments above that sum. Such a move would have mitigated the impact on affluent investors, most notably wealthy Russians who had deposited around twenty billion euros on the island. But in return, the deal would have represented a massive financial blow to ordinary citizens. Not surprisingly, the Cypriot public was outraged, and widespread protests ensued. People rushed to banks and cash machines to get as much money out before the legislation might come into force. Banks subsequently were forced to close and a maximum cash withdrawal of 100 euros per day was imposed. But Anastasiades failed to get his package through parliament. A desperate attempt to reach out to Moscow for further financial support also failed. And the ECB added further pressure by threatening to switch off liquidity to Cyprus's banks if a deal with the troika was not concluded swiftly.

The government ultimately backed down and reached an agreement on a series of measures. The struggling *Laiki* bank was closed and the island's biggest commercial bank, the Bank of Cyprus, restructured. Deposits over 100,000 euros were subject to an eye-watering haircut of up to 80 percent in order to raise the money required for the "bail in," but at least less-affluent investors saw their assets untouched. Usual austerity measures, such as tax rises and spending cuts completed the package.[16] In the end, Cyprus needed only 7.25 of the earmarked 10 billion euros and returned to growth in 2015. Two years later, the country seemed stable. The reorientation of the economy toward tourism (the island is a year-round destination for sun-seekers), shipping, construction, and business services, such as consulting or accounting, paid surprising dividends. As shown in table 2.7, in 2018, the economy grew by a respectable 3.7 percent,[17] which silenced critics of the rescue plan who had predicted an economic meltdown.

The Cyprus deal was the first bailout package to hit savers and thus represented a marked departure from the previous models applied in Greece, Portugal, Ireland, and Spain. In these cases, the troika offered liquidity in return for austerity measures and sustainable public finances. In Cyprus, the government first had to apply tax rises and spending cuts before the financial lifeline arrived. This left a lasting impression, since in any future bailouts privately held bank accounts could now form part of the equation. The Dutch finance minister Jeroen Dijsselbloem, chair of the so-called Eurozone group of EU members who had adopted the single currency, admitted that the Cyprus rescue was "pushing back the risks." Referring to the struggles of Cyprus's two biggest banks *Laiki* and Bank of Cyprus, he argued: "If the bank can't do it, then we'll talk to the shareholders and the bondholders, we'll ask them to contribute in recapitalizing the bank, and if necessary, the uninsured deposit holders."[18]

Dijsselbloem certainly made a valid point, arguing that it would be unfair to European taxpayers to continue to pick up the tap for bank losses. Cyprus's economic model certainly played a prominent role in the thinking of the Eurozone countries, but also within the IMF and the Commission. For years, the island was a persistent thorn in the eye of its European partners. Allowing laundered cash to enter the EU might have been highly lucrative for Cyprus, but it also enhanced the geostrategic position of Russia and thus was not welcome by most member states. The bail in / bail out nature of the package fundamentally undermined that status. Cyprus had built a reputation based on confidence in its banking sector. That confidence was now shred to pieces in a fatal blow to the country's status as a low regulation and low-tax haven. Even more so than in Greece, this was policy making by coercion. It did the financial trick: the Eurozone was kept intact, and a rogue state had come to heel. But the Cyprus saga also provided ample evidence of a divided union where prosperous northern European states under the leadership of Germany, EU institutions such as the ECB and the Commission, as well as the IMF are able and willing to shape a country's economic and financial structures. It is too early to determine whether Cyprus represents a special case, or indeed a new template. For this, a new financial crisis of an EU member needs to occur.

THE SOVEREIGN DEBT CRISES IN SPAIN, IRELAND, AND PORTUGAL

Unlike Greece and Italy, Spain, Ireland, and Portugal have seen a relatively swift return to growth and more stable finances. Yet, the reasons behind the downfall of so many of the Eurozone's economies were startlingly similar. Across the region, the arrival of the euro resulted in low interest rates and a stable currency, which prompted an economically hyperactive spending and consumer boom. In Spain, greedy banks handed out ever cheaper mortgages. At one stage, the Spanish construction industry accounted for a quarter of the country's GDP, counting on the illusion, that an ever-increasing number of foreigners and affluent Spaniards would snap up more and more holiday and retirement homes. With the subprime mortgage crisis of 2008 and 2009, this economic model proved to be short sighted and foolish. By 2012, one out of five Spanish workers were without a job, and in a country of forty million, one million families had no steady source of income. Gradually a tale of corruption and mismanagement emerged; just prior to the collapse of their banks, executives had received multimillion payouts. Some board members—often politically driven appointees—admitted that they did not possess the necessary skills to read balance sheets. In the case of the *Caja de Ahorros del Mediterraneo* (CAM), senior executives and their families were granted loans of 161 million euros. The board of CAM included a sociologist, a check-out worker, a dance teacher, an artist, and a psychologist, which did not suggest an abundance of accounting financial or legal expertise.[19] Not surprisingly, the government of socialist prime minister José Luis Rodríguez Zapatero experienced an electoral meltdown. In November 2011, Zapatero was replaced by the conservative Mariano Rajoy who, like Papandreou in Greece, embarked on a brutal austerity course in order to cut the public deficit to 3 percent by 2013.[20]

The conundrum for Spain was similar to that of Greece: Where could growth come from? The country suffered from extremely high unemployment, which prompted widespread social unrest. Furthermore, Spain's banks were shackled by the excesses of the previous property boom with balance sheets that were full of properties, which no one wanted to buy. The markets reacted accordingly. Bond yields rose steadily to over 7 percent, a rate widely regarded as unsustainable. The Spanish bailout of 100 billion euros to shore up the country's financial sector therefore did not take the EU by surprise.[21] By 2014, austerity had done what it had set out to do. Public finances were balanced and after years of a contracting economy, growth returned, averaging round 3 percent between 2015 and 2017. But healthier public finances were accompanied by declining real wages, and unemployment remains a worrying and widespread phenomenon. Yes, in 2018, the figure had dropped to 14.1 percent (see table 2.6), but for young people, the future remained grim with just around one-third of workers under the age of twenty-five without a job (see table 2.7).

In Ireland, it was once again banks, working cozily in tandem with the political establishment and the construction industry that failed to read the signs on the wall and foolishly believed in a never-ending economic miracle fueled by low Eurozone interest rates. At the peak of the property boom, Dublin had become Europe's most expensive city. Irish people were now paying the price for this megalomania: in November 2010, the EU bailed out this small country of some 4.5 million people to the tune of eighty-five billion euros, thirty-five billion of which was spent on recapitalizing failing banks,

Table 2.6 Financial and Economic Data in Crisis-Hit EU Countries, 2012 and 2018

	GDP Growth (% Change from Previous Year)		*Unemployment (%)*		*Annual Deficit (% of GDP)*		*Government Debt (% of GDP)*	
	2012	2018	2012	2018	2012	2018	2012	2018
Cyprus	−2.9	3.7	11.2	7.4	−5.6	−4.4	80.1	110.9
Ireland	0.2	5.0	14.5	5.3	−8.1	0.1	119.9	68.8
Italy	−2.8	0.6	9.8	10.5	−2.9	−2.2	123.4	133.0
Portugal	−4.0	2.1	15.3	6.7	−5.7	−0.4	126.2	125.0
Spain	−2.9	2.4	24.1	14.1	−10.5	−2.5	85.7	98.3
Germany	0.5	1.2	5.6	3.2	0.0	0.8	79.9	61.0
EU average	−0.4	1.8	10.2	6.5	−4.3	−0.7	83.8	80.8

Source: Eurostat.

Table 2.7 Youth Unemployment in Crisis-Hit EU Countries, 2007 and 2017

	2007 (%)	*2018 (%)*
Greece	22.7	39.9
Spain	18.1	34.3
Italy	20.4	32.2
Portugal	21.4	20.3
Cyprus	10.2	20.2
EU Average	15.8	15.2

Unemployment of people aged fifteen to twenty-four.
Source: Eurostat.

ten billion was needed to pay for on-going commitments, while forty billion was set aside to keep the country afloat for the next three years. In the meantime, the government had embarked on massive spending cuts (a notable 18 percent pay cut for civil servants) and tax rises, with the aim of bringing the annual public deficit, which ran at 13 percent at the end of 2011, in line with the Stability Pact's target of 3 percent. Three years on, in 2013, Ireland told the IMF that its help was no longer needed.

Before the crisis, Ireland had a much-admired economic model by establishing a knowledge-based economy that attracted multinationals because of the country's rock-bottom corporate tax rate, which at 12.5 percent is one of the lowest across Europe. Once the banking system was liquid one more time and sustainable public finances were restored, the country was able to simply tap into the successful formula of pre-crisis times. But a return to growth came at a harsh price. Although unemployment levels dipped below 6 percent in 2018 (see table 2.7), this was not achieved by establishing more jobs, but instead through widespread emigration of young workers. The Irish public was reminded of an almost-forgotten time prior to the establishment of the

Celtic tiger economy at the turn of the century, when financial security was often only achieved by sending family members abroad.

Portugal, a laggard economy, largely based on small, family-run businesses, had already found it difficult to compete within the Eurozone and the Single Market and was further exposed by the credit crunch. The EU came to the rescue in May 2011 with a package of seventy-eight billion euros and demand for widespread privatization, resulting in a swift exit of the bailout program three years later in May 2014. The fortunes of Portugal took an impressive turn with the election of socialist prime minister Antonio Costa in 2015. Costa departed from the austerity course of his center-right predecessor Passos Coelho, and increased the minimum wage, pensions and civil servants' salaries. The economy grew by 2.1 percent in 2018, aided by the creation of 350,000 jobs, which pushed unemployment down to 6.7 percent; the lowest level since 2000.[22] These highly positive indicators were achieved without excessive public borrowing and Portugal's annual budget deficit stayed well within the limits of the Stability Pact (see table 2.7). High overall debt levels, however, remains a concern and could potentially affect the public finances in the future in case a loss in market confidence results once more in higher bond yields.

All three countries had just about managed to avoid a financial meltdown, but except for Ireland, describing these economies as healthy might be a step too far. Still, the prospect of any of these countries leaving the Eurozone or bringing the single currency to its knees is highly unlikely. The crucial difference from Greece was the structural cause that started the crisis. Spain, Ireland, and, to a lesser extent, Portugal had excessive housing booms, fueled by banks that could have done with more regulation and supervision, and more financial prudence and restraint when lending to customers. Although house prices in Greece also increased, it was that country's unsustainable public finances and irresponsible wage and salary growth, which descended into financial chaos. The absence of these in Spain, Ireland, and Portugal explained the relatively short-lived nature of the bailout programs, and why the process to stabilize Greece lasted that much longer.

EU RESPONSES TO THE CRISES

The credit crunch of 2008 and 2009, which was caused by a massive contraction of the world's banking system, forced European governments to reconfigure economic and monetary institutions even before the extent of the Greek malaise became known. As such, at the March 2009 summit, EU leaders discussed new mechanisms to regulate and supervise the financial sector. Electronic money, credit agencies, the solvency of insurance companies, as well as capital requirements for banks and cross-border payments were featured on the agenda. More important than these discussions, however, was the establishment of the so-called High Level Group on Financial Supervision under the chairmanship of the former French central banker Jacques de Larosière. At the end of their deliberations, the group advocated the establishment of a European Systems Risk Council (ESRC), an early-warning unit that operates under the guideline of the ECB with all EU countries as members.[23]

The Larosière plan would have resulted in a supranational setup, which offered advice and guidelines, but also would have formed a coherent supervisory body with direct powers to regulate the banking and insurance sectors of the member states. The plan prompted instant criticism, most notably from the UK, which saw its highly lucrative hedge fund industry under threat. At first, the EU only partially agreed with Larosière: the Systems Risk Council as a supranational authority was indeed put in place. But Larosière's idea of granting this body the supranational power to supervise national financial markets was downscaled to mere supranational advice, thus giving the member states the final say in the regulation of their national banking, insurance, and securities sectors. It was not until the summit of June 2012, that Eurozone leaders finally agreed to establish a supranational supervisory system for banks. UK prime minister Cameron, however, stated that his country would not be part of such a setup.

Larosière's initiative paved the way for the gradual formation of a *European Banking Union*. As of 2019, significant steps have already been taken. For a start, Eurozone countries agreed to the establishment of a so-called *Single Supervisory Mechanism* (SSM), which gave the ECB the power to monitor the implementation of a single rulebook for all Eurozone banks.[24] The SSM entered into force in November 2014. Step Two consisted of a *Single Resolution Mechanism* (SRM) financed through a *Single Resolution Fund* (SRF), which ought to reach fifty-five billion euros by 2024. The fund receives its contributions by charging a 0.8 percent leverage on the deposits of all Eurozone credit institutions. The SRM aims to help banks in trouble by going through a process of restructuring and potential bailouts. Most importantly, and heavily influenced by developments in Cyprus, the SRM applies a new procedure on how to deal with a financial collapse: a failed bank must first approach its shareholders, followed by its creditors. Only then will other depositors be asked to shoulder any potential losses. In any case, the first 100,000 euros of every person's assets in a bank remain untouched. If all these collected assets are still not enough to shore up a bank, then and only then will the SRF come to the rescue.

With regard to the sovereign debt crises, the first 30 billion euros rescue package for Greece resulted in the establishment of the EFSF with a volume of 750 billion euros. Agreed in May 2010, the fund included contributions of 60 billion euros from all EU members (even those that do not share the single currency), 440 billion euros from Eurozone members, as well as 250 billion euros from the IMF.[25] It is important to note that the fund offered loans, not grants. Hence, countries contributing to the fund would receive their money back (default permitting), including interest. In December 2010, the EFSF was placed on a firmer, long-term footing with the establishment of the *European Stability Mechanism* (ESM). Operational since July 2012 and with a lending capacity of 500 billion euros, the fund can be tapped into only as a last resort. The ESM required a change to the Lisbon Treaty and was established as an intergovernmental institution located in Luxembourg, thereby giving future bailout mechanisms a firm legal base. The ESM, however, is not a stimulus package, as countries in financial distress first have to look for other refinancing sources, such as through borrowing money on the international money markets.

Beyond bailout mechanisms, the EU and the tandem of Angela Merkel and Nicolas Sarkozy convinced their European partners to agree to a set of structural reforms, which aimed to prevent a recurrence of the unsustainable economic models as witnessed above all in Greece. Negotiated in March 2011, the *Euro Plus Pact* addressed three key elements: Sustainable public finances, financial stability, and tax policy coordination.[26] The Pact was yet another example of the ever-increasing asymmetry within the EU, as not all countries signed up to it. Sweden, Hungary, the Czech Republic, and the UK—all of which are outside the Eurozone—decided for yet another opt-out. All other countries, including the non-Euro users Bulgaria, Denmark, Latvia, Lithuania, Poland, and Romania, signed the Pact and abided to what could cynically have been referred to as Merkel's and Sarkozy's dictum on sound economic governance.

Given the continued liquidity problems in many member states, the autumn of 2011 was preoccupied with much discussion on the next necessary steps to prevent the European house from collapsing. After frenetic consultations, an emergency summit in October 2011 agreed on the *Euro Rescue Deal*,[27] which further wrote down Greek debt by 50 percent. The agreement also gave specific guidelines for the recapitalization of European banks, while also asking state investment funds (and here in particular those in China) for a boost to the EFSF.[28]

The almost perpetual summitry of the previous two years continued with the gathering in Brussels in December 2011. Merkel and Sarkozy (by then often simply referred to as "Merkozy") aimed to enforce tighter budgetary rules on Eurozone members. After the usual acrimonious negotiations lasting long into the night, the so-called *Fiscal Compact* allowed EU institutions to enforce austerity measures should a Eurozone member overspend its budget. Countries were now obliged to get their debt to below 60 percent of GDP by the end of 2013. If not, automatic fines would be imposed. Moreover, in order to reach the 60 percent mark, Eurozone members had to have an annual reduction of one-twentieth of the difference between that target and their actual debt. At a follow-up summit in January 2012, when the *Fiscal Compact* was signed, member state governments further agreed to empower the ECJ as the enforcer of these fiscal rules, by giving it the right to impose fines.

The summit became notorious for the veto used by UK prime minister Cameron.[29] President Sarkozy very much wanted this agreement to be part of a new EU treaty. However, Cameron in return insisted on concessions for the UK's finance industry in the wake of potentially stricter EU regulations. His demands were flatly refused, and the EU—minus the UK and the Czech Republic—simply signed an international, bilateral agreement among twenty-five participatory states that is now outside the confines of the EU treaty architecture. The *Fiscal Compact* therefore marked the true arrival of a two-speed Europe. While opt-outs (e.g., for the Human Rights Charter or the Schengen agreement on passport-free travel) have been common for nearly thirty years, the Eurozone was now moving toward a fiscal union with uniform budget rules. The Stability Pact of the Maastricht Treaty was also toughened up by imposing a regime of fiscal discipline that further undermined fiscal and monetary national sovereignty.

Not only European governments tried in an increasingly desperate fashion to prevent the crises from spinning out of control. The performance of the ECB also came under intense scrutiny. The ECB had acted slowly in lowering interest rates when the first effects of the credit crunch started to come to the fore. While the US Federal Reserve lowered rates for the first time on September 18, 2007, it took the ECB a further three weeks (October 8) to respond. Also, both the US Fed and the Bank of England used quantitative easing as a widespread method to add liquidity to struggling economies. Quantitative easing in the EU, however, was more complicated given that the ECB had to look after the monetary well-being not just of one, but of nineteen entities. This meant that if the ECB had decided to help, for example, Greece, then countries such as Portugal or Ireland justifiably would have argued for help too. Furthermore, quantitative easing had to be agreed by all Eurozone members, and it therefore came as little surprise that this financial vehicle was only used to limited effect.

On a more positive note, the ECB made three very significant liquidity injections. In June 2009, the bank set aside 442 billion euros worth of cheap loans for EU banks, which had to be repaid within one year. This was during the height of the credit crunch when banks had stopped lending to one another and to businesses, resulting in a shortage of cash. An even more ambitious injection took place in December 2011 under the tutelage of newly appointed

ECB president Mario Draghi. On this occasion, 489 billion euros were made available. Given the very low interest rate of 1 percent and a generous repayment period of three years, 523 financial institutions across the continent applied. In contrast to the first injection two years earlier, some of the money was invested straight away in buying government bonds from distressed Eurozone members, such as Spain or Italy. In the end, Draghi's move not only helped banks and businesses, but also the struggling under performers of the Eurozone, who saw their borrowing costs coming down. A couple of months later, in February 2012, Draghi made available a further 529 billion euros under the same conditions in what the ECB referred to as its "Long-Term Repo Operation" (LTRO). Again, borrowing costs on the international markets fell for the crisis-ridden states, as banks bought up sovereign debt, which offered higher returns.

Proper quantitative easing, often referred to as the "bazooka" of central bank instruments, arrived on Eurozone shores in January 2015, when Draghi stunned the finance world with a stimulus package estimated to be at least 1,100 billion euros, aimed at buying up government bonds to the tune of 60 billion euros a month. Consequently, the cost of borrowing for governments decreased even further.[30] His actions were highly welcomed by EU members as balancing their books now became just that little bit easier. The main impact, however, was seen in the currency devaluation of the euro. While the dollar traded at 1.35 euros in the summer of 2014, the US currency rose to 1.13 euros after Draghi's announcement and remained at that level until the end of 2018. The cheaper euro boosted exports across the EU. But the program went way beyond its anticipated duration of two years and was only stopped at the end of 2018, nearly four years after its inception. Sluggish wage growth was cited as the main reason for this slow recovery.[31] And it was not only the time scale that needed to be expanded. The same applied to the size of the stimulus, which ultimately reached a staggering 2,500 billion euros.

THE FUTURE OF EMU

If one believes in European integration, in giving up certain aspects of a country's national sovereignty for the sake of European solidarity, in improved relations among neighbors, in shared and sustained prosperity across the continent, then EMU had the potential to form a vital cornerstone for such idealism. But EMU in its present shape dramatically jeopardized European integration and threatened the very viability of such a vision. What if Greece (or Italy) had decided to leave the euro, as was advocated by a growing number of politicians and commentators? Economic meltdown and a financial collapse would almost certainly have been the outcome. Proponents of a Greek exit often cited the example of Argentina, which at the beginning of this century unpegged its Peso from the US dollar, prompting a massive devaluation of its currency. It worked for Argentina, chiefly because the country possessed significant deposits of minerals, which it could now sell cheaply within a booming world economy. The country, unlike Greece, had something viable to offer to global markets.

If Greece had left the euro, the value of a reinvented drachma would almost certainly have collapsed in relation to the euro, maybe by as much as 50 percent. The country would have found it impossible to meet its credit commitments (which were in euros, thus potentially doubling government debts). This would have brought about more bank collapses and subsequent nationalizations across the EU as Greek debt was now practically worthless and would have to be written off. Surviving banks, which throughout the crisis were reluctant to lend, would have had to reduce their exposure even more, resulting in a further credit crunch. Investors would have pulled out of Greece, the ECB would have intervened by buying up Greek drachma in order to keep that currency at an artificially higher level, hitting the ECB's currency reserves hard. Capital controls would have had to be imposed and borders would have closed down in order to prevent money from pouring out of the country. There might also have been a run on the euro as investors began to speculate which country would be the next victim.

Given this apocalyptic scenario, the only viable alternative was to reform EMU; for the sake of the financial and economic survival (not just of Greece but of all EU countries), as well as for the moral sake of the entire European integration project, which after all rests on the notion of European solidarity, on a mindset, which ought to transcend purely national interests. The EU therefore had no choice but to move ever closer toward fiscal and economic harmonization. *The Euro Plus Pact* of March 2011, as well as the *Fiscal Compact* of January 2012, prescribed a narrowly defined path on how national economies must be organized. The former introduced tighter rules on public finances, pensions, health care, and other welfare provisions, which now have to be translated into national law. The latter concentrated on a balanced budget rule that if violated results in automatic fines and a loss of budgetary sovereignty. Furthermore, the *Banking Union* established a single rulebook, which every EU bank must now abide by. The ECB is also now the single supervisory body, which monitors the implementation of those rules. There is also a clear procedure in place on how to restructure or even bailout failing banks, backed up by the SRF. So far so good.

What EMU still needs, however, is a mechanism that can facilitate the transfer of money from richer European states to their poorer southern partners. The ESM offers a last-resort credit facility for countries in financial peril. However, this might not be enough. One might want to look at the example of German unification, where a poorer entity (eastern Germany) was shored up by a richer one (western Germany). The government organized this by imposing a so-called solidarity tax, which was deducted at source from capital investments and pay slips of western employees. Thirty years after unification, workers in the West continue to pay this tax with latest figures reaching almost eighteen billion euros annually. The total money the country spent on rejuvenating the east now stands at over 2,000 billion euros. Incidentally, the total amount that the German government transferred to Greece was 914 million euros.[32]

But having a straightforward fiscal transfer from richer northern taxpayers to poorer southern governments might be impossible to achieve given the growing EU skepticism among European electorates. The fact is that the EU already transfers money—albeit in a limited fashion—through its cohesion and agricultural policies. The EU budget is financed through member state contributions, and this pot of money is then handed out in large parts to farmers, and to economically backward regions. In 2012, former French president François Hollande called on other leaders to agree to an increase in the seven-year EU budget for 2014–2020. The chorus for growth-stimulating measures grew louder with Spanish prime minister Mariano Rajoy and Italian prime minister Mario Monti backing Hollande's call. Even ECB president Mario Draghi argued that the *Fiscal Compact* ought to be complemented by a "Growth Compact." In the end, the EU budget was only tweaked a little without any substantial increases. The EU spends just under 100 billion euros annually on redistributive programs. For a failing national economy, such an amount would merely represent a drop in the ocean. Budgets also have to be agreed on a unanimous basis by all member states. Therefore, there is every reason to doubt a massive increase in the EU's next financial perspective, which runs from 2021 to 2027.

Given the limited options available to the EU, it was unsurprising that commentators and political leaders frequently called upon the ECB to assume a more pivotal role. Granted, ECB president Draghi embarked on a more proactive course than his predecessor Jean-Claude Trichet when he injected liquidity into southern Europe by offering 1,000 billion euros in bank loans, and by applying the bazooka of a 2,500-billion-euro program of quantitative easing. But bazooka and liquidity injections ought to be temporary remedies. What the EU needs is a central bank that is capable of issuing Eurobonds, which are guaranteed by the Eurozone members. This would enable countries like Greece or Italy to access money at a cheaper rate than those offered by the international financial markets. Germany, however, was vehemently opposed to such an idea as it would undermine the ECB's independence; a sacrosanct relic that had its origins in the way the German *Bundesbank* was set up, which in itself was a reflection of the financial collapse of the Weimar Republic that resulted in the rise of Nazi Germany. However, if Germany (and indeed other EU countries) is committed to a supranational EMU, then supranational mechanisms ought to be put in place to alleviate discrepancies in the economic structure of other Eurozone members. Simple rules on how to run an economy are not enough. This ought to be complemented by financial mechanisms that allow for a transfer of funds. A straightforward solidarity tax along the lines of Germany's financing of unification might be a step too far for the mindsets of European citizens. But call it fiscal federalism or call it financial solidarity, the EU has to find established and permanent ways of transferring money from richer to poorer parts for EMU to succeed.

THE DILEMMA

The sovereign debt crises demonstrated that a number of countries had embarked on utterly unsustainable economic models. Easy access to cheap money and low interest rates proved too much of a temptation for politicians and citizens alike. Instead, some countries embarked on a spending and consumption spree without looking at the fundamental working mechanisms and potential flaws of their national economies. Instead of improving economic parameters, investing in research and education, building up coherent infrastructures, and establishing conducive industrial relations, the order of the day was spent, spent, spent without worrying how countries might fare during an economic downturn. This behavior was irresponsible.

But irresponsible behavior was not only confined to the governments in the countries affected by a sovereign debt crisis. Across the continent, other governments but also EU institutions turned a blind eye to what was going on. What had been agreed at Maastricht, when the key principles of EMU were set out in the Stability Pact, represented a worthless piece of paper that no one felt obliged to adhere to. Ever since the start of EMU in 1999, France and Germany had persistently violated the Stability Pact by accumulating more debt than was allowed. The Commission would have been entitled to impose fines, but failed to do so, fearing a tarnished reputation for the young currency on the international markets. And if France and Germany regarded the Stability Pact as more of a guideline than a legal obligation, why should other countries have obeyed?

The financial sector too enjoyed a period where regulation was shockingly neglected. How else can one explain the arrival of the now infamous 110 percent mortgages given out to bank customers without sufficient capital collateral? The euro worked fantastically well in a time of economic plenty. For many governments and their citizens, the realization that EMU was shockingly ill-equipped to handle a financial crisis came too late. EMU ought to have been a firm prescription on how to keep spending and inflation under control, but instead it turned into a temptation to give in to easy access to cheap money. It all ended in unsustainable economic models, unbalanced growth, wage and spending excesses, and a reliance on bubble revenues.

The rationale of politics and of politicians is to improve people's lives, to guarantee peace and safety, to secure standards of living and—now more than ever—to offer environmentally sustainable conditions. For a great part of its existence, the EU and member state governments did precisely that. The founding treaties of the 1950s ushered in a period of peace among former enemies. Free trade across borders brought a remarkable level of prosperity. The Maastricht Treaty of 1993 paved the way for the reunification of a once divided continent. But EMU? It inflicted potentially irreparable damage to the European idea and a loss of moral authority. What started out as a project to achieve an ever-closer union brought hardship to many. Behind the unemployment statistics and falling GDP levels are people who had lost their livelihoods, whose businesses went bankrupt, whose pensions had been eroded, whose welfare state had become sclerotic. Who would have thought that eighty years after the implosion of the Weimar Republic in Germany—one of the historical memories, which after all prompted European governments to set up the EU—we would see the return of fascists marching in the streets (of Athens)?

The sad case of Italy laid bare the current twin challenges of the European project: protecting the economic and financial livelihood of Eurozone members while maintaining a core set of values and norms shared by all governments. Salvini toyed with the idea of embarking on a path to destroy both. In a world of growing iron-fist, nationalist, isolationist, and anti-globalist politics, the EU ought to represent a haven of reason, of international collaboration, of evidence-based policy making; something that is hard to achieve with politicians of the ilk of Salvini. But Italy has also shown that large parts of the European electorate have lost faith in their politicians. Populist, right-wing movements have a firm grip on power not only in Italy, but also in Poland and in Hungary and are causing political turmoil in the UK, in Finland, Sweden, Denmark, Germany, the Netherlands, Austria, and France. It seems as if the one thing that unites a lot of European citizens is their disdain for Brussels (and for rich and austerity-imposing Germany).

The longer the union has been together, the more the people are distancing themselves from its objectives of unity and transnational cooperation; a paradox, which European populists, united only in their hatred for Brussels, are only too keen to exploit. The EU's austerity-enforcing handling of the Greek crisis and an Italian economy, which according to Salvini is suffocated by EMU rules, provided the starting gun for the oratory boost that these very worrying developments needed in order to gain such widespread support. Austerity measures are never popular and always seem to offer political opportunities for demagogues. Political insanity could yet return to Europe with even greater force should politics fail in its attempt to bring the economic and financial situation under control. What leaves a sour taste is also the fact that Greece and Italy were governed by unelected officials during the height of the crises—hardly a ringing endorsement for legitimacy and democratic accountability.

In the run-up to the start of EMU, many analysts and in particular the economists of the German *Bundesbank*, warned that the Eurozone would not be an OCA where economic structures and financial parameters of the participating countries are by and large in line with one another. The *Bundesbank* warned repeatedly against the inclusion of such countries as Greece or Italy. Both were allowed to join despite the fact that one of the key ingredients of EMU—an overall budget deficit of no more than 60 percent of GDP—was not met. Furthermore, an OCA relies on labor mobility. In the United States, a recession in one part of the country might be offset by workers moving to a more prosperous one. Because of language barriers, labor mobility in the EU is very limited and only 3.8 percent of citizens live in a member state other than their country of birth.[33] An OCA also requires some form of mechanism to transfer funds from one region to another. The EU budget, however, is very limited (only about 1 percent of each member state's GDP), while Germany agreed to EMU under the explicit condition that fiscal union would not be part of it. In the United States, monetary union took place alongside a political (and thus fiscal) union. German and other leaders, however, argued that a monetary union could be established without the accompanying unifying political measures. They were proven wrong.

A decade later, the doomsday preachers of the *Bundesbank* had won the argument. The key point here is that with a single currency, countries lose their monetary autonomy. It seems too obvious to mention, but once you are a member of the Eurozone, you lose a crucial instrument on how to keep your economy competitive: that of devaluing your currency. Hence, once a country adopted the euro, it could no longer compete by offering lower prices. It had to compete on quality and innovation, which turned out to be next-to-impossible, given the high levels of efficiency, innovation, and productivity of northern European economies, such as Germany, the Netherlands, Luxembourg, or Finland. In return, these countries enjoyed a benign competitive advantage based on the exchange rate parity, which allowed them to build up a vast trade surplus on the back of consumption-hungry yet less competitive southern Eurozone partners. Blaming irresponsible governments and greedy citizens in crisis-affected countries did not solve the euro dilemma. The fact remained that the struggling member states were not in a position to get out of their economic and financial mess by themselves. The option of devaluation does not exist in EMU. Defaulting on debt would have affected banks and governments across the EU, while a collapse in demand would have consequences for export orientated member states such as Germany. The EU therefore had no choice but to stay the course.

Given the current set of instruments available to the ECB and the troika, Italy might be too big to be rescued. The volatile political situation might result in two scenarios. One the one hand, Italy could continue with austerity, which would be against the political will of most Italians, and also against the majority of members of the Italian parliament. On the other hand, the government could give in to demands from its citizens to end the cycle of tax rises and spending cuts, which might prompt a panic by international financial markets. In both scenarios, the future of Italy's membership of the Eurozone, and that of the single currency project altogether, could be at stake.

At the moment, every country in the Eurozone is responsible for managing and servicing its own debts. There is no European solidarity fund, which helps countries in crisis. What had been set up was a bailout fund that injects liquidity in return for harsh austerity measures. But what Europe needs is a different approach in the shape of the third, and so far, unimplemented step of the *Banking Union*: a common system for deposit protection. Money markets buy up government bonds based on a country's perceived economic and financial health. The worse the state of a country, the higher the bond rates, and therefore, the higher the costs for that country to service its debts, pay wages, or invest in infrastructure. More importantly, money markets also speculate against the potential collapse of a national economy. A solidarity fund, which goes beyond the fifty-five billion euros reserved for any bank collapses, could put an end to this. No investor will place a bet for the financial implosion of governments or banks in the knowledge that a trustworthy European fund would come to the rescue of ailing actors.[34] The betting would most likely stop, thereby offering a steady refinancing of the country on the bond market. A storm has been brewing in Italy for some time now. Yet the Eurozone is still ill-equipped for its potential rescue, whether politically or institutionally.

The crisis in Cyprus has resulted in a new formula on how to deal with failing banks. These used to be kept alive, while the assets of creditors and shareholders were largely unaffected. This was excellent news for players on the international money markets and for financial institutions in London or Luxembourg who could count on the fact that governments and thus taxpayers would foot the bill for gross financial mismanagement. Ever since the collapse of *Laiki*, this is no longer the case. In Cyprus, the Eurozone demonstrated for the first time, that the onus of dealing with a collapsing bank should first fall on shareholders and creditors of that bank. Cyprus set a precedent for how collapsing banks worldwide might be dealt with in the future. This approach was also fair and long overdue, as was the establishment of the SSM and the SRM, which now gives the ECB concrete powers on how to deal with bank failure. The decision to protect the first 100,000 euros of assets also provides much-needed security for less privileged investors.

But the crises also revealed a darker picture, most notably in Greece. The single currency works very well for northern European countries, in particular Germany. The low euro-exchange rate brought about by the long-lasting economic downturn benefited German exports. In return, the fact that most European countries have adopted the single currency meant that poorer countries have lost the option to devalue their former national currencies and thus to regain competitiveness resulting in an uneven playing field, which once again benefits Germany. Even more striking, it was the reckless behavior of political elites in Greece, Ireland, and in Spain that brought about the debt crises. But these were also galvanized by reckless lending from banks in France and Germany. And what was most of the bailout money used for? Not for invigorating the economy, not for an increase in infrastructure spending, not for investment in science, research, and education. It was spent mostly to meet creditor demands. The *Euro Plus Pact* of 2011 and the *Fiscal Compact* of 2012 demonstrated that Keynesianism—the proactive engagement in the economy to address its shortcomings—is practically dead, at least for now. *Syriza* and Alexis Tsipras tried to convince their EU partners that a new approach was desperately needed. They failed. The crises management—in Greece and elsewhere—was done through austerity at the expense of national sovereignty. It does not bode well for the European project that the explicit wishes of the electorates in Greece and in Italy were steamrollered in such a fashion.

A monetary union without a fiscal and thus political union is the *Gründungsfehler* (the German word for design fault) of EMU. This is the term used by Angela Merkel when addressing the German parliament in 2011. She was right. On the one hand, we have advocates of consolidated public finances, of adhering to the Stability Pact. For countries like Germany, the Netherlands, Finland, Austria, Estonia, Latvia, Lithuania, and Ireland, the stability of the Eurozone is paramount, which is why budgetary rules ought to be followed regardless of any negative repercussions this might have on a national economy. But then we also have countries like France, Italy, Spain, and Greece that regard Maastricht as a dictum that strangulates national sovereignty and the political will of its citizen should they choose to elect a more left-leaning government. Germany and Merkel were caught in the middle. As pillars of European integration, a conflict with France and Italy (at least before Salvini was voted into office) would seem an anathema to Berlin. Yet, Germany was also on the same ideological side as northern and eastern European member states. In the end, the handling of Greece resulted in a harsh compromise. The country was allowed to stay in the Eurozone, and the European project was—at least for now—safe. This pleased the governments in Paris, Rome, and Madrid. But the other EU partners were also taken on board with the insistence on severe austerity measures, despite ignoring evidence, that the economic and fiscal measure imposed on Greece had highly counterproductive elements (e.g., a rise in sales taxes), which made a recovery all the harder. This formulaic approach to solving the Greek crises was subsequently also applied to Ireland, Spain, Portugal, and Cyprus. The deeper, and essential question, of whether a single currency is practical for states with such diverging economies, but also with a different understanding of the rationale of Maastricht's Stability Pact, remained unanswered. What the EU ought to have done was to reach a compromise, which allowed for a fiscal consolidation of crisis-ridden countries accompanied by measures that facilitated economic growth. It remains to be seen whether the potentially much more serious and devastating case of Italy might force a rethink across Europe. Austerity does not guarantee prosperity. Greek citizens were made to suffer for this misconception and there might come a breaking point when European citizens reach the end of what they are willing to bear.

Instead of pushing for an "Ever Closer Union" as advocated by Maastricht, the crises made countries drift further apart. Old war-time antagonisms reemerged, and the EU did not become more European, but paradoxically more nationalistic. Brussels—as the incarnation of the EU's faceless unelected institutions—had little say in the handling of the crises. This was intergovernmentalism par excellence with member states at the center of crucial decisions. Throughout these challenging years, the role of Germany and its position within the European integration project was heavily scrutinized. For decades, the country had been content to offer generous funding while leaving the institutional and policy design of the EU to member states like France and the UK. Germany only really got on board (with chancellor Kohl as a subsequent enthusiastic supporter) when France pressured Germany into starting negotiations on a single currency in return for agreeing to German unification. With Kohl leaving office in 1998, the country's often ambiguous attitude toward EMU was further exacerbated by his successor Gerhard Schröder who treated the Stability Pact of the Maastricht Treaty merely as a loose guideline on how to organize the country's finances. When Angela Merkel replaced Schröder in 2005, the Stability Pact's benchmarks on public debt and annual deficits continued to be violated for a further four years. This was hardly a country assuming leadership in the most pivotal of EU policies. But all this changed with the advent of the Greek crisis in 2010. Together with French president Nicolas Sarkozy, Merkel was instrumental in the design and ratification of the Euro Plus Pact (2011) and the Fiscal Compact (2012). In tandem with her Finance Minister Wolfgang Schäuble, she led the union in imposing tight austerity measures in particular on Greece and Cyprus. Prompted by the sovereign debt crisis, Germany—arguably for the very first time—firmly controlled the reins of European integration. Many commentators inadvertently drew parallels to World War II; the last time Germany had exercised a hegemonic power over the continent and a historic question then quickly reemerged: How to deal with the might of Germany in order to avoid the country's dominance over the continent? But the focus of this inquiry is too narrow. Europe witnessed the widening of the union in the first decade of the twenty-first century. But member states—Germany included—still have not found an answer to how to define the deepening aspect of the European project. Instead, the sovereign debt crises provided a ruthless testimony on the state of European integration. This was not a Europe built on consensus; instead it was one of coercion.

NOTES

1. In 1998, the BBC broadcast a documentary entitled "The Money Changers" that charted the development of the EMU project. Over three hours all key actors involved in the design and implementation of Europe's single currency went on record, apart from Margaret Thatcher (whose foreign policy advisor Charles Powell was interviewed instead) and Helmut Kohl (whose advisor Horst Teltschick shed light proceedings). When asked about EMU, some politicians could not hide their contempt. Germany's Finance Minister Gerhart Stoltenberg (1982–1989) was against it in principle (in German: "*In der Sache dagegen*"). His successor Theo Waigel (1989–1998) could only be convinced of EMU by a long convergence process (agreement on EMU came at a summit meeting in Maastricht in November 1991, yet the start of EMU was not until January 1999). Jacques Delor's chief of staff during this time was Pascal Lamy who subsequently was EU Commissioner for Trade (1999–2004), and the director general for the World Trade Organization (WTO) (2005 to 2013). He paraphrased Stoltenberg's and his finance ministry's attitude by saying that European integration and EMU according to the Germans do not belong into the same boat (in French: *au même bateau*).

The documentary is still accessible on YouTube. Viewers might want to focus on the second part, which can be accessed at: https://www.youtube.com/watch?v=BuzXkib8nTQ.

2. Quantitative easing (QE) is a process whereas a central bank is buying up assets—most often government bonds—from banks and other financial institutions, such as pension funds. The aim is for banks to use the generated cash to increase their lending to private households and to businesses. Thus, QE is a way to inject cash into a struggling economy.

3. The inflation target of the Eurozone was for countries to have price increases of no more than 1.5 percent above the average of the three best performers.

4. Ireland's annual debt of 13.1 percent was the highest, although this figure was a marked improvement to the 32.4 percent for 2010, when the country was forced to bail out its entire banking sector.

5. According to Bloomberg, the interest rates for a ten-year bond in November 2011 were: Greece 31.0 percent, Portugal 14.01 percent, Ireland 8.21 percent, Italy 7.04 percent, Spain 6.67 percent, France 3.68 percent, the UK 2.13%, and Germany 2.13 percent.

6. The bailout came with the following conditions:

- 30 billion euros in loans up to a maximum of 110 billion euros.
- Interest rate of 5.2 percent (which was reduced in March 2011 to 4.2 percent)
- Privatization of fifty billion euros worth of public assets
- Raising the retirement age to sixty-seven for men and sixty-five for women
- Tax increases on cigarettes, alcohol, and fuel
- Higher sales tax
- Demands to tackle tax evasion, to cut health care and pensions provisions
- Involvement of the EU's statistical office Eurostat in monitoring Greek accounts
- Loss of control over tax and spend should Greece fail to meet these conditions by March 2012

7. Bail out money was not paid out in one installment. Instead, it was divided into several tranches, which were released at certain intervals and subject to the bailed-out country meeting its tax and spend commitments.

8. The terms of the deal were harsh and included the following:

- Acceleration of privatization of state-owned businesses
- Slashing of 150,000 public sector jobs by 2015
- Cut in the minimum wage by 22 percent for new employees
- Public spending cuts of 3.3 billion euros in 2012

9. The privatization fund was heavily influenced by Germany. During the country's unification in the 1990s, all assets of the now defunct German Democratic Republic were organized into a public trust fund called *Treuhand*, with assets subsequently being sold off to the private sector. When the program was disbanded in 1994, a staggering 14,000 businesses had been transferred in such a manner.

10. See: Seumas Milne. "*The crucifixion of Greece is killing the European Project.*"

The Guardian, July 17, 2015, p. 33. www.theguardian.com/commentisfree/2015/jul/16/crucifixion-greece-killing-european-project-debt-colony-breakup-eurozone.

11. The EU did not have to go back too far in history to find a precedent. In 1953, West Germany secured a debt forgiveness of fifteen billion *Deutschmark*, much of it accrued as part of the reparations emanating from World War I. The remaining debt only needed to be repaid, once the country ran a trade surplus. It therefore was in the interest of western powers for the German export machine to kick into action, and the deal was widely regarded as offering the impetus for the German economic miracle of the 1950s.

12. At the outset of the crises, Greece had debt levels of around 120 percent of GDP. By 2018 that figure had risen to 180 percent. Welfare payments were slashed by a devastating 70 percent. Wages shrank by a fifth since the start of the crisis. The public sector was reduced by a fourth. At one stage, unemployment rose to an eye-watering 27 percent with youth unemployment (those aged twenty-five and under) climbing to over 50 percent. In a country of ten million people, one million had lost their job. In 2015, levels of extreme poverty affected 15 percent of the population. In comparison to pre-crisis levels, the economy had shrunk by a quarter.

13. This assessment was offered by Loukas Tsoukalis, a prominent scholar of EMU from the University of Athens. See www.theguardian.com/world/2018/jul/15/greece-exit-final-international-bailout-debt-catastrophe. The article furthermore offers a haunting account of the devastating effects of the crisis on the Greek people.

14. Ever since the end of World War II, Italian politics had been undermined by the plethora of political parties that managed to gain seats thus making the formation of viable coalition governments an often-insurmountable challenge. Renzi's proposal would have given those parties gaining more than 40 percent of votes a higher share of seats. Renzi linked his political career to the passing of a referendum on these electoral reforms. With Italian citizens voting down his proposal, he was left with little choice but to resign from office.

15. See: https://tradingeconomics.com/italy/government-budget.

16. Cyprus agreed to tax rises (most notably an increase of the country's rock-bottom corporation tax from 10 percent to 12.5 percent and a rise in the tax on interest from 15 percent to 30 percent), as well as cuts to pensions and welfare benefits.

See: www.ft.com/content/118d8034-e49f-11e5-ac45-5c039e797d1c.

17. Cyprus's annual deficit in 2018 was –4.4 percent of GDP, which was a violation of the Stability Pact. However, this setback can be explained by the structural reform of the banking sector in that year. In 2017, the country had a budget surplus of 1.8 percent of GDP.

18. See: *The Guardian*, March 26, 2013, p. 30.

19. See: *The Guardian*, June 9, 2012, p. 4. The article can be accessed at: www.theguardian.com/world/2012/jun/08/spain-savings-banks-corruption.

20. Rajoy's first budget called for twelve billion euros worth of spending cuts and fifteen billion euros of tax rises with the aim of bringing the annual deficit down to 5.5 percent in 2012 and to 3 percent a year later; the latter being an EU-wide benchmark to which Spain had agreed to in the *Fiscal Compact* of January 2012. This amounted to 570 euros of either spending cuts or tax rises per citizen. Government departments were asked to slash their budgets by 17 percent. The wages of civil servants, which had been reduced by 5 percent in 2010, were kept frozen.

21. Shortly after asking for bail out money, Rajoy announced further spending cuts and tax rises amounting to sixty-five billion euros in austerity measures. The sales tax was raised by 3 percent and civil servants saw their salaries reduced. The reduction of social security contributions, which had been Rajoy's only stimulus to the economy, was scrapped.

22. See: https://www.spiegel.de/international/europe/antonio-costa-a-socialist-success-story-in-portugal-a-1288837.html.

23. De Larosière also pressed for the establishment of European Supervisory Authorities (ESAs) based on a European System of Financial Supervisors (ESFS). Members of the ESFS are representatives from the twenty-seven national supervising authorities with the objective to oversee micro-prudential risks. The ESAs consist of three sub-bodies, namely, the EBA (European Banking Authority), EIOPA (European Insurance and Occupational Pensions Authority), and ESMA (European Securities and Markets Authority).

24. While all financial institutions inside the Eurozone were automatically subject to the ECB's authority, non-eurozone countries could also seek a close collaboration.

25. During the crisis, Christine Lagarde, the Head of the IMF asked for an increase in contributions from its members. Between 2011 and 2012, she managed to raise the Fund's lending resources by 430 billion US dollars, 200 billion of which came from the eurozone. The largest shareholder of the IMF, the United States, declined to contribute more money at that particular moment.

26. With regard to public finances, the fiscal rules of the Stability Pact of the Maastricht Treaty had to be written into national law. Pensions, health care, and other welfare state provisions had to be kept at financially sustainable levels. As to financial stability, the debt for banks but also for households and nonfinancial firms had to be sustainable and were monitored by the recently established European Systemic Risk Board. Lastly, the pact aimed for the development of a common corporate tax base, and the common tackling of fraud and tax evasion, although direct taxation would remain under the competence of national governments.

27. The key points of the *Euro Rescue Deal* were as follows:

- The writing down of Greek debt by 50 percent with the remaining debt to be secured by member states.
- A recapitalization of European banks with the requirement to raise their capital ratio to 9 percent. Banks were required to raise their capital by first going to private markets. If this initiative proved to be unsuccessful, banks were then obliged to apply to their national governments for financial support. The European Financial Stability Fund (EFSF) was seen as the last resort in order to reach the 9 percent target.
- Increase the resources of the EFSF: by establishing a so-called Special Purpose Vehicle, EU leaders aimed to raise money by approaching wealthy state investment funds (e.g., those held by China) to boost the ESFS's capacity to 1,500 billion euros.

28. In the immediate aftermath of the summit, the response by global investment funds, in particularly those of China to become involved in the EFSF was at best lukewarm, which made the target of 15,000 billion euros look rather ambitious.

29. It was not only the UK that did not sign up to the treaty. The Eurosceptic governments of the Czech Republic, Hungary, and Sweden all indicated that they first had to consult their national parliaments. We therefore saw the emergence of the awkward acronym CHUKS for four countries that did not commit to tighter budgetary rules. In the end, it was only the UK and the Czech Republic who decided on the latest opt-out of the EU's treaty agenda.

30. On the day of Draghi's announcement on January 22, 2015, the rate of ten-year German bonds fell to a new low of just 0.377 percent. France's thirty-year yield dropped to just 1.5 percent, while that of Italy went below 3 percent for the first time ever.

31. See: www.ft.com/content/c55dbfaa-a6c8-11e8-8ecf-a7ae1beff35b.

32. Germany has done very well out of the Greek crisis. Ever since the start of the economic downturn, the German government bought up Greek bonds. In total, Germany collected 2.9 billion euros interest during this time.

See: www.euractiv.com/section/economy-jobs/news/germany-earned-2-9-billion-euros-from-greeces-debt-crisis/.

33. Source: Eurostat, May 2018.

34. See: Henrik Enderlein: "*Noch ist Zeit, aber nicht mehr viel.*" Der Spiegel, No.23, June 2, 2018, pp. 18–19.

Chapter 3

Migration

In 2016, humanitarian crises of shocking and devastating proportions frequently hit the news headlines. In Syria, around thirteen million people, or a little over half of the prewar population, had been displaced. Iraq was facing the threat of ISIS terrorism and the separation of the Kurdish and Shia Muslim minorities. Libya had descended into anarchy with multiple tribal governments laying claim to the succession of Colonel Muammar Gaddafi's regime. In Yemen, the religious antagonism between Sunni Saudi Arabia and Shia Iran was acted out to vicious effect with fifteen million people facing a humanitarian disaster. The Kenyan government shut down the world's largest refugee camp in Dadaab, which at one point had accommodated 600,000 people, and refugees were sent back to their countries of origin, mainly to Somalia. In Nigeria, Boko Haram continued to commit terrorist acts including kidnaping children in the most vicious manner. The young state of South Sudan saw widespread human rights violations. US engagement in Afghanistan entered its sixteenth year. The Ebola virus in West Africa claimed many innocent lives, as did the super typhoon in the Philippines and the Zika virus in Brazil. According to the International Office for Migration (IOM), around 180 million people in Africa alone lived in crisis-affected areas. And Europe was the destination of choice for many. Seeking a better future might in some cases be driven by material concerns; more often, however, it is a desperate act of survival.

TYPES OF MIGRATION

The free movement of people is enshrined in the Treaty of Rome as one of the fundamental principles of EU integration. Holding a passport of any EU member state entitles citizens to live, work, study, or retire anywhere within the bloc without the need for a visa or the approval of their new host state. Since 1985, free movement is complemented by passport-free travel within the *Schengen* zone,[1] which makes crossing borders as easy as traveling from one US state to another. As seen in table 3.1, the percentage of EU citizens living in another EU member state is relatively small at 3.3 percent (or 16.9 million people). Citizens of certain member states, however, have taken an astonishing advantage of the free movement of people. In 2017, a staggering 19.7 percent of Romanian citizens were living in other EU member states, followed by Lithuania (15 percent), Croatia (14 percent), Portugal (13.9 percent), Latvia (12.9 percent), and Bulgaria (12.5 percent).[2]

In the run-up to the Brexit referendum of 2016, Prime Minister David Cameron secured a remarkable set of concessions from his fellow heads of

Table 3.1 Share of Non-Nationals in EU States, January 2017

EU Member State	*Total (%)*	*Citizens of Other EU Member States (%)*	*Citizens of Non-Member Countries (%)*
EU average	7.5	3.3	4.2
Luxembourg	47.6	40.7	6.9
Cyprus	13.4	12.9	3.5
Austria	15.2	7.5	7.7
Estonia	15.0	1.3	13.7
Latvia	14.3	0.3	14.0
Belgium	11.8	7.8	4.0
Ireland	11.8	8.9	2.9
Malta	11.8	6.6	5.2
Germany	11.1	4.8	6.3
Spain	9.5	4.2	5.3
UK	9.2	5.5	3.7
Denmark	8.3	3.5	4.8
Italy	8.3	2.5	5.8
Sweden	8.2	3.1	5.1
Greece	7.5	1.9	5.6
France	7.0	2.4	4.6
Slovenia	5.5	0.9	4.6
Netherlands	5.3	2.9	2.4
Czech Republic	4.9	2.0	2.9
Finland	4.4	1.8	2.6
Portugal	3.8	1.1	2.7
Hungary	1.5	0.8	0.7
Slovakia	1.3	1.0	0.3
Bulgaria	1.1	0.2	0.9
Croatia	1.1	0.4	0.7
Lithuania	0.7	0.2	0.5
Romania	0.6	0.3	0.3
Poland	0.6	0.1	0.5

Source: Eurostat.

governments in order to curb EU migration. As such, the UK did not grant any social benefits (such as income support) to EU migrants for the first seven years, thus effectively treating them as second-class citizens. The Cameron government also refused to pay child benefit for family dependents who remained in their EU country of origin. Longer re-entry bans for rough sleepers, beggars, and fraudsters were introduced as well. However, Cameron's proposal to reject EU citizens who were not in possession of a firm job offer was dismissed by the other member states, as was the idea to deport EU citizens within six months, should they fail to secure gainful employment.[3]

In addition to citizens moving to other member states, there is legal migration from outside the EU. Over the past ten years, the annual flow of non-EU nationals moving to the continent has been relatively steady and in January 2017 accounted for two million people, bringing the total figure of non-EU foreigners to 21.6 million; a mere 4.2 percent of the overall population (see table 3.1.) As mentioned earlier, only 16.9 million EU citizens are living in a member state, other than their country of birth. Hence, out of a total population of 512 million, only 38.5 million people (or 7.5 percent) can be classified as foreigners.[4] Once again, the UK was the member state most keen to bring immigration figures down. Government circles were increasingly alarmed by persistently high net migration figures.[5] This fueled an anti-foreign rhetoric in the media and resulted in the rise of UKIP, which became the most popular party in Great Britain in the elections to the European Parliament in 2014. While the UK government could do very little about the EU's free movement of people, Cameron and his Home Office Minister Theresa May embarked on an ambitious policy to curb non-EU migration, underlined by the perpetually repeated electoral mantra of bringing migration down from the hundreds of thousands to the tens of thousands. Tougher visa rules were implemented, which meant, for instance, that non-EU students were forced to leave the country within days of graduating from their UK programs. Bogus colleges that were merely designed to give students an entry visa but without offering any academic courses were shut down in droves. Tighter naturalization laws, for instance, of relatives from UK citizens, were also imposed. The measures, however, did not work, and in 2018, a staggering 248,000 people from outside the EU immigrated to the UK; the highest figures for fourteen years.[6]

The statistics show that the EU by and large is still quite homogenous. Granted, some countries mainly in the western part of the EU are more diverse than others. The UK, for instance, has a large nonwhite population of about 13 percent—legacy of their colonial empire. According to the 2011 census, Germany is now home to 2.7 million Turks, and the picture in larger, western European cities is one of multiculturalism and ethnic diversity. By contrast, Poland and many other EU member states in central and eastern Europe are highly homogenous whether from an ethnic, cultural, or religious perspective. It is obvious that the EU is an attractive destination in an increasingly mobile and globalized world economy. But statistics offer very little support to those critics who might see the cultural integrity of some European countries jeopardized. The fact remains that the EU in its entirety does not have that many migrants—whether from within or from outside the EU—and if so, migration hotspots tend to be in western European cities, with the national character of many states completely unaffected.

Far from being a strain on a country, migrants provide a vital boost to the economy as consumers, but also as taxpayers who contribute to the funding of welfare provisions. For years, European states have been suffering from a demographic deficit, with historically low birth rates and consequently an ageing population; a process, which endangers long-term economic prosperity. By 2080, the total EU population is projected to increase only marginally from 510 to 518 million.[7] While the UK will see its population swell from sixty-five to eighty-two million people, many countries will see a decline in the number of citizens, including Poland (−8.9 percent), Italy (−7.0 percent), Romania (−5.2 percent), Germany (−4.4 percent), and Greece (−3.5 percent).[8] Clearly, without migration, the economic and social parameters of certain EU countries will be affected in a highly significant fashion.

But it is non-legal migration into the EU—whether economic migrants seeking a more prosperous future on European shores or political refugees fleeing their war-ravaged homes—that hit the headlines in recent years. The migrant routes from Africa into Spain or Italy have long been established. But the civil war in Syria, which began in 2011, and the subsequent exodus of large parts of the population exacerbated a crisis, which had already reached worrying dimensions. According to the International Office for Migration, in 2014, a total of 280,000 refugees arrived in the EU. A year later, the figure had increased dramatically to 2.1 million, with at least 3,700 people being lost at sea. By 2018, and with entry into the EU now much more difficult, there were still over 100,000 people that had crossed the Mediterranean, with over 2,000 feared to have perished.[9]

MIGRATION FROM AFRICA

Managing the migration routes from Africa into Italy and Spain was initially handled by individual member states without co-ordination at EU level. Italy, for instance, ran a full-scale rescue mission referred to as *mare nostrum*. The government claimed that between October 2013 and October 2014 alone, 140,000 people had been rescued at a cost of nine million euros per month to the Italian taxpayer. In November 2014, *mare nostrum* was replaced by *Triton*. Now orchestrated by the EU border agency Frontex, it did not possess its own boats or planes and thus relied heavily on the financial support, staff, and equipment of volunteering member states. The budget for *Triton* was also considerably below that of *mare nostrum* at a mere three million euros per month. Even more astonishing, given the large number of people trying to reach Europe, rescue missions were now no longer conducted in international waters but were restricted to a thirty-mile zone off the coasts of Italy and Spain.

By the spring of 2015, migration had reached crisis levels. At a summit in May of that year, member states agreed to raise more money (although the summit's conclusions failed to provide specific sums) with more ships and planes deployed with the aim to destroy trafficker boats and networks and to improve border controls and surveillance. The measures were largely inward looking, designed to face the growing anti-migration sentiments that had emerged in countries like France, Germany, or the UK. They tackled symptoms but did not address the root causes of the refugee crisis. Moreover, the plan did not work. The numbers of ships and planes coordinated by Frontex were insufficient, while the tackling of trafficker networks proved to be an almost impossible task, as criminal networks often relied on boats, which had been fishing vessels one day and were carrying refugees the next. Trafficking people into the EU was also highly lucrative with people smugglers being able to earn up to 40,000 US dollars per trip. Outsourcing the control of migrants—as practiced by Australia and Indonesia—was also not a viable option, as those states with which the EU could have collaborated (such as Libya and Tunisia) were highly unstable. To this day, a reduced, but nonetheless steady trickle of people from Africa embark on the dangerous voyage across the western Mediterranean.

MIGRATION TO SOUTH-EASTERN EUROPE

In contrast to migration from Africa, the refugee crisis in south-eastern Europe was handled by the EU in a much more proactive fashion. By 2015, the sheer numbers that had started to arrive on European shores (see table 3.2)

Table 3.2 Migrant Arrivals into Europe, 2014–2018

Year	*Italy*	*Greece*	*Spain*	*Total*
2014	111,197	209,457	2,166	319,000*
2015	153,052	847,048	3,845	1,004,356
2016	179,525	173,244	5,445	358,403
2017	119,310	29,595	21,663	171,635
2018	181,436	173,561	8,162	363,504

Source: Office for International Migration.
* estimate.

Table 3.3 Migrant Deaths at Sea, 2014–2018

	Western Mediterranean Route (Spain)	*Central Mediterranean Route (Italy, Malta)*	*Eastern Mediterranean Route (Greece, Cyprus)*	*Total*
2014	23	2,326	83	3,279
2015	74	2,892	805	3,771
2016	69	4,410	434	4,913
2017	223	2,832	61	3,116
2018	128	4,581	434	5,143

Source: Office for International Migration.

simply necessitated a rapid reaction. Most of the refugees taking this route from Turkey into Greece or Bulgaria came from Syria, with additional people pouring in from Afghanistan, Iran, Iraq, or Pakistan. But it was the vicious civil war in Syria, which caused a migration stampede on a scale that Europe had not experienced since the end of World War II. By 2018, out of a total population of 13.5 million people, around 5.6 million Syrians had fled the country and a further 6.2 million had been displaced within Syrian territory.[10] There was barely a person left that had not been affected by the civil war in one horrific way or another. Many people made it across the border into Jordan, and by February 2018, this small country housed over 650,000 Syrian refugees; close to 9 percent of its total population. Many more, however, were looking to escape to Europe and fled to Turkey before trying to cross the sea into Greece. Table 3.3 lists the shocking number of fatalities and in 2015 alone, 805 people had died making this perilous journey.

Others entered the EU via land borders in either Greece or Bulgaria. By the summer of 2015, thousands upon thousands of people made their way through the Balkans toward the more prosperous parts of Europe further north. On leaving Greece or Bulgaria, the trek then snaked its way through Macedonia and into Serbia (both non-EU countries) before reaching the EU border in Hungary. By June, the flow of migrants had become so large that the Hungarian government tried to seal its border with Serbia by erecting a metal fence. Refugees then looked for an alternative by entering Hungary's neighbor Croatia, before moving onward through Slovenia, Austria, and ultimately Germany. By September, those borders too, were all closed.

The rush to reach northern European countries was exacerbated by German chancellor Angela Merkel, who on August 25, 2015, announced to an astonished public that the country was willing to accommodate one million refugees. By early September, Germany was taking in migrants who had been stranded in Hungary by the train load. News of this extraordinary generosity started to spread to other migrants, and even more people made their way up north. By mid-September, Germany had to strengthen controls on its border with Austria. Managing the tide of people proved to be a great organizational and administrative challenge for German municipalities. Shelter, clothing, food, and schooling needed to be provided, which stretched authorities to the limit of their capacities. Resentment also started to grow resulting in the worrying rise of the xenophobic party *Alternative für Deutschland* (Alternative for Germany). Still, the German people deserve much praise for their response to Merkel's call for action. The summer of 2015 provided memorable scenes of overcrowded train stations in southern German cities, to which people had flocked with drinks, food, and welcoming signs. Many were reminded of their own family's history. At the end of World War II, some 20 percent of Germans had to abandon their homes and had become refugees themselves. This collective memory provided for an astonishing buffer of emotional readiness to follow Merkel's rallying cry of "*Wir schaffen das*" (We can do this). But the Merkel government did not properly consult other EU countries affected by the refugee wave. Welcoming Syrians into Germany is one matter. But how can refugees get to their final destination? Most people made the journey by carrying all their belongings with them. To reach Germany, walking was very often the only viable option, and that meant crossing other EU countries. Hungary, Croatia, Slovenia, and Austria were not best pleased by Merkel's unilateral approach.

EU RESPONSES

Since 1997, the legal mechanism of the EU for dealing with refugees has been the Dublin agreement. Updated in 2003 and 2013, it stipulates that refugees entering an EU state must be administered by that country—which involves fingerprinting and registration, providing food and shelter, or schooling for children—before any potential asylum application could be processed. Refugees making their way to another member state would then have to be sent back to the country where they first entered EU territory. In this way, multiple applications could be prevented. On August 25, 2015, however, Merkel, decided to suspend Dublin for all Syrian refugees. This meant that migrants from that country would not be send back to the original state of EU entry (in most cases Bulgaria and Greece). Describing her decision as a sense of national duty, Merkel thereby granted protection to hundreds of thousands of refugees. Even two years after the peak of the migration wave, Germany continued to be the member state, which processed by far the most asylum applications in the EU with 524,000. This was in sharp contrast to the similar-populated UK, which merely handled a twentieth of that number.[11]

It was not until the end of September that the union tried to establish a more multilateral and coordinated approach by passing a raft of measures.

A structural strengthening of EU borders was agreed upon. Financial assistance was offered to Jordan, Lebanon, and Turkey with the clear aim to keep Syrians closer to home and thus to avoid the long and dangerous march across Europe. This approach also had the undisputed benefit of making a return to Syria much easier, once the country returned to a degree of stability. The UN also received a financial boost of one billion euros to improve conditions in their refugee camps. Most importantly, the summit proposed to distribute 120,000 refugees across the EU that were currently stranded in Greece and in Italy. The proposal was met with fierce resistance from Hungary, Romania, the Czech Republic, and Slovakia—often referred to as the *Visegrad* group—who cited their lower economic development in comparison with richer western European countries, and a consequent massive strain on public finances. But Merkel was unrelenting and even threatened that during future budget negotiations, Germany would veto additional agricultural and cohesion funds for those countries. In the end, the objecting states were outvoted by the remaining EU members, which left a highly bitter aftertaste, based on the notion that smaller member states saw their concerns overridden and ignored by Germany as the mighty arbiter of EU policy. It was widely regarded as an obtrusive act of meddling in national affairs.

But the implementation of the refugee distribution was a farce. By 2016 and with numbers now having increased to 160,000, only a paltry 6,000 people had been reallocated. Other matters, most notably Brexit, had assumed a higher priority and the Slovakian presidency of the EU in the second half of 2016 understandably made no attempt to revisit this issue. Irrespective of the suitability and coherence of this policy, it nonetheless represented binding EU law, which was widely ignored. The Visegrad countries remained stubborn and by the end of 2017, with only 27,000 people finding new homes, the program was quietly shut down.

THE EU-TURKEY JOINT ACTION PLAN

Since attempts to resettle migrants across the whole of the EU were largely failing, much hope was pinned on the EU-Turkey Joint Action Plan, which came into effect in March 2016. In return for six billion euros, the promise of enhanced enlargement talks and more visa-free travel for its citizens, Turkey agreed to take in refugees who had reached Greece by sea. The government also promised to improve human rights and conditions for refugees in Turkey and to use its security forces to intercept migrants and prevent boats from leaving its shores. On the EU side, for every person returned to Turkey, the bloc would accept a Syrian refugee for resettlement. However, the envisaged resettlement across the EU failed to materialize. Furthermore, in the aftermath of the failed coup of July 2016, Erdogan's actions became increasingly autocratic, which nullified any expectations of an improved human rights record. Still, almost instantly after the deal came into force, the number of refugees across the south-eastern Mediterranean route began to fall sharply. While in 2015, over 800,000 people had arrived in Greece, the figure dropped to some 170,000 (see table 3.2) as Turkey began to sharpen up its security measures.

But this did not mean that refugees stopped coming to Europe. Instead, an ever-increasing number of refugees looked for an alternative, longer, and, thus, more dangerous sea crossing in order to circumvent the Turkish fortress. As seen in table 3.3, deaths occurring at sea on the central Mediterranean route to Italy and Malta jumped from 2,832 in 2015 to 4,410 a year later. The problem was not solved, but it merely shifted to other shores. There were also no significant developments on behalf of Turkey to improve its human rights record while enlargement negotiations continued to be stalled, with the visa regulations for Turkish travelers into the EU also unchanged. The deal lowered the number of refugees entering Greece and Bulgaria, but it did fall short in delivering on the other aspects to the agreement. It therefore can best be described as the attempt to contain a precarious situation.

THE DILEMMA

Throughout the migration crisis, affected member states were intent on moving the human tide along to the next member state as quickly and comprehensively as possible. Any notion of European solidarity, of finding a continental solution, was absent. Angela Merkel's government was the notable exception by welcoming Syrian refugees with an astonishing degree of generosity. But Merkel was also the catalyst for growing tensions at EU level. Her open-door policy was announced without much consultation with those member states that were most affected by the refugee stampede. Her aggressive behavior in making the Visegrad countries come to heel over an agreement to spread out the burden of accommodating refugees went down very badly in the capitals of Hungary, Romania, Slovakia, and the Czech Republic. There was no evidence of European solidarity, nor was there much consensus building.

The causes of the human tide were not addressed, merely its consequences. With the help of Russia, Assad resumed his authoritarian and unchallenged position as Syria's leader. The UN—despite the EU's one billion euros cash injection—continued to be underfunded and its efforts, for instance, in the refugee camps in Jordan and in Lebanon, were greatly compromised. Given the gravity of the civil war in Syria, the EU had a humanitarian obligation to help refugees. But how about refugees from other countries, such as Afghanistan or Iraq, who might also have a legitimate claim to seek a haven?

Those people were not given shelter, simply because the Syrian numbers were so overwhelming.

Attempts by the EU to get a grip on the crisis never focused on how to bring refugees in and thus safeguard them from the potentially perilous trek up north. EU actions, as evidenced by the EU-Turkey deal, instead focused on how to keep people out. The crisis brutally demonstrated the consequences of lacking an effective EU immigration policy. Instead, we had an incoherent, uncoordinated mish mash of national approaches, with affected member states fiercely guarding their sovereignty. An EU-wide approach, whether implemented through intergovernmental collaboration or coordinated by supranational EU institutions, simply did not exist.

Ever since the migration tide reached crisis levels in 2014, the EU was behind the curve, desperately, yet futilely catching up with developments. At best, the bloc was just about able to handle African migrants, although the death tolls on the central and western Mediterranean routes certainly tell a different story. But Brussels and national capitals were hopelessly ill-prepared once Syria started to implode in the aftermath of the Arab Spring of 2011. It is as if Europe had stuck its head in the sand, hoping for an increasingly insurmountable problem to just disappear.

EU actions have also been divisive. Germany had used threatening language over future EU funds to bring about an agreement to re-distribute refugees in a more widespread fashion, which in any case was never implemented in sufficient numbers. The government of the Czech Republic had argued that compulsory refugee quotas were illegal and demanded a clarification through the ECJ. Such a clarification was provided by the court in September 2017 by confirming that the refugee relocation scheme was indeed valid and legally binding. The verdict came amid legal procedures, which the European Commission had initiated against the Czech Republic, but also against Poland and Hungary over their refusal to accommodate migrants in sufficient numbers.[12] In June 2018, Italy's incoming populist government had turned away two rescue boats. The first one, carrying 630 stranded migrants, was rerouted to Spain, with Interior Minister Matteo Salvini claiming victory in his ongoing feud with other EU countries over a fairer distribution of refugees. The second boat with 224 passengers was also turned away, this time to Malta. The ships were operated by aid organizations that had rescued migrants in open waters and were aiming for the nearest coast, which happened to be the Italian one. Salvini went on to describe them as "taxi services that finish the job of the smuggler organizations." In response, Mission Lifeline, which operated the second vessel, argued that many of its passengers were fleeing torture, rape, and slavery.[13] Salvini escalated tensions by threatening to withhold his country's contributions to the EU budget if it does not receive more support on the migrant issue.

The sovereign debt crisis in Greece demonstrated that a supranational management of the EU—even for a supranational policy such as the Euro—was no longer deemed to represent a viable solution. Intergovernmentalism was the order of the day and within this process, it was Germany that was taking the helm in a hitherto unseen fashion. Up until 2010, the country was quite content to support and finance European integration, without taking too much of a proactive role in designing the key policies or institutions. Of course, being the economically most powerful player in the union always meant that its voice carried a stronger resonance, but it would have been far-fetched to describe Germany as the architect of the EU. Other countries, most notably France but also the UK were far worthier of such an accolade. But 2015, with the restructuring of the Greek economy in the spring and the refugee tide in the summer, ushered in a period of German hegemony. Welcoming Syrian refugees gave Chancellor Merkel the moral high ground. Coercing fellow EU governments into an agreement on refugee distribution, however, did not.

The unprecedented nature of the migration tide might have sown the seeds of a tentative EU refugee policy. Germany liked to see a replica of its own asylum system being spread out across the EU, whereby migrants are distributed more evenly while also considering prosperity levels, unemployment, and population density of affected member states in order to reach a fairer formula. The Commission was backing Germany's agenda, but the potential damage to the union was clear for everyone to see. Forcing countries to take people that they don't want, while asking migrants to go to places they don't want to settle in could have disastrous consequences for inner peace and social stability.

The migration crisis turned into yet another identity crisis for the EU. The European project has always been built on solidarity. In days gone by, before the Big Bang enlargement of 2004, a member dealt with a problem, which arrived at its border for the sake of the EU. Nowadays, once a problem arises, the first cries are for help in solving the problem. These are two utterly different conceptualizations of solidarity. Pursuing a common notion of a European destiny centers on the belief that the interests of the member states are intertwined and that peace and prosperity for all depends on giving up a degree of national sovereignty. It is highly questionable whether such an understanding is at all alive in many EU capitals. The refugee crisis revealed a tension between the interests of the EU (which was managing the crisis as swiftly as possible) and the interests of most of the member states (which was passing on the problem to other member states as swiftly as possible). In the end, we had a chaos of nationally driven, short-term remedies.

One reason for this new mindset might be found in recent developments surrounding the Eurozone crises. More and more people from countries that were affected by economic collapse moved from poorer to richer member states, sparking a gradual increase in anti-migration rhetoric, which was exacerbated by the astronomical bailouts for Greece, Spain, Ireland, Portugal, and Cyprus. These emerging nationalist sentiments then fueled much of the debate surrounding the migration tide. It seems that Europe—more than ever since the Big Bang expansion of 2004—suffers from utterly different notions on how to integrate people. In western Europe, past forty years saw an ever-increasing move toward multiculturalism. In the new member states of central and eastern Europe, however, such a concept was always regarded as potentially disruptive to social cohesion. The concept of multiculturalism as practiced by the West was expressed by Angela Merkel's offer to house Syrian refugees and to demand a more even distribution of them across more member states. The response to her actions, however, and the resentment of being bullied by Germany were the expression of some of the new member states' belief that multiculturalism is a failure.

Borders can't be sealed. European leaders ought to have been aware of this considering the relatively recent dismantling of the Iron Curtain. And the Turkish-Greek border, with its very large Turkish coastline and hundreds of Greek islands is particularly hard to seal. So is the Italian border with many islands close to African shores. The refugee tide might continue for years to come, if the Middle Eastern region continues to remain unstable. If the risk of fleeing is smaller than the risk of dying, then people will leave their homes behind. At the moment, Greece and Italy are housing most of the migrants, with refugee camps now permanently in place, since people cannot be moved on, unless a coherent EU distribution quota is implemented. This is not a solution, but merely a stop gap. What is needed is a common EU migration policy with common asylum rules applicable across all participating member states.

But Europe also ought to address the causes of the problem. Fewer refugees mean fewer refugee distribution, less costs, less antagonism between member states, and more inner peace and social stability. Investing more heavily in crisis-affected countries therefore seems paramount and international charities have for years called for more financial resources for food security, healthcare, and job creation or to tackle government corruption. The problem is not new, it has only been exacerbated recently, but the solutions have been plain to see for many years. Now might be the time to significantly upgrade the UN spending target for development aid of a paltry 0.7 percent of GDP.

In concrete terms, and in addition to promoting sustainable economic development, the EU could fund reception centers where people are fed, housed, clothed, and schooled. Financing ought to be done not by national governments as is the present practice, but by the EU budget and thus by financial contributions from all member states. An agreed quota system could then allow for a coordinated resettlement of migrants across Europe while considering different prosperity levels of EU members. More EU funds should also be made available to shut down trafficking networks while assistance to Jordan, Lebanon, Serbia, and North Macedonia who also house significant refugee numbers would seem a justified action. After all, refugees are human beings, and helping them is a moral and humanitarian imperative—a notion that is one of the founding legacies of the EU.

NOTES

1. Schengen refers to the very small town in Luxembourg where in 1985 the governments of France, West Germany, Belgium, the Netherlands, and Luxembourg agreed to abolish border controls. Over the years, many EU but also non-EU countries joined this bilateral agreement before the Treaty of Amsterdam (1997) formally integrated Schengen into EU law. All EU member states except for Ireland, Croatia, Bulgaria, Cyprus, and Romania are part of Schengen. Outside the EU, Iceland, Switzerland, and Norway also do not impose border controls to the traveling public. Given its Eurosceptic credentials, it comes as little surprise that the UK was never part of this agreement, often citing the danger of terrorism, and the consequential need to screen anyone entering the country's territory. Despite its international character, Schengen represents pure intergovernmentalism. As such, any government can at any stage suspend Schengen and reinstate border controls. This occurred on a widespread scale during the Syrian refugee crisis in the summer of 2015. In the immediate aftermath of the Al-Qaeda attack on Madrid commuter trains in 2004, Spain dropped out of Schengen. Germany did the same when hosting the FIFA football championships in 2006.

2. The member states with the smallest share of its citizens living in another EU country were Germany (1.0 percent) and the UK (1.1 percent). Source: Eurostat.

3. In November 2014, the ECJ supported Britain's assessment of the potential abuse of the free movement of people. The city of Berlin had refused to pay welfare support to a female citizen from Romania who had moved to Germany, but without showing any intention of looking for employment. The ECJ sided with Berlin, stating that a member state must "have the possibility of refusing to grant social benefits to economically inactive EU citizens who exercise their right to free movement of people solely in order to obtain another member state's social assistance."

4. In 2016, the top five countries from where people acquired EU citizenship were Morocco (101,300), Albania (67,500), India (42,700), Pakistan (32,900), and Turkey (32,800). For more information on a range of migration statistics please refer to: https://ec.europa.eu/eurostat/statistics-explained/index.php/Migration_and_migrant_population_statistics.

5. Net migration refers to the difference between the number of people entering the UK, and those leaving the country. This figure started to rise after 2004, when the UK government—unlike all other western EU member states except for Ireland and Sweden—allowed EU citizens from the new member states of central and eastern Europe to come to its shores. During the peak of the recession in 2012, net migration

(including EU and non-EU migrants) dropped to 177,000, only to rebounded strongly in the year ending in June 2016 with 336.000. The annual figure for the year ending June 2018 was 273,000.

6. By contrast, Germany, with an ageing population and low birth rates, embarked on a pro-migrant policy by issuing US-style green cards for professionals in the high tech and IT sectors. The policy had little success, however, mainly because of language barriers.

7. To access the full table, please refer to: https://ec.europa.eu/eurostat/statistics-explained/index.php?title=File:Demographic_balance,_1_January_2016-1_January_2080_(thousands)_PITEU17.png.

8. To access the full table, please refer to: https://ec.europa.eu/eurostat/statistics-explained/index.php?title=File:Demographic_balance,_1_January_2016-1_January_2080_(thousands)_PITEU17.png.

9. See: www.unhcr.org/europe-emergency.html.

10. See: www.worldvision.org/refugees-news-stories/syrian-refugee-crisis-facts.

11. Source: Eurostat. In 2017, the numbers for asylum applications for the top five EU countries were Germany (524,000), France (111,000), Italy 78,000), Sweden (61,000) and Austria (56,000). In marked contrast other countries accepted far fewer applications, including the UK (28,000), Greece (25,000), Belgium (24,000), the Netherlands (16,000), and Spain (13,000).

12. The relocation scheme required member states to pledge available places for relocation every three months. Hungary had not taken any action at all since the scheme had started. Poland had not relocated anyone and not pledged since December 2015. The Czech Republic had not relocated anyone since August 2016. See: europa.eu/rapid/press-release_IP-17-5002_en.htm.

13. See: www.independent.co.uk/news/world/europe/migrant-crisis-italy-rescue-ships-matteo-salvini-libya-spain-latest-mission-lifeline-a8412591.html.

Chapter 4

Brexit

No one saw it coming: not the pollsters who confidently predicted that British citizens would vote in favor of staying in the EU; not Prime Minister David Cameron who—despite running a lackluster campaign—saw no reason to instruct his government to make contingency plans for a possible EU exit; not the financial markets, which had confidentially invested in British assets in the safe assumption that the referendum debate will soon become an unpleasant footnote to British political history. But on the morning of June 24, 2016, Europe awoke to the astonishing news that the UK had decided 52 percent to 48 percent in favor of leaving the EU. The truth is that Britain's relationship with its continental neighbors had always been characterized by conflicting interests and a fundamentally different understanding on how collaboration between European governments could best be achieved. In the end, the decision to leave the EU was a political outcome that was waiting to happen ever since the country joined the bloc in 1973.

THE AWKWARD PARTNER

Back in 1950, when the first tender shoots of European integration started to sprout, Britain had been invited to join the nascent Coal and Steel Community. The governing Labour Party was in the process of nationalizing key industries—including coal and steel—and felt no desire to give up control to a supranational entity after finally succeeding in bringing these industries into public ownership. Just a couple of years later, in 1955, the UK once again snubbed efforts to help unite the continent by leaving the Messina conference, which eventually set up the ECC, the forerunner to the EU's Single Market. This reluctance to come on board seemed to a certain extent justifiable. After all who could have predicted that a project centering on the two arch enemies France and West Germany could ever succeed? Better then to rely on the special relationship with the United States, which had served the country so well during two world wars. And why trade with war-torn economies when the countries of the former empire, which after all were not directly affected by the European theatre of war, continued to provide vital markets across the globe? Such reasoning revealed a certain feeling of superiority. Britain, albeit with massive financial and military support from the United States, emerged victorious from World War II. The logic of getting together with the "losers" was simply not compelling.

By 1960, however, British thinking had performed a U-turn. While the UK was still emerging from years of austerity, growth rates on the continent were impressive and easily outclassed those across the Channel. The feeling of superiority gave way to a sense of inferiority. A country that had won the war was about to lose the peace, and the greatest empire, which the world had ever seen was in the process of being dismantled. But political circumstances were not on Britain's side. In the 1950s, a great number of continental politicians argued that European integration would be incomplete without the participation of the British.[1] A decade later, however, French president Charles de Gaulle regarded European integration as less important than close bilateral ties between his country and West Germany, and dismissed the UK as an "American Trojan Horse" that would water down European ambitions. He twice vetoed Britain's application; in 1961 and then again in 1967.

It took a change in French politics and a staunchly pro-European UK prime minister to finally get the country into the bloc. Georges Pompidou replaced de Gaulle in 1969 and a year later Edward Heath led the Conservative Party into government. The stars were aligned for a speedy integration, and the UK joined in 1973, with both sides not worrying too much about any policy consequences. But the haste with which negotiations were concluded would soon backfire. Britain had previously started to drill for oil in the North Sea and given the precarious nature of the state's finances, the country was rather reluctant to share its new-found wealth with its European partners at preferential rates. Membership of the EU's Common Agricultural Policy resulted in higher food prices, because cheaper products from New Zealand or Australia were no longer given easy access to UK markets, and were now replaced by more expensive European ones. The biggest bone of contention, however, was the UK's budget contribution.[2] While it was in line with that of other member states, the EU spent most of its budget on supporting farmers. But Britain only had a very small farming population, which meant that the country emerged as the biggest net contributor to the EU's finances. No wonder, with Heath losing the 1974 elections, the Labour government almost instantly called a referendum on whether to leave the European Community (as it was then called) merely two years after joining. Although the outcome was 2 to 1 in favor of staying, it left commentators on the continent bewildered by such conflicting and seemingly fluid identity messages. Staying outside of Europe was not good enough, but neither was joining the European project. It was as if feelings of superiority and inferiority were forever conspiring to form a combustible political brew.

The "awkward partner"[3] truly emerged with the arrival of Margaret Thatcher in Downing Street in 1979. As education secretary in the Heath government, and subsequently as opposition leader she never shied away from beating the drum for European integration, once famously sporting a piece of fetching knitwear that proudly displayed the flags of the nine individual member states. Once in power, however, her differences in opinion over how European collaboration could be achieved, and what European integration should, and more prominently should not entail became very pronounced. It was her government that emerged as the key proponent for the completion of the Single Market with the ratification of the Single European Act in 1986. But beyond this groundbreaking initiative, Thatcher was adamant that Europe should not develop a social dimension where workers' rights were regulated at European and not at national level. The disproportionate budget contribution was finally, yet acrimoniously settled in 1984, with the UK receiving a rebate, financed by the other member states, of two-thirds of the difference between the standard member state contribution and the funds earmarked for the UK. Any moves toward an erosion of national sovereignty, and the establishment of a European super state were vehemently opposed. Thatcher's antipathy toward Economic and Monetary Union (EMU) reached almost paranoid levels, while her crass and antagonistic diplomacy in the run-up to the Maastricht Treaty of 1992 eventually resulted in her being ousted from office by her own cabinet colleagues.

Thatcher's successor John Major found out to his disadvantage how Europe continued to divide public opinion and that of his own governing Conservative Party. Major managed to negotiate an opt-out on EMU, easily the most contentious policy of Maastricht. But this impressive achievement was more and more undermined by Eurosceptic voices within the media and the Conservative Party, which questioned the democratic credentials of the European project, and the loss of national sovereignty of an "Ever Closer Union" as set out by Maastricht. In the end, a deeply unpopular and divided government lost by a landslide in 1997 to be replaced by the more Europhile Tony Blair.

Under New Labour, and for the first time since Thatcher's push for the completion of the Single Market, the UK found itself at the center of policy innovation. Stunned by the disintegration of Yugoslavia, European leaders had come to realize that without the military capacities of NATO and in particular the United States, an independent military engagement was next to impossible. It was Blair, together with French president Jacques Chirac, who instigated the Rapid Reaction Force; a 50,000-strong army made up of national military units. Blair was also an outspoken advocate of EU expansion to the former communist countries of central and eastern Europe and sorted out the budget row on how to finance this so-called "Big Bang enlargement" during the UK's tenure as the EU's presidency in the second half of 2005. In the end, the controversial participation in the war in Iraq in 2003 cut his premiership short, but for a brief period, Britain under Blair was very much the driving force of European integration.

A return to a more cautious approach came with the arrival of Blair's former chancellor Gordon Brown, who became prime minister in 2007. Coinciding with the signing of the Lisbon Treaty in the same year, Brown argued that this major reorganization of EU policies ought to be the last treaty for a long time. His government had also negotiated yet another opt-out from the recently introduced Charter of Fundamental Rights. This apprehensive attitude came as little surprise, given that from early on, Brown had been very dismissive of EMU, arguing that the economic cycles of the UK and of its continental partners were simply not aligned and thus a single currency would bear too much of a risk for the UK.

Brown's tenure as prime minister was short lived. The ramifications of the global economic crises resulted in a 2010 election loss to a coalition formed by the Conservative Party of David Cameron and the Liberal Democratic Party under the leadership of Nick Clegg. Cameron had made several striking moves to please the Eurosceptic wing of the Conservatives. In 2009, and as leader of the opposition, he ordered his party colleagues in the European Parliament to leave the pro-European center-right party grouping. As a result, instead of collaborating with parliamentarians from fellow conservative and Christian democratic parties, Tory politicians were now forming an alliance with occasionally rampant Europhobes. Once in power, Cameron came to realize that public opinion in the UK, fueled by often exaggerated media reports, continued to be more and more Eurosceptic. EU rebels within his party kept diverting attention from pressing reforms and Cameron felt that his agenda of economic renewal, austerity, and balancing the budget was hijacked by an ever-present insistence on cutting ties with the continent. Still, the announcement in January 2013 that the British people must "have their say" with an in/out referendum took many commentators by surprise.

Cameron's tactics were vindicated by the election results to the European Parliament in June 2014. The UKIP, under the charismatic and populist leadership of Nigel Farage, came out on top in the polls with the Conservatives a distant third. Anti-EU backbenchers in Cameron's party continued to be ever more vocal, and the prime minister, with some justification, feared that the upcoming national elections of 2015 might result in significant electoral losses, with UKIP potentially outflanking the Tories on the right with an anti-EU and anti-immigration rhetoric. Cameron was not an outright Eurosceptic, but he held strong views that EU integration and, in particular, the recent migration from many central and eastern European countries imposed vast and sudden economic and cultural changes, which many UK communities struggled to cope with. His previous attempts at bringing immigration down to the tens of thousands from the current 200–300 thousand had failed, largely caused by the EU's Single Market and its cornerstone of a free movement of people, which allowed not only workers but also students and pensioners, in fact, anyone holding an EU passport to settle on British shores. So, Cameron rolled the dice, announcing to the British people that he would renegotiate the UK's membership terms with a subsequent referendum on those new terms scheduled for June 2016.

When looking at those new terms, however, one cannot but feel distinctly underwhelmed. Cameron had set his sights on benefit tourism, where EU citizens from countries with less advanced welfare systems settled in the UK to receive more generous social allowances. To fend off any potential welfare scroungers, Cameron negotiated a four-year period during which no social benefits at all were given to recent EU migrants, thereby in fact treating fellow Europeans as second-class citizens. This was an astonishing concession granted to him by the other member states. More reasonably, child benefit to EU migrants could now only be claimed when the dependents in question were also residing in the UK. Cameron also received assurances that those countries which at this stage had not adopted the Euro (Poland, the Czech Republic, Hungary, Bulgaria, Romania, and Croatia) or which had negotiated a Euro opt-out (apart from the UK, this also applied to Denmark and Sweden) ought not to be disadvantaged by any developments emanating from reforms of the Single Market. On a final note, Cameron also reiterated his refusal to sign up to an "Ever Closer Union"—a rather empty rhetoric that pandered to the anti-EU wing of his party, as any moves toward more federalism would in any case require the approval of every individual member state, thus giving the UK a de facto veto power.

But that was it. What was heralded as a major renegotiation of EU membership did not address the fundamental issue that gave such prominent rise to anti-EU feelings among the UK electorate. Ever since 2004, when the EU had welcomed eight countries from central and eastern Europe, the UK has seen the arrival of around 1.5 million EU migrants.[4] Such high numbers were great news for the economy. GDP growth was impressive, productivity went up, skill gaps were closed, and inflation was under control. All this against the backdrop of unemployment figures that were very low when compared with the likes of France or Italy.[5] But many people were also astonished by the speed of change that migration had brought. While Britain had a long history of integrating migrants, there was now a sizeable number of citizens who found themselves on the losing side of an ever more Europeanized and globalized economy. In migration hot spots, such as in bigger cities, or in rural areas with large agricultural businesses, people realized that their wages had stagnated and public services—from schools to hospitals and day care centers—were stretched to bursting. But even in areas without any significant migration pressures, a fervent media stirred up notions of discontent and the UK witnessed the recurrence of a bewildering social phenomenon: that of xenophobia despite the absence of foreigners.

Reflecting on over forty years of EU membership, the accolade of the "awkward partner" has a distinct truth to it. Several UK governments had fundamentally different conceptions of how EU integration ought to be organized and what kind of Europe should be established. All prime ministers, from Harold Wilson (1974–1976) to David Cameron (2010–2016) had resisted any developments toward a more federal Europe that could one day become a European super state along the lines of the United States of America. Discussions about potential increases in financial contributions, and, in particular, the perennially controversial Common Agricultural Policy, were met with fierce resistance. What the UK essentially aimed for was a glorified trading union with easy market access, coupled with political cooperation, not necessarily through the EU but potentially merely through bilateral collaboration, in such vital areas as security, defense, and foreign policy. For most of the political establishment, this was as far as the UK's European ambitions could be stretched.

On the other hand, giving up sovereignty on social policies, the welfare state, or on military capacities and a foreign policy that would replace their national equivalents, or indeed on a European bureaucracy with far-reaching powers over national governments and equipped with a substantial budget, was viewed as attacks on the UK's national interest. One must remember that the UK had finished World War II with a sense of tremendous national pride and achievement. A lot of continental countries, however, were invaded (with heavy losses of civilian lives and destroyed towns and cities), or as in the case of countries in central and eastern Europe, colonized by communism. The belief that the postwar era should therefore aim for a radical departure from the status quo to avoid such economic, political, and human catastrophes from ever happening again, never gained much traction within the UK's public discourse. The country's entry in 1973 was the reluctant admission that from an economic perspective, the EU had made impressive strides. The rationale for a political union, however, escaped most members of the political establishment. Nonetheless, the "awkward partner" was instrumental in many policy innovations and on certain occasions shaped the union into a more integrated entity. Thatcher's government was the driving force in the eventual implementation of the Single Market and its associated free movements of goods, services, capital, and people. Agreed in the 1950s, it had been undermined by national derogations for thirty years, and it took a forceful UK prime minister to finally help create a truly European economic sphere. On a less spectacular but nonetheless decisive level, the EU's cohesion policy, designed to offer financial support for struggling regions, would not have been implemented without the UK's insistence upon the country's accession in 1973. And Tony Blair's role in shaping the EU's post–Cold War era—from the push toward a sweeping enlargement to central and eastern Europe, to a budget overhaul, and on to a more proactive foreign policy—made him the biggest catalyst for integration among all his fellow European leaders during his time in office. The "awkward partner" was on occasion surprisingly collaborative.

Looking at voting records at EU level also reveals a picture that is far less anti-EU than the referendum campaign made people believe.[6] True, in the Council of Ministers, which consists of representatives from all national governments and which together with the European Parliament passes EU legislation, the UK was on the "losing side" of legislative initiatives the most times of all EU members. The figures reveal a marked jump from 2.6 percent between 2004 and 2009 (the Blair/Brown years) to a staggering 12.3 percent between 2010 and 2015 (the Cameron years). By contrast, the second most outvoted countries (Austria and Germany) found themselves on the losing side only on 5.4 percent of occasions during the Cameron period. Viewed from a different perspective, this also means that the UK supported 97.4 percent of EU legislation between 2004 and 2009 and still 87.7 percent between 2010 and 2015. It is therefore incorrect to portray the United Kingdom as a country that was forced to participate in a union, which aimed for fundamentally different objectives that ran counter to the British national interest.

THE REFERENDUM CAMPAIGN

In the run-up to the referendum, British citizens had to embark on a process of soul searching. There was the Eurosceptic side who regarded sovereignty as a zero-sum game and the more the EU was organizing British lives, the less British citizens were in control of their own destiny. Many people were worried about a threatened notion of democracy that was severely curtailed by the power of unelected Brussels officials. For them, European integration and the institutions and policies that it had created over the past seventy-five years had failed and being a member of the EU no longer served the national interest. On the pro-EU side, many felt that despite the considerable shortcomings of the EU, twenty-first-century challenges could only be met through multilateral cooperation, with any loss of national sovereignty more than compensated for the sharing of sovereignty with European neighbors. For Europhiles, relinquishing a degree of national autonomy still served the national interest best, arguing that being a European means more than consuming French wine or holidaying in Spain, but instead requires a formalized and structured way of interacting with other states and their citizens.

Ever since David Cameron announced the date of the referendum in January 2013, there were feverish discussions in parliament, in the media, and among voters. The government, except for a handful of cabinet members (including the minister for Justice Michael Gove), argued in favor of staying. So did the Liberal Democratic Party and the Green Party. Most businesses also supported Cameron's cause. As to the Labour Party, the recently elected leader Jeremy Corbyn and his shadow chancellor John McDonell had argued throughout their political careers that the EU favors big business, and although Corbyn campaigned for "Remain," his support was at best lukewarm, and at worst non-existent.[7] The "Leave" campaign relied to a large extent on former London mayor Boris Johnson; easily the most charismatic UK politician with a huge support base among Conservative voters. Most mainstream politicians organized themselves under an umbrella organization called "Vote Leave" and refused to collaborate with the UKIP. It had for years campaigned for an EU referendum, and subsequently started its own "Leave.EU" campaign, with Nigel Farage putting every ounce of his considerable rhetoric skills into what he believed to be an historic opportunity.

The concessions, which Cameron secured from his European partners in the run-up to the campaign became almost instantly immaterial to the public debate. Some changes to welfare claims of EU migrants, an assurance that countries that opted out of the continent's single currency will not be discriminated against, and a commitment toward a more competitive European Single Market made virtually no impact on voters' perception. Cameron's strategy to return from Brussels with an improved deal, which he could then confidentially present to the British public and which subsequently would sail through parliament misfired in spectacular fashion. What was at stake was not a tweaking adjustment to existing membership terms but an overall assessment of the country's relationship toward Europe. The "Remain" camp stressed economics and financial security based on the fact that the UK could influence the regulation of Europe's Single Market and could freely trade with its 500 million consumers. Exiting from this market would result in job losses and a massive fall in prosperity levels. Finance Minister George Osborne turned the rhetorical screws very tight by announcing that a "Leave" vote would result in an immediate budget adjustment to account for the subsequent loss in government revenue caused by lower economic output and less foreign investment. In short, the EU might not be perfect, but it was certainly preferential to the uncertainties of a Brexit Britain. But the scare-mongering rhetoric of the government, as well as of some business leaders and the Bank of England, was completely overblown. Yes, given the drastic restructuring of the British economy, which Brexit would necessitate, economic indicators such as GDP growth, employment levels, and tax revenues would certainly be affected. But the scenario of an economic Armageddon that would transport Britain back into the Stone Age started to look ludicrous, and only heightened the belief among many voters that the government was not sincere. No wonder the "Leave" campaign mocked its counterpart by referring to its campaign as "Project Fear."

Responding to this rhetorical swipe, "Remain" then argued that its case for staying in the EU was more about "Project Fact." And indeed, Brexiters failed conspicuously to paint a concrete picture of what an independent UK would look like. Some preferred the "Norwegian" option; being a part of the EU's Single Market without being a member of the EU. While such an approach might have freed a country from the political subordination to Brussels, meeting Single Market regulations that were only set by EU members would most certainly have resulted in a loss of economic sovereignty. It would turn the UK from being a rule maker (of the EU's Single Market) into a rule taker. Hence, the "Canada" option also gained some traction: being outside of but negotiating trade deals with the EU on an ad-hoc basis, as a free trader, guided by bilateral trade agreements that were complemented by the rulebook of the WTO. Unfortunately, while trading inside the EU's Single Market came tariff free, the same did not apply to free traders and other WTO members where, depending on the type of product or service and the volume of trade, tariffs, and customs duties are charged. Not a problem, said the Brexiters. These increased costs would be more than compensated for the fact that the UK would now be free to negotiate its own trade deals and would not have to collaborate with EU countries on reaching agreements with the likes of the United States, China, India, and other emerging economies. As a result, new trade deals would be more in line with the UK's economic strengths, and independent from the trade agenda of the likes of France and Germany. There was, however, a significant level of doubt whether such a calculation would result in a net gain. After all, the EU is a powerhouse when it comes to world trade and thus has significant negotiation leverage; something that the UK might struggle or even fail to achieve when going it alone.

Given the difficulties in establishing an economic case for Brexit, political arguments relating to national sovereignty featured prominently within the "Leave" camp, with its catch phrase of "Taking Back Control." Here the Brexiters had a compelling case: while new EU treaties (as well as the accession of new members) must be agreed unanimously by all member states, the large majority of EU legislation now only requires the approval of a majority of states (55 percent, which must represent at least 65 percent of the total EU population), as well as a majority of EU parliamentarians. This means that countries no longer have a veto, and on occasion, must accept what other countries have agreed upon. By being part of the EU, a country has given up a certain degree of national sovereignty. On the other hand, leaving the EU would also mean a loss of shared sovereignty. On occasion you will be overruled as an EU member, but in other instances, your own view, once it has the support of most of bloc's countries, might be superimposed on others. In any case, the question of national sovereignty is greatly compromised by the way the world works in the twenty-first century. The empire is no longer, and the days when Britain was a global power had long faded into a distant memory. Moreover, there isn't a single European country that could call the shots when dealing with Russia, China, or the United States. Collaboratively, however, the EU still has a voice in international affairs. Any notion of a perceived increase in national sovereignty outside the EU should have taken these matters into account.

Every now and then "Remain" also highlighted security concerns from IS terrorism, as well as migration from the Middle East and Africa, which could only properly be addressed through a pan-European approach. This was a precarious strategy. London and Paris had just been the subjects of terrorist attacks, and images of the summer of 2015 when hundreds of thousands of refugees crossed the continent to escape the conflict in Syria were still fresh in the mind of many voters. "Leave.EU" further fueled tensions when Nigel Farage posed in front of a large poster depicting a line of refugees and migrants on the Croatia-Slovenia border under the headline of "Breaking point: The EU has failed us all." Disregarding the facts that the civil war in Syria was beyond the control of the EU, and that EU enlargement and the refugee crisis are two separate matters, Farage then claimed, further EU enlargement to countries such as Turkey would result in further mass migration to the UK, conveniently ignoring the fact that the integration of Turkey was many years if not decades away, and that in any case, every EU member state including the UK had the right to veto such a move. Farage opportunistically stoked up xenophobic sentiments, but the image of a Britain overcrowded with refugees stuck in the mind of many voters.[8]

"Don't you like democracy?" historian Simon Schama was asked by the crime writer and "Leave" supporter Dreda Say Mitchell during yet another television debate just days before the referendum. The distinguished academic offered an answer suitable to his profession by concentrating on the intricate institutional structures of Brussels, but his opponent was able to bring across some hard-hitting points: The EU is bad for democracy, unelected officials determine the destiny of every EU member state, and the umbilical cord between citizens and their elected representatives was severed because of too much European integration. This was powerful stuff, and arguments over a loss of national sovereignty were the strongest points for "Leave." Nigel Farage was not alone in wanting "our country back" (the official slogan of UKIP's campaign) and "to take back control" (the official catch phrase of the "Vote Leave" campaign). Many people agreed.

On the other hand, an improvement of the state of democracy could easily have been achieved by constitutional amendments, which were long overdue. An unelected House of Lords, an electoral system that disproportionally benefits larger parties and disregards the votes for smaller ones,[9] or the lack of representation for English regions are just some of the democratic shortcomings of the UK. Also, comparing the EU with a national polity is comparing apples with oranges. The EU is a vehicle of integration and collaboration between countries, and not a super state along the lines of the United States of America. It certainly has its democratic weaknesses, but successive treaties have strengthened the role of the European Parliament, while checks and balances carried out by the member states to curb some of the legislative and executive enthusiasm of the Brussels bureaucracy had been strengthened over the years. It is uneven to compare the EU with a nation-state. A comparison with an international organization would be more appropriate, and from this perspective, the EU has made significant democratic strides, unlike the OECD, the IMF, the World Bank, or the UN, for example, where the involvement of citizens is all but absent.

The image that best captured the demand for a return of national sovereignty was the "Vote Leave" campaign's tour bus, which proudly sported the slogan "We send the EU £350 million a week. Let's fund our NHS instead." Here was the headline-grabbing financial conundrum of EU membership. Instead of funding vital domestic causes such as the National Health Service (NHS), the UK instead was paying an inflated sum to a Brussels' bureaucracy that spent UK taxpayers' money according to their own objectives. The day after the referendum, journalists asked leading Brexiters when and how the money will be pumped into the NHS. To the consternation of many, not a single politician was willing to take up the pledge, and indeed it was unceremoniously dumped by Cameron's successor Theresa May. The figure of £350 million per week also requires further clarification. It is true that the UK paid about 18 billion pounds per year into the EU budget (or 350 million pounds per week). This is the price of EU membership, and every member state, not just the UK, contributes to European integration. What "Vote Leave" failed to mention was that around 50 percent of this money went back into the UK to support farmers, poorer UK regions (such as Wales, Scotland, and Northern Ireland), as well as science and research. Hence, not only did the slogan raise false hopes for the financial consolidation of a much-loved UK institution, the claim was simply untrue. It nonetheless managed to bring a vital point across:

an expensive and wasteful EU bureaucracy prevented UK citizens from shaping their own destiny.

Beyond money and national sovereignty "Leave" was also able to win sympathy among many voters who felt that the pace of change caused by EU migration was too fast. Ever since the "Big Bang" Enlargement of 2004, the UK accommodated large numbers of citizens from other EU countries who settled in Britain, taking advantage of one of the founding principles of the EU: the free movement of people. By the time of the 2016 referendum, the UK's population continued to grow at a significant rate: from sixty-five million to a predicted seventy-five million by 2050, with around two-thirds of the population increase attributed to EU migration. As a compact island, Britain would have found it very difficult to absorb and integrate that many people. Overcrowded schools and hospitals and a continued housing shortage were cited, as were concerns about the national cultural character, where in the words of Nigel Farage, in some parts of many British cities, English was no longer spoken. These sentiments were not new. In fact, they went back to a debate that the UK had in the late 1960s when leading Conservative politician Enoch Powell called for compulsory repatriation. Some fifty years later, these issues also found resonance in France, Germany, and the Netherlands. But as far as numbers were concerned, only one-eighth of UK residents were born abroad, which didn't even make the country the most multicultural place in Europe (see table 4.1). Mainstream politicians—whether in the era of Powell or during the Brexit referendum campaign—often ridiculed and misunderstood such perceived xenophobia and racism, which did not foster a productive debate about a cultural sense of belonging. Lamenting the rapid pace of change, the influx of new cultural, social, and political norms was not necessarily racism. It could also merely have been a genuine and entirely legitimate concern about fundamental changes to one's way of life.[10]

Table 4.1 Foreign-Born Population in EU Countries in 2016

Top 8	*Percent (%)*	*Bottom 8*	*Percent (%)*
Luxembourg	45.2	Portugal	8.4
Cyprus	20.4	Finland	6.0
Austria	18.2	Hungary	5.1
Sweden	17.0	Lithuania	4.5
Ireland	16.9	Czech Republic	4.1
Belgium	16.3	Slovakia	3.3
Germany	13.3	Romania	1.8
United Kingdom	13.0	Poland	1.6

Source: Eurostat, March 2017.

The high percentage of foreigners in Luxembourg can be explained by the attractiveness of the tiny country as a financial hub and magnet for multinational corporations. Figures for Cyprus are increased by large numbers of Turkish Cypriots claiming citizenship in the Republic.

In arguing the case for "Remain," Cameron relied on his election advisor Lynton Crosby who in the past had become notorious for his negative campaign style. This worked well in the referendum on Scottish independence in September 2014, and a significant number of voters were swayed to remain in the UK for fear of the economic uncertainties surrounding the creation of an independent Scottish state. The tactic also showed positive results in the general elections of May 2015 when Cameron warned of a "coalition of chaos" fronted by Labour leader Ed Miliband. But it backfired in the London Mayor poll of May 2016 as many voters were appalled by the often-racist attacks of the Conservative candidate Zac Goldsmith who had linked the eventual winner Sadiq Khan—a senior Labour politician with Pakistani roots—to alleged Islamic extremists.[11] During the EU referendum campaign, it was simply astonishing that Cameron once again relied on Crosby's tactics by establishing a horror scenario of what the UK would look like outside the EU. But positive and affirmative messages of a Britain inside the union, and of the EU's past achievements were almost absent from his campaign rhetoric. Bringing prosperity to Europe, unifying the continent after the Cold War, offering a mechanism to establish democratic stability for previously autocratic regimes, being capable of handling twenty-first-century challenges such as global warming or terrorism were just a few points from which Crosby could have drawn inspiration. In the end, Cameron's team merely portrayed EU membership as the lesser evil.

The government never contemplated the possibility of losing the referendum. Government departments, ministers, and the Conservative Party hierarchy did not draw up plans of what type of Brexit should be negotiated in case "Leave" won. Cameron simply did not have a plan B. Steps that ought to be taken to assure the markets, timelines for negotiations, the identification of negotiation positions on contentious issues such as Gibraltar, the border with the Republic of Ireland, the role of the City of London as the most powerful seat of finance in the EU, the introduction of additional border and custom controls or the provision of budget contingencies, and the list goes on and on, but nothing of that sort was planned for a potential Brexit D-Day. In the end, Cameron cast a tragicomical figure when announcing his resignation just hours after the results came through, leaving not only his party but an entire country utterly unprepared for the monumental challenges that lay ahead. The moment outside his residency in Downing Street on the morning of June 24, 2016, will forever define his six years at the helm of the UK government: a moment of defeat tinged by a strong underlying current of arrogance and complacency. Months later, when touring the US lecture circuit, a journalist asked how he slept at night. "Like a baby," responded Cameron. "I wake up every hour and cry for my mum." At least Cameron maintained his sense of humor; something that cannot be said of his political credibility.

Britain had always justifiably been proud of its political culture: an inquisitive, scrutinizing, and by and large trust-worthy media; a well-informed public; politicians willing to engage with voters; and a general discourse that treasures public debate and allows for the exchange of arguments. Not on this occasion. For a start, the political discourse often had menacing, divisive, and venomous undertones. Some politicians reverted to a questionable war-time rhetoric.[12] On the night of the referendum, Nigel Farage proudly proclaimed that victory was won, without "a single bullet being fired," which was a shockingly insensitive comment in the light of the murder of the Labour MP Jo Cox by a deranged extremist just a week before. On an almost daily basis, Brexiters and Remainers fought shouting battles outside the Houses of Parliament, and many members of parliament became figures of hate. The UK had not experienced such vitriol in the postwar era.

Knowledge of European affairs was surprisingly patchy, not only among the public but also among senior political figures. While watching television debates and reading news reports in the run-up to referendum day, one cannot but have felt astonished by the fabrications of some members of the political establishment—whether on the "Leave" or the "Remain" side. The case of Andrea Leadsom was remarkable. With Cameron's resignation, she emerged as one of two front runners for the leadership of the Conservative Party, which would have turned her into the UK's prime minister. In the aftermath of the referendum, Leadsom suggested that Britain should leave the EU straight away, thereby showing a complete lack of appreciation of how EU rules (over 170,000 pages of them) are instrumental to the organization and functioning of a country. One might not like some of the rules, but first one might want to assess the consequences of those rules, and subsequently one might want to replace them with one's own rules to prevent a certain degree of anarchy. Under Leadsom's scenario, no air passenger or indeed airline would have had any legal recourse upon leaving EU air space and entering that of the UK. One would very much doubt whether airlines at all would have been willing to take such legal risks, thus resulting in the grounding of air traffic. Or think of the poor people of Dover, Britain's busiest port. Instead of enjoying the free movement of goods, trucks now would have to be thoroughly inspected by custom officials (who given their increased workload would also have been severely understaffed), resulting in mile-long tailbacks. To give another example, the UK exports around 1.27 billion pounds worth of animals, processed meat, and other food products to Europe's biggest port in Rotterdam.[13] Yet, the Dutch port had neither the facilities for the personnel to inspect the animals. Hence, a sudden Brexit, but also a rash no-deal Brexit, would interrupt entire supply chains, with dramatic consequences not just for food supply, but also for medicine (e.g., for cancer patients) or the manufacturing sector.

Leadsom would have been well-advised to have collected conducive intelligence on countries that are outside of the EU. The case of Croatia, which joined the EU in 2013 springs to mind. The country's northernmost province of Istria has a lively fishing industry and is located right next to a prosperous and sizeable market: The Italian region and tourist magnate of Veneto. Prior to EU integration, Istrian fish could not be sold in Italy as "fresh" given the long delays at the Croatian-Slovenian border. Now imagine the organizational and administrative nightmare of an EU external border between Calais in France and Dover in the UK. And it is not Croatian fish that is at stake but a multitude of products for a country fifteen times the size of Croatia. Of course, with time, sufficient preparations can be made to accommodate such a changing regulatory environment. But these changes take many months if not years to implement, and certainly cannot happen overnight. The UK therefore can be grateful when Leadsom's leadership ambitions came to a merciful end, prompted by her less than fortunate assertion that having children made her a better candidate to be prime minister.[14] This paved the way for the childless Theresa May to become the unopposed leader of the Conservative Party.[15] Countries deserve more competent and knowledgeable politicians than Andrea Leadsom.

If knowledge on EU affairs was on occasion found wanting among the political class, it comes as little surprise that the general public at times also struggled to comprehend fully the pros and cons of EU membership. Granted, European integration can be a fickle, complicated, confusing, abstract and technocratic business, but the union's history, politics, or economics were not taught at UK schools. Instead, education on Europe often ended with World War II. Unlike in other member states, news reporting on EU matters stood in marked contrast to the impact that the EU had on domestic life. While members of the European Parliament in Italy, France, or Germany could regularly be seen on TV channels, only conservative MEP Daniel Hannan and—of course—UKIP MEP Nigel Farage were known to the wider public. In the run-up to the referendum, speculation as to what the EU does (and succinctly what it does not do) was rampant, and real knowledge rather thin on the ground. The Brexit vote was therefore often a vote on one's assessment of life in general. If one's wages were too low, if government was not listening, if the NHS was underperforming, if jobs were hard to come by, the EU found itself an easy target for one's frustration.

The example of Sunderland is a telling one. As a highly Eurosceptic electoral district (61 percent voted "Leave"), the city in the north-east of England had suffered from years of industrial decline in particular to its shipbuilding industry. In the 1980s, European integration, however, offered a lifeline when the Japanese car giant Nissan decided to establish a massive plant there, designed to serve the EU's Single Market. Nissan produced about 2,000 cars every day, giving employment to over 7,000 people, not counting jobs in subsidiary industries. In a town of 275,000 inhabitants, it was by far the biggest employer. Yet, voters showed little concern that in a post-Brexit world, and with potential tariffs imposed on cars, Nissan might move the plant to the continent, where most of its European market was located.

Amid all this hyperbole of speculation, false information from both sides was all too prevalent. The media, the presumed bastion of accountability, and public service had much to answer for. During what seemed endless TV or radio debates, journalists were often all too keen to avoid taking sides. This can be laudable but being neutral does not mean that lies should be left unchallenged. And this is precisely what happened all too often, thus only further augmenting the lack of reliable facts. A one-on-one interview granted to Brexiter and justice secretary Michael Gove summed up the mode of the campaign. When confronted by Sky News journalist Faisal Islam with an exhaustive list of organizations that supported "Remain," Gove responded by claiming that the British people "have had enough of experts." This was an extraordinary comment, especially when considering Gove's former role as education secretary, where he surely appreciated the importance of expertise and evidence-based analysis.[16]

THE REFERENDUM RESULT

A week before the vote, Nigel Farage, with an air of restrained confidence, announced that "Leave" might just win it. To the astonishment of the financial markets, political leaders, and commentators, he was right: 51.89 percent versus 48.11 percent with a voter turnout of 72.2 percent. But regional differences were sharp. In Scotland, 62 percent voted "Remain." Northern Ireland too voted in favor of the EU (56 percent). On the other hand, England (53 percent) and Wales (52 percent) wanted out. Age was also a highly defining factor. Among the younger group of voters (those aged between eighteen and twenty-four), a staggering 75 percent supported "Remain." By contrast, 61 percent of voters over the age of sixty-five wanted nothing to do with the EU. Education levels were equally decisive. Of those with a university degree, 71 percent supported "Remain." Among those with a high school degree as their highest academic attainment, 68 percent wanted out.[17] Socioeconomic factors could also not be discounted. For statistical purposes, the UK government organizes its population into five categories ranging from A (the highest class) to E (the lowest). Here too, one could find a clear trend in that the lower your class, the higher the likelihood for opting out of the EU. Of the top fifty areas, with the highest DE concentration, only three (London, Liverpool, and Leicester) voted "Remain." Equally telling, almost all areas that had more than 30 percent non-UK born residents supported the EU, indicating that the

Table 4.2 Results of the UK Referendum

Entity	*Result*
UK wide	52% Leave
Scotland	62% Remain
Northern Ireland	56% Remain
England	53% Leave
Wales	52% Leave

The higher the level of academic attainment, the more "Remain."
The younger the voter, the more "Remain."
The lower the social-economic class, the more "Leave."
The less multicultural environment, the more "Leave."

more culturally diverse one's life experience, the more favorable one's stance toward EU integration.

The referendum results brought up many legitimacy issues. The UK, as the name suggests, is a union made up of four distinct nations: Those of Scotland, England, Wales, as well as the Irish contingent living in Northern Ireland.[18] A union ought to represent the wishes of its constituent parts. Yet, two of the four nations of the UK now found their political will fundamentally compromised by the UK-wide referendum (see table 4.2). It therefore came as little surprise that Scotland's first minister and leader of the Scottish National Party, Nicola Sturgeon, instantly resurrected the possibility of a new Scottish referendum on independence, which would allow the country to stay in the EU. Many Scots felt justifiably outraged. One of the key arguments in the 2014 referendum was that leaving the UK would also mean leaving the EU. Having voted to stay in the UK, many Scots now found that the other side of the bargain was not kept.

Londoners too found that the vote on Brexit ran counter to their beliefs. Sixty percent of UK citizens living in London voted "Remain." However, the city has by far the largest concentration of foreigners of any place in the UK, and in 2015, 36.8 percent of its population were foreign born. Given that a very high number of this contingent was not eligible to vote, because they were not UK citizens, and assuming that most appreciated the benefits, which EU membership bestows on non-nationals, one can safely state that around three-quarters of people living in London might have been against Brexit.

The situation was even more delicate in Northern Ireland. The Good Friday Agreement of 1998 brought an end to thirty years of violence between British Protestants and Irish Catholics. In the aftermath of the referendum, constitutional experts were clear that Brexit would compromise the Agreement as one guarantor country (the UK) would now be out of the EU, while the other (the Republic of Ireland) would remain. This would make a cross-border collaboration as enshrined by the agreement very difficult, and as such "Good Friday" might lose its constitutional validity, thus requiring a further referendum, which could ultimately lead to Northern Ireland joining the Republic in the south.

If this was not damaging enough, constitutional commentators were aghast at the low referendum threshold, which Cameron had agreed upon. He merely decreed that whichever side secured most votes would win the referendum. But referendum questions of such utmost and historical importance usually come with extra caveats in order to make sure that a populace is certain of the new direction, which a country is embarking on and thus, referendums ought to avoid cementing a fluctuating state of opinions that could easily have a different outcome when asked a week later or in different meteorological conditions.[19] As such, some referendums, for instance, the one held to finalize the independence of Montenegro from Yugoslavia in 2006 simply raised the threshold to 55 percent of votes. "Leave" did not reach that figure. Another example is provided by the referendum on Scottish devolution in 1979. Here the UK government stated that not only the majority of votes cast but also at least 40 percent of registered voters had to pass that motion. Hence, although most Scottish votes were in favor of devolution, only 64 percent of registered voters turned out, and only 33 percent of registered voters wanted devolution. Under this formula, a simple calculation reveals that the Brexit vote only accounted for 37.46 percent of the registered electorate; little more than a third, thus hardly showing an overall large majority. David Davis, Brexit secretary, frequently referred to the fact that the vote to leave the EU represented the biggest (absolute) popular vote in the history of the UK, since 17.4 million citizens opted for "Leave." He conveniently forgot to mention the 16.1 million people who had voted "Remain," which was the second biggest of such votes ever recorded. In the end, the UK embarked on potentially the most far-reaching transformation process the country had ever witnessed in the postwar era, based not on crystal-clear support from its electorate but on a momentary assessment of its mood.

The biggest controversy, however, surrounded the wording of the referendum itself. "Should the United Kingdom remain a member of the European Union or leave the European Union?" An analogy might serve to illustrate the mess, which Cameron heaped on his people. Imagine a group of 100 tourists visiting London. Every night this group goes out for dinner at a Chinese restaurant, and voices from within the group start to argue in favor of a different culinary experience. Group leader Dave then holds a vote on whether to remain with or abandon the Chinese option. Twenty-six people of the group are indifferent and do not vote. Thirty-eight vote passionately against eating Chinese, while thirty-six express their satisfaction with the current arrangement. Dave accepts the result of the thirty-eight to thirty-six majority and declares that the group will not be eating Chinese. He resigns in protest, and it now falls to a new tour leader (let's call her Theresa) to identify what "not eating Chinese" means. Very quickly, some of the anti-Chinese voices declare that what they don't like about the previous dining experience is the use of rice and noodles. For them, not eating Chinese means steak and potatoes, quickly termed the Polish option. Others, however, begin to argue that they like noodles and rice, but don't like the sweet and sour taste of some Chinese dishes. For them, a Thai option would certainly be feasible. In the end, the tour group cannot reach a compromise, and Theresa loses her job for failing to live up to her promise to deliver a non-Chinese dining option.

What prevented a coherent group decision was the prevalence of a false choice between Chinese and non-Chinese dining. But what ought to have been done in this fictitious example is to present the group with clear alternatives: Polish, Thai, or Chinese. Or after the initial decision not to eat Chinese, the group should have moved on to another vote between the two non-Chinese options. This is the story of the Brexit referendum. A majority of the voting public—but not of all registered voters—reached a decision on what they don't like. But the identification of the country's alternative to existing EU membership was never asked. It was a ridiculous failure of democracy.

THE FUTURE RELATIONSHIP WITH THE EU: WHAT'S AT STAKE?

Leaving the EU requires a massive readjustment of a country's economy. Trade relations with erstwhile partners conducted with hardly any barriers need to be recalibrated. Closer relations with trade partners in the non-EU world need to be explored. Entire industrial sectors might require government support in order to adjust to new regulatory regimes. Exiting the Single Market and thus the free movement of people necessitates the establishment of a new visa regime. The list goes on and on. Some key aspects will suffice to demonstrate the complexity of a Brexit process that was walking a tightrope: delivering on the referendum result of leaving the EU, without jeopardizing growth, prosperity, and jobs.

Migration and the Rights of EU Nationals

All EU citizens are entitled to take advantage of one of the key ingredients of the Single Market: The free movement of people, which allows anyone to settle in any EU country, whether as a pensioner, as a worker, as a student, or simply as a private person, as long as they hold a passport of an EU member state. After the Big Bang enlargement in 2004, many citizens from new member states sought a better economic future and moved abroad, with the UK being one of the most attractive destinations.[20] Over the next twelve years, close to 1.5 million EU citizens settled on British shores, bringing the total number of EU foreigners living in the UK to 2.9 million people.[21] But the UK also needed to be watchful of any notions, which might undermine the status quo of the 1.2 million British citizens that had settled in EU countries, as any migration or visa deal would almost certainly be reciprocated.

Migration is a fickle business. Up until the referendum, it was very good for the UK as it closed vital skills gaps. Migrants also worked jobs, which Brits were often hesitant to take up.[22] The employment rate of migrants from the EU was also higher than that of UK citizens,[23] and tax revenues and productivity improved accordingly. Wages and thus inflation were also kept under control, which was great news for business, consumers, the government, and the Bank of England. Hence, the economic boom prior to the financial crash of 2008 and the subsequent recovery would not have been possible without migrant workers. On the other hand, low wages disproportionally affected low-income workers. In areas with high migration, public services, such as schools, health centers, and hospitals, came under severe pressure. But these shortcomings were also the result of governmental inactivity and could not necessarily be blamed on migrants. More spending on public services and a fairer tax distribution would most certainly have been better remedies in the long term. Still, managing these considerable migration pressures in the short term proved very challenging, and a hospital for example can't just be built overnight. In the end, many citizens' capacities to absorb the extent and speed of change was severely stretched.

If the UK intended to keep prosperity at comparative levels, migration post-Brexit would have to continue. Any country, and particularly one that now intended to brand itself as "Global Britain," needs global talent. But some restrictions, some quotas, some visa policy still needed to be implemented. For years, Nigel Farage heralded the Australian system, which welcomes migrants depending on the type of skills that they possess. However, in the aftermath of the referendum, the UK government never explicitly stated which system it preferred. In addition, although the free movement of workers (i.e., those with jobs) might cease, the free movement of people (which also includes tourists) will not stop. Hence, any migration control could only relate to workers and as such, the UK would most likely see a drastic increase in the number of illegal workers with the added disadvantage that those disappearing into the black economy would not contribute to tax or national insurance revenues. Finding a coherent balance between a free movement of workers and people, therefore, represents a formidable challenge.

Even worse, any visa regime might deter high-skilled workers. How about the spouse? How about older children who would soon enter the job market? Would they be allowed to be economically active? And how about those high-skilled workers who arrive at the border without a confirmed job offer? Those skills could hardly be assessed at a border crossing. Visa regimes are also notoriously difficult for businesses to administer and plan. Say, for instance, a business has a certain quota for low-skilled jobs. But what if one low-skilled employee proves to be a big success? The business might not be able to promote the worker as there might not be any visa vacancies in the higher job category. Managing migration is therefore terribly complex. It is about finding a balance between lower migration numbers (after all, this was one of the underlying currents for the "Leave" vote) and migration that sustains productivity, skills, and growth (which is what businesses but also many voters want).

In the end, migration in a post-Brexit Britain might cease to be an issue rather quickly. After all, who would like to move to a country, which is not welcoming to migrants and which might be about to enter a period of economic decline. Migrants came to the UK because it was a successful country, because it was a job machine, and because it had one of the lowest unemployment levels in Europe. But some foreign workers will not come, and some that are based in the UK might return to their country of origin, if these positive economic factors are no longer. Nigel Farage and many Brexiters would welcome this. Life is after all "more than just economics, it is also about culture."[24] One cannot be sure whether this notion would be shared by many voters, who might see their jobs disappear and their living standards compromised.

The Border with Ireland

Relations between Britain and its former colony Ireland were always highly sensitive. In the rest of the Empire, London adopted a more laissez-faire approach, which allowed for a degree of self-government as long as trade and strategic benefits were not deemed to be compromised. But because of the close geographical proximity of Ireland, this option was not feasible as any trouble in the colony could have spilled onto the British mainland. This meant that the UK's handling of Ireland was always heavy-handed. Furthermore, the antagonism in Northern Ireland (which is part of the UK) between British, Protestant settlers, and native Catholics resulted in a civil war that lasted some thirty years and was only ended with the Good Friday Agreement of 1998. The guarantor states of this agreement are both the UK and the Republic of Ireland, and any changes to its legal prerogatives might require a further referendum. Given that a clear majority of voters in Northern Ireland had chosen "Remain," it would not have been unthinkable, if the province would leave the UK and join the Republic in the south. Furthermore, the EU stood firmly behind Ireland, which was only logical given that the country was a member of the club and the UK would soon not be.

After the Good Friday Agreement, there was a profusion of cross-border cooperation, with people working on the "other side" and supply chains developing across the former divide. Bus networks were aligned, as were energy provisions, and Irish businesses invested in the north and vice versa. These developments were largely made possible by the establishment of the EU's Single Market in 1993, which enabled the seamless crossing of borders, for goods, services, capital, and people. For Ireland and Northern Ireland, membership of the EU meant that the concept of a border—establishing barriers between peoples—lost its meaning and galvanized the peace process. Northern Ireland leaving the EU would thus automatically reintroduce such a concept.

From an economic perspective, the vast majority of Irish exports ended up in the UK. Any hard border would have had drastic consequences for the Republic and thus it was no surprise that the permanence of an open border was a red line for the EU. But an open border as envisaged by Ireland and the EU would have been difficult for the UK government. For Brexiters, leaving the EU, of course, meant leaving EU policies, most notably the Single Market but also the customs union, which regulates trade with non-EU partners. But leaving those policies would logically result in a hard border as the free movement was no longer.

The Brexit Divorce Bill

The budget of the EU is a curious construct. It is agreed for seven-year periods, and prior to the start of each so-called financial perspective, all budget items are agreed upon in advance. The problem emanating from Brexit was that the referendum and a possible EU departure fell during the financial perspective of 2014–2020. This means that prior to this budget cycle, the UK made a legally binding commitment to the financing of EU programs and policies. But what if the Brexit date did not coincide with the end of a financial perspective, which was in December 2020? Would the UK be liable to continue to pay its annual contribution? In addition, throughout its forty-plus year membership of the EU, the UK had accrued additional financial commitments, most notably the payment of pensions to EU staff. Would these liabilities be added to the divorce bill?

Currency

Assessments of the UK's currency in the post-referendum era were mildly optimistic. For years, Sterling was a magnet for speculative international financial capital. In the absence of attractive yields for commodities, stocks, and government bonds, the UK had experienced a property frenzy, and an overvalued Pound meant a loss of competitiveness. The Brexit referendum resulted in an immediate drop in value of 30 percent against the US dollar and 20 percent against the euro and thus corrected this overvaluation in a speedy fashion. Sterling was now more leveled, British goods were now more competitive internationally, and the argument started to prevail that any upcoming potential costs of accessing the Single Market might be offset by lower exchange rates. Still, the UK is an import economy with a trade deficit of 200 billion euro. In the months following the referendum, import prices went up. So did inflation, and with it the purchasing power of wages declined. In any case, the performance of currencies is impossible to predict. While the euro was on a high post-referendum, the situation could easily turn once the sovereign debt crises in the Eurozone hit new heights, for example, with the implosion of the Italian economy.[25] Under this scenario, the UK could be hit by a double blow: a more expensive Sterling complemented by restricted and more costly access to EU markets.

Overall Trade

But currency indicators paled into insignificance when compared with the paramount importance of trade. For four decades, British firms and businesses had unfettered access to its European trade partners. The EU share for British trade in goods reached 56 percent just before the referendum. For services, it was 40 percent. Yet, with Brexit, trade relationships would have to be redefined almost from scratch. Monique Ebell, economist at the National Institute for Economic and Social Research,[26] gave a stark assessment of the potential risks of leaving the EU's Single Market. A hard Brexit, that is, trade with the EU on the terms established by the WTO, would result in a loss of 60 percent for EU trade in goods and also 60 percent for EU trade in services. The UK's cash cow, the finance industry, would be particularly affected. Should the two sides agree on a specific trade deal (a so-called Free Trade Agreement or FTA) the losses would be slightly lower for goods (40 percent) but the same for services (60 percent). The consequences for UK trade would be astonishing. Taking into account EU and non-EU trade, dealing with the EU through WTO rules would mean a drop of 35 percent for goods and 25 percent of services. An FTA would not remedy the situation with a loss of 22 percent for goods and 25 percent of services.

Brexiters, most notably the MEP Daniel Hannan but also Trade Minister Liam Fox, reiterated that any loss of EU trade would be more than compensated for by a gain in non-EU trade. The argument was simple: leaving the EU would allow Britain to enter free trade negotiations with economic power houses, such as the United States, China, Japan, and India; something which under the EU regime was governed by the Common Commercial

Policy (CCP). The Brexiters saw enormous economic potential, given that the Eurozone's growth prospect had been largely flat while non-EU markets promised higher returns. But Ebell did not share the Brexiters' optimism and bluntly stated that any gains cannot compensate for the losses emanating from a hard Brexit. Her report argued that the gain in services would be close to zero, although she did acknowledge a potential for trade in goods citing an increase of between 26 percent and 66 percent.

In any case, such trade deals would require years of painstaking negotiations. The 2017 trade deal between Canada and the EU took over seven years of brokerage. Granted, the UK post-Brexit and the EU would have much more of a regulatory alignment, which would help in speeding up the process, but the task of establishing special trade relationships with a host of countries would take many, many years and even after their conclusion might not guarantee the same degree of trade that the pre-Brexit status quo offered. In the end, establishing new trade relationships would almost certainly represent a formidable risk to jobs and economic stability.

Manufacturing

In the globalized economy of the twenty-first century, labor mobility and the absence of trade restrictions are key to the establishment of an outward looking, international economy. Take, for instance, London's highly prestigious fashion industry. At the high end, fashion houses need to recruit top designers, who might not all be born in the UK. At the lower end, garments then need to be fabricated by using dressmakers from, for instance, lower-wage economies in eastern Europe. Or take the car industry: a Bentley limousine starts life in the Slovakian capital of Bratislava where the car is fitted with a German engine. Financing arrives from Dublin, while English workers apply the chrome parts. Honda's factory in Swindon in the southeast of England represents another good example. The company had adopted a far-reaching supply chain model where parts are only stored in Swindon for a very short production cycle of under two hours, with new parts constantly being restocked by around 380 daily trucks, which arrive from across the European continent. It is easy to see that trade restrictions would necessitate a complete rethink of how products are manufactured across the UK. Even goods, which fall under the free trade regime of the WTO would be affected, albeit to a much-lesser extent. Although tariffs are not applicable, the increased time spent at border controls would still severely disrupt the just-in-time nature of any supply chain. Hence, industries such as, computers, telecommunication, information technology, pharmaceuticals, and aerospace might not encounter any new trade restrictions, as they fall under the WTO free trade scheme, but the production process would still be subject to delays. But the situation is far worse for those sections that face a steep imposition of WTO tariffs. These include cars (10 percent), chemicals (4.6 percent), machinery (between 1.7 percent and 4.5 percent), steel (between 8 percent and 30 percent), or agriculture (on average 16 percent but higher for certain products such as beef, which faces a 40 percent surcharge).

Cars

A more specific picture of just how massively the manufacturing sector will be affected by a new trade regime is offered by the car industry. Over the past decade, UK-based car makers have gone from strength to strength and at the time of the referendum, the country produced two million cars per year, which made it Europe's largest manufacturer. But 80 percent of those cars ended up in the EU. This was a consequence of the Single Market and its free movement of goods, which allows manufacturers to set up plants anywhere in the EU with unrestricted access to all EU markets. Britain was brilliant in luring non-EU manufacturers to its shores, including the likes of Nissan, Honda, BMW (which produces the highly popular Mini), Volkswagen, and Tata Motors (which makes Jaguar and Range Rovers cars). A post-Brexit UK has to consider that British-based manufacturers imported 40 percent of their steel (at a WTO tariff of between 8 percent and 30 percent depending on type and quality). Once a car comes off the production line, a further 10 percent tariff is applied when selling it offshore. It does not require much imagination to envisage board room discussions at German or Japanese car companies. Why produce automobiles in Britain and be charged high tariffs when selling the product to a market of 440 million Europeans? Better to produce (and sell tariff free) on the continent and accept the tariffs when selling to the smaller UK market of sixty-five million consumers. Not surprisingly, BMW, Honda, Toyota, and Nissan all reiterated a Brexit deal, which would see tariffs imposed on the industry had a drastic impact on their companies' investment in the UK, and soon many foreign car companies started to announce the scaling back of their UK operations.[27]

Banking

The City of London is the financial center of the world and much of the UK's tax revenues, as well as 500,000 jobs depend on it. A large proportion (30 percent of its activity) focuses on EU markets and Brexit provided "the City" with a high degree of uncertainty. Will London maintain the so-called passporting rights to the EU, which would allow it to continue offering services to EU-based economic actors? The same applies to some US and Swiss banks that currently are gaining EU access through their London-registered branches. In November 2017, the EU decided to move the European Banking Authority from London to Paris. But to what extent will the industry follow? Will it establish headquarters in Frankfurt, Amsterdam, Paris, Dublin, or Madrid? Or will it merely open smaller branches on EU territory, which would then qualify for an EU finance passport? And if this is the case, will the EU impose benchmarks as to the size of the operation to avoid being "infiltrated" by non-EU finance houses? What is at stake for Britain is to maintain an epic market share, with alternative locations snapping opportunistically at its heels.

Security

The fight against organized crime and terrorism is still the domain of national governments, and collaboration between EU states proceeds in an intergovernmental fashion, thereby largely side-lining the supranational European Commission.[28] But the European security landscape has changed drastically since Al Qaeda bombed commuter trains in Madrid in 2004. We now have a network of EU agencies that allow for a much-improved transnational interaction of security agencies, through the sharing of information, joint actions, or the handing over of criminals through the European Arrest Warrant. During the referendum campaign, Richard Dearlove, the former head of the UK's intelligence agency MI6 claimed that the country would be much safer outside the EU, by comparing some EU states to "leaky ships" when it comes to the collaboration through Europol.[29] This assessment was vehemently criticized by Rob Wainwright, the British director of Europol who argued that the UK had a "far stronger capability to fight crime" by being a member of the law enforcement agencies of the EU. As this spat illustrates, a clear assessment of the security landscape that a post-Brexit UK is about to enter was not straightforward. Should the country go it alone and deal with security threats in a unilateral fashion? Or should the UK form a bilateral relationship with its erstwhile partners? And if so, how much would such a relationship cost the UK taxpayer? This lack of clarity seemed astonishing, given the pernicious effects of terrorism, organized crime, and cybercrime on a country's safety.

POST-BREXIT SCENARIOS: TRADE DEAL OPTIONS

We ought to remind ourselves that the referendum merely asked whether voters would prefer to "Remain" in the EU or wanted to "Leave." At no point did the campaign on both sides address the specific nature of post-Brexit trade relations with the continent. Many people simply assumed that Britain would continue to be part of the EU's Single Market: a so-called soft

Brexit. But such an option would necessitate that Britain remains under the jurisdiction of the ECJ, and Brexiters argued that such a scenario could not be described as "Leaving" the EU as stated in the referendum result. Hence, a hard Brexit option—leaving all EU policies and reclaiming total national sovereignty—became ever more prominent. But this would mean leaving the Single Market and thus potentially jeopardizing Britain's fundamental economic parameters. What models could the British government call upon before the start of negotiations?

Norway

The affluent Scandinavian country had on two occasions flirted with the idea of joining the EU but referendums in 1972 and 1994 marginally rejected such a notion. Still, Norway is to some extent part of the EU. Together with Iceland and Liechtenstein, it forms part of the European Economic Area (EEA) and accepts the key ingredient of European integration, the Single Market with the free movement of goods, services, capital, and labor, but without having a say in the formulation of Single Market regulations. This also means that Norway accepts the jurisdiction of the ECJ in Single Market matters. In return, this setup gives the country unfettered access to 500 million consumers. For the privilege of being part of the Single Market, Norway pays into the EU budget, but remains outside of the big budget policies, namely cohesion (which offers financial support for struggling regions) as well as agriculture and fisheries (where European farming and fishing are financed solely through the EU budget). As such, the Norway option would allow for the seamless continuation of trade. This would provide economic certainty, which is vital for jobs and foreign investment. But budget contributions would need to be made and, in the end, these might be higher than the 1 percent GDP membership fee, which the EU currently collects from every state. Furthermore, Britain's sovereignty would be severely curtailed. The country would have to follow Single Market rules over which it has very little influence, while British courts would still be subjugated to the ECJ. The UK would be an EU rule taker, but not a rule maker as Single Market regulations are agreed upon exclusively by EU member states. On the plus side, Britain would be in a position to conduct its own trade deals with the non-EU world, as Norway is not part of a customs union, and does not participate in the EU's CCP.

WTO

At the other end of the spectrum, Britain could just walk away from the Brexit negotiations and organize trade based on its membership of the WTO. All EU countries are also members of this organization, which regulates trade across the globe. Ever since its inception in 1995, the WTO has come a long way and now around 40 percent of trade in goods is free from any tariffs or other restrictions. But the WTO has failed recently in its attempt to liberalize the market for services. Intellectual property rights, inventions, and patents also found it difficult to be elevated onto a WTO platform, and certain areas (e.g., agriculture) are still subject to massive tariffs. As a fallback option, it would provide the UK with an almost instant boost for national sovereignty. Non-EU trade deals can be negotiated with any WTO member without the interference of Brussels. This is very tempting for hard-line Brexiters, but it does carry enormous risks to a UK economy that for years basked in the glory of the EU's Single Market.

Turkey

Facing the economic uncertainty of establishing a new trade regime, the Turkey option might also offer a solution. Although Turkey has been an EU candidate since 2005, negotiations have stalled recently and as long as President Recep Tayipp Erdogan remains in power are unlikely to resume. Still, the country is part of the EU's Customs Union. A logical spillover of the Single Market, the CCP presents the rest of the world with a united EU front when it comes to trade. Individual member states cannot form their own trade deals, which would make a bilateral trade deal, for instance, between the United Kingdom and the United States impossible. Any external non-EU trade must go through the supranational policy of the CCP. While this compromises national sovereignty, it provides a potent leverage when dealing with mighty trade partners, such as China, Japan, and the United States. Hence, given the prize of accessing the enormous European market, the EU can afford to play tough and negotiate more favorable deals than individual member states could by themselves. This would be beneficial to the economic standing of the UK, but the downside, of course, is the continuation of a perceived deference to Brussels in external trade matters.

Canada

Norway and Turkey represented choices that were too compromising to the notion of national sovereignty and hence were not acceptable to many Brexiters. Instead, the Canada option was regarded as a more accurate reflection of the public's will to "Leave." In 2017, the EU signed its most wide-reaching FTA so far, entitled the "Comprehensive Economic and Trade Agreement" (CETA). Both sides claimed to have eliminated 98 percent of tariffs, resulting in a free trade zone between 500 million Europeans and 35 million Canadians. But the deal also had limitations that might make this option unsuitable for Britain. While CETA offers tremendous opportunities for trade in goods, the service sector is severely compromised. With regard to the finance industry, which after all represents the most lucrative area of the UK economy, CETA cannot stop Canadian and European regulators from maintaining specific licensing and regulatory requirements. As such, a bank, for instance, would only gain access to a new market by establishing a substantial presence. This falls far short of the current passporting rights that UK banks enjoy in Europe. This fundamental structural deficiency explained why Brexit minister David Davis argued for a Canada plus, plus, plus option.[30]. But the UK government might find that the EU will not share its enthusiasm. Under what circumstances would the union grant unilateral access to its most successful achievement, the Single Market? And what would it demand in return? What would be the point of EU membership if countries can enjoy the benefit of the free movement of goods, services, and capital without taking on board the commitments of European integration (most notably the EU's membership fee). "Having the cake and eat it," as then foreign secretary Boris Johnson had put it in characteristically blunt fashion, would, of course, represent a highly attractive outcome of Brexit.

BREXIT MEANS BREXIT: BUT WHAT DOES BREXIT MEAN?

With Cameron's resignation in the immediate aftermath of the referendum, the Conservative Party needed to elect a new leader who would then automatically assume the premiership and define the Brexit process. Given the outcome of the vote, it seemed compelling, that a "Leave" supporter would assume this mantle. Yet one by one, leading Brexiters—from former London mayor Boris Johnson to the justice minister Michael Gove could not garner enough support among their Conservative parliamentary colleagues. In the end, it was the tacit "Remain" supporter and home secretary Theresa May who won the race. She seemed a safe pair of hands largely because of her competent track record as home secretary in Cameron's government. Her cabinet included prominent Brexiters: Johnson became foreign secretary, Gove was given the environment portfolio, while the crucial role of Brexit minister was handed to the outspoken Eurosceptic David Davis, with the former Conservative Party chairman and prominent right-winger Liam Fox responsible for working on trade relations in the post-EU world.

But what type of Brexit did May want to pursue? The referendum had merely asked the British people whether they would like to remain or leave the EU but did not mention at all what kind of relationship the country would like to establish with its European counterparts. During the campaign, it was very easy to identify what you were exiting from, but now it was much more difficult to pinpoint what you are exiting toward. May's rhetoric did not help as she kept referring to "Brexit means Brexit," without clarifying further what type of divorce deal she was embarking upon. Her speeches were often vacuous, exemplified by her nonsensical claim to see through a "red, white and blue Brexit" (the colors of the UK flag).

Over the course of the summer of 2016, government ministers and EU hardliners within the Conservative Party started to fill the void. Instead of a "soft" Brexit, which would have allowed for a continued membership of the EU's flagship policy the Single Market, more and more red lines emerged. Finally, in a speech at Lancaster House in January 2017, seven months after the referendum, May outlined her vision on how to leave the EU. She intended to depart from the Single Market and the EU's customs union. The free movement of people needed to be stopped, since the large numbers of EU citizens moving to the UK over the recent decade was with some justification interpreted as one of the reasons why people expressed such strong EU aversions. Leaving the jurisdiction of the ECJ and thus regaining a substantial degree of national sovereignty was also regarded as instrumental, as was the reduction, if not total elimination of any contributions to the EU's budget. Hence, May's interpretation of the referendum result was very much in line with the slogan of the "Leave" campaign: take back control of UK borders, of the country's budget and of its sovereignty; a "hard" Brexit indeed.

May and Davis intended to pass a very complex and in-depth legislative agenda without much parliamentary scrutiny, arguing that the referendum vote had given the government the legislative authority to shape Brexit in any way it sees fit. At one stage, Davis even pronounced that the government would not offer a "running commentary" of its negotiations with Brussels This extraordinary intended power grab, which undermined parliamentary sovereignty as one of the key principles of the UK's constitution, was stopped by the courageous activist and business woman Gina Miller, who took the government to court. In November 2016, the Supreme Court agreed with her that indeed the final Brexit bill required parliamentary approval.[31]

Worse was to come for Theresa May. In the spring of 2017 and bolstered by encouraging polls and the poor performance of opposition leader Jeremy Corbyn, she called an early election, in the hope of increasing her slender majority in parliament, accompanied by her decision to ask the UK parliament to trigger the so-called Article 50 of the EU's Lisbon Treaty, which required a country to leave the EU within two years. Parliament did so on March 29, 2017, with a thumping majority of 413 to 202. But the election was a disaster for the prime minister. Instead of increasing her majority, May was now forced to form a minority government supported by parliamentarians from the Democratic Unionist Party (DUP) of Northern Ireland.[32] Unlike in the referendum, Corbyn had fought an inspiring campaign, and although he lost the election, made substantial gains and was now widely regarded as a viable alternative prime minister. But Article 50 proved to be a severe strait-jacket. At that stage, the government astonishingly still had not identified the finer details of a Brexit deal. Impact assessment studies on the effect on the economy, on security, or on migration were either not commissioned or still outstanding. Yet the government proceeded to set itself a tight deadline; the meeting of which could at best be described as optimistic. It was as if someone confidently announces to jump into the sea, without knowing one's capability to swim, or indeed the potentially treacherous nature of the water. One must remember that discussions with former EU partners, with individual countries or with the negotiation authorities of the EU bureaucracy and the EU parliament were still at an exploratory stage, without knowing precisely what the UK's position on all vital aspects was, and how those positions would be perceived by the EU and its individual member states.

Davis in particular was often nebulous in his statements to parliament, while frustrating his European counterparts with shifting or unclear UK positions. Frequently arguing that "nothing is agreed, until everything is agreed," his strategy was a holistic one, addressing as many issues as possible simultaneously, and inching them forward toward a possibly positive outcome. But this is not how the EU works, and Davis as former junior Europe minister in the government of John Major (1990–1997) ought to have known better. Multiple EU enlargement negotiations have shown that the EU does sectoral negotiations, concentrating on issues one by one, while following a clear list of priorities. As such, the EU chief negotiator—the former Single Market Commissioner Michel Barnier—canvassed the priorities of the European Parliament (EP), which must give its final consent on any deal, as well as all member states before establishing EU positions on every issue. These positions were then used as the EU's negotiation platform. A flexible approach as desired by Davis, where issues are lumped together, and compromises are reached by looking at the whole picture and not just at individual items is simply not workable for the EU as it would require Barnier to constantly go back and forth between the UK team, and the individual member state governments and the EP. As evidenced by any EU enlargement process, negotiations occur among EU member states on what to expect from any potential EU candidate, with the input of the latter kept at a modest level. And likewise, with Brexit, the EU first had to negotiate among itself what to expect from the UK, before it could begin the process of negotiating a deal.

Triggering Article 50 without having concrete positions, without evaluating options and alternatives, and without knowing the impact, which such options would have on the UK, was therefore an extraordinary act of casualness that imposed a needlessly tight deadline on a highly complex process.[33]

"So what?" exclaimed the Brexit hardliners in the Conservative Party, arguing that no deal is better than a bad deal, and the UK could always just walk away from the negotiations. Ignoring the fact that a bad deal could be avoided by diligent preparations on behalf of the UK government, the overwhelming evidence gathered by think tanks, government departments, and business associations stated ever more clearly that a failure to secure a deal would result in a cliff-edge scenario, with drastic reverberations for the British economy and potentially catastrophic consequences for investment and jobs. Unlike the government, the House of Lords, the country's unelected second legislative chamber, did its homework and had commissioned a sixty-page report on a failure to secure a deal.[34] It provided for grim reading. "It is difficult, if not impossible, to envisage a worse outcome for the UK," was only one of many remarkable phrases. No deal would mean that the UK would henceforth trade with the outside world (including the EU) on terms agreed through the WTO. Such a move would have catastrophic consequences ranging from a 20 percent rise in food prices, grounded airline flights, the loss of 75,000 jobs in the financial industry, to a loss of eight to ten billion pounds per year in tax revenues. Poignantly summing up the report, the Lords pointed to the crucial cause of this mess: "The key factor adding to the risk of 'no deal' is the lack of time." One would be hard pressed to find a worst example for government incompetence and recklessness in the postwar history of the UK than the start of the Brexit negotiations. Michel Barnier and also Guy Verhofstadt, his counterpart in the EP and the individual member state governments, were, of course, aware of the impossible situation that May and Davis had navigated themselves into. The UK needed a deal, but instead of assessing the Brexit process in all its fine detail, May had decided to start the clock prematurely, needlessly compromising the outcome of Brexit, which—if one needs reminding—was one of the most radical transformations of the UK in its modern history.

THE FIRST PHASE OF NEGOTIATIONS: THE DECEMBER 2017 AGREEMENT

Fully aware of its superior negotiating position, the EU from the start insisted that three vital issues needed to be clarified, before the real deal of identifying a future trade parameter between the UK and the EU could be discussed. For Brussels, the divorce needed to be finalized first, before a new relationship could be negotiated (see table 4.3). As such, out of the lengthy list of items, which needed to be addressed in order to form an eventual new modus operandi, the EU focused on the issue of the border between the Republic of Ireland (an EU member state) and Northern Ireland (a UK entity), the UK's

Table 4.3 The First Phase of Brexit Negotiations: Key Points

Citizens' Rights	EU citizens in the UK and UK citizens in the EU maintain rights to live, study, and work until the day of Brexit and are protected by ECJ jurisdiction until 2027.
	Citizens are allowed to bring family members to live with them, but not future spouses.
	A decision on rights of Expat Brits to move to another EU country than the one they are currently residing in was postponed.
Border with Ireland	No hard border.
	The whole of the UK including Northern Ireland will exit EU policies.
	UK will maintain "full alignment" with EU rules in areas that are relevant to the Good Friday Agreement, but a decision on how to achieve this was postponed.
Divorce Bill	Forty to forty-five billion euros, but a final figure was difficult to assess because of ongoing pension liabilities.

divorce bill and how to account for the UK's budget commitments, which were given before Brexit, as well as the rights of EU citizens in the UK (and vice versa, the rights of British citizens residing in EU member states). It took both sides an awfully long time, nine months after Theresa May had triggered Article 50, to reach a first tentative agreement, but finally, on December 8, 2017, both sides issued a joint statement described by the Irish prime minister Leo Varadkar as the "end of the beginning."

With regard to EU citizens moving to the UK, free migration would come to an end with Brexit. The December 2017 agreement confirmed that EU citizens living in the UK, and their UK counterparts living in the EU would continue to enjoy the benefits of the free movement of people but only until the day of Britain's exit from the EU. As such, anyone from the EU who might arrive before that day would not see their rights compromised. In an extraordinary concession, which alarmed several Brexiters, these rights would not only be enshrined in UK law, but furthermore would be protected by the superior jurisdiction of the ECJ up until March 2027.[35] However, EU nationals would lose their rights of residency should they live outside the UK for more than five years. In addition, those UK citizens who have enjoyed their retirement on a Spanish costa would not be forced to move back to the UK, as long as they had resided in an EU country before Brexit day.[36] As to a visa regime in the aftermath of Brexit, the government often referred to a salary threshold of at least 30,000 pounds, upon which a visa application would be seen in a preferential light. Against a predicted worker shortage in schools, hospitals, or the hospitality industry, where a great deal of jobs pay less than this figure, it remained very likely that further government revisions would be on the agenda for many years to come.

Negotiations over border between Ireland and Northern Ireland were complicated by the role handed to Northern Ireland's DUP after the general election in June 2017. The Conservative Party fell well short of an overall majority and Theresa May needed the backing of the ten DUP members of the UK parliament to secure a working majority. Given the crucial role of the DUP in maintaining her government, it therefore came as an embarrassing surprise that May had never consulted her Northern Irish colleagues over a Brexit deal. With the December 2017 agreement ready to be signed, the DUP's leader Arlene Foster announced that she could not support a deal, which would treat the province differently from the rest of the UK. But this was exactly what May's team had planned: A special status for Northern Ireland that would prevent the establishment of a hard border, and thus would not contravene the terms of the Good Friday Agreement. May therefore had no choice but to leave the negotiations and return to London to liaise with Foster. She returned to Brussels three days later with an agreement, which deferred this crucial issue to a later stage. However, the agreement affirmed that there would be no hard border across the island, and that the whole of the UK (including Northern Ireland) will leave the EU and with it the customs union and the Single Market. But on the other hand, the agreement also stated that the UK would maintain "full alignment" to EU rules in those areas, which were affected by the Good Friday Agreement. These areas are vast and total 142 issues of cooperation between Northern Ireland and the Republic. How the British government would be able to square this circle remained a mystery. It seemed fanciful to exit an EU policy such as the Single Market, yet simultaneously maintain the rules of precisely that policy. The agreement on the Irish border was therefore a fudge, which offered no legal clarity and was designed to enable both sides to move onto the next negotiation stage in the hope that some miraculous political solution might emerge.

With regard to the divorce bill, the EU insisted that the UK's financial commitments of around twenty billion euros per year needed to be met until the end of 2020. In addition, Barnier tabled further financial commitments, most notably the payment of pensions to EU staff.[37] These too ought to be met, bringing the proposed overall figure to around forty-five billion euros. "The EU can go whistle," was the undiplomatic response of foreign secretary Boris Johnson, and leading Brexiters claimed that Britain should leave the EU without any payments, and that once again, no deal would be better than a bad deal, which would carry such a hefty divorce settlement. In the end, sanity prevailed, as a failure to meet legal financial obligations would have been very detrimental to the UK's international standing. The December 2017 agreement therefore stated that the UK would meet all future financial commitments, thereby giving in to EU demands. As such, the divorce bill included a—seventeen to eighteen billion euros budget contribution in both

2019 and 2020. There were further twenty-one to twenty-three billion euros on unpaid bills, as well as—two to four billion euros on other liabilities including pensions. The exact and final figure would not be known for years, as pension payments could stretch far into the future. In the end, the EU only made one concession on financial matters. Because of Brexit, two EU agencies were moved from London to EU locations. The European Medicines Agency would now be in Amsterdam, and the European Banking Authority in Paris. In the December Agreement, Barnier—in what can hardly be described as a generous gesture—no longer insisted that the UK should pay for the cost of the relocations.

The agreement laid bare the fundamental negotiation dynamic in the Brexit process. It was the EU, which had negotiated among its members and institutions what to demand from the Brexit process. Barnier reiterated this notion time and time again: The UK is leaving the EU and thus the onus on the costs of leaving should be with the departing country. It was "take it or leave it" time for Theresa May. And she took it.

THE SECOND PHASE OF NEGOTIATIONS: THE WITHDRAWAL AGREEMENT

"Having the cake and eat it" would have been a near-perfect negotiating target for May's government. Access to the Single Market but without the commitment to allow for the free movement of people would have pleased many Brexit supporters, as EU migration would have been brought under control without too many adjustments required for the UK's economic model. It was a pipe dream from the start. A mere week after the December Agreement, chief negotiator Barnier gave a taste of matters to come, indicating once again, that the EU had strict red lines and that Brexit would have strong legal, financial, and economic implications. As such, the UK's intention to leave the Single Market would be all encompassing, and any moves to maintain the highly lucrative rights of UK banks to do business in the EU would have to be sacrificed. Furthermore, in addition to free trade deals on goods, Barnier only saw potential in three further areas: those of judicial cooperation, defense, and security, as well as aviation. Both sides, therefore, entrenched themselves around strict red lines, which seemed irreconcilable. Let battle commence.

In the UK, Brexit discussions continued at fever pitch, but were held largely in private between May and a small group of advisers. Senior Conservative Party colleagues, members of the cabinet, but also opposition parties or representatives from Scotland, Wales, or Northern Ireland were largely excluded. The public and the media as well were often kept in the dark and received updates only in a sporadic fashion, on how May planned to balance her Lancaster House speech with the demands set forth by the EU. Matters reached a temporary impasse at a heated meeting at the prime minister's country retreat at Chequers in July 2018. As to Northern Ireland, May tried to square the circle with the proposal of a fancifully called "facilitated customs arrangement." Such an arrangement would have avoided a hard border on the island of Ireland. But this would also have meant that goods coming into the UK would be tracked and charged different tariff levels depending on whether those goods stayed in the country or were moved on and into the EU. May also intended to end the free movement of EU citizens coming into the UK.

But in a departure from Lancaster, the prime minister also argued for the UK to stay in the Single Market for goods and to accept EU norms on food. Her plan also spelled out leaving the EU customs union (essentially EU rules on how to trade with non-EU partners), while simultaneously phasing in a new and vaguely termed "combined customs territory" (of presumably harmonized rules on how to trade with the rest of the world). This arrangement would have greatly facilitated trade with existing European partners, but in return would have seriously compromised the country's national sovereignty, and its ability to make its own laws and trade relationships. Brexit minister David Davis resigned two days after the summit, followed a couple of hours later by Foreign Minister Boris Johnson, who claimed that May was planning to reduce the UK to the "status of a colony," with "large parts of the economy still locked into the EU system."[38]

Over the summer, May's government embarked on a charm offensive by visiting several national capitals, in an attempt to try and find support for the Chequers compromise. But "divide and conquer" failed in an abysmal fashion, as the EU formed a unified front in its rejection of her proposal. From the outset, Barnier and other EU leaders expressed their concerns whether a technology, which would facilitate the customs arrangement in Northern Ireland actually existed, while also pointing to the potential of fraud, smuggling, and red tape. It could also have meant that UK manufacturers could potentially import parts from non-European countries cheaper than their EU counterparts (since the UK customs regime could offer a lower tariff than the EU) before selling the product customs free to Europe, thereby gaining a significant competitive advantage. Most bizarrely, Chequers would also have meant that the UK was to collect customs duties for an entity (the EU) of which it would no longer be part of, and whose judicial authority (the ECJ) it no longer accepted. But apart from these considerable practical, legal, economic, and technical concerns, Barnier with much justification also kept reiterating what he and fellow EU leaders had been stating all along: The Single Market—the cornerstone of European integration centering on the free movement of goods, services, capital, and people—could not be cherrypicked. Otherwise, the Single Market would unravel, as other member states might follow suit in discarding those elements that might not be conducive to a country's political or economic agenda. The UK either had to agree to all four freedoms or to leave the Single Market altogether.

Ultimately, the proposal antagonized everybody. On the domestic side, trade and thus economic prosperity were not properly safeguarded since Chequers failed to address trade in services (thereby leaving 80 percent of the UK economy outside of any arrangements). It also did not deliver on enhancing national sovereignty. The idea of adhering to EU food and product standards would have turned the country into a rule taker. Chequers also failed to establish a practical and technologically workable solution for Northern Ireland. The continued cherry picking of the Single Market caused consternation, which subsequently turned into irritation at an EU summit in Salzburg in September 2018 when May was told in no uncertain terms to come back with a better idea. May's negotiating gamble of coming up with a proposal that did not take on board the views of the EU and of her senior cabinet colleagues and then presenting Chequers as the only solution backfired in an embarrassing fashion.[39] Her plan was simply unworkable.

May ploughed on, replacing Davis with Dominic Raab, referred to as "the brain" by some of his party colleagues. Such an accolade might have been regarded as a quaint manifestation of a sarcastic British sense of humor when Raab admitted he "hadn't quite understood the full extent of this . . . but we are particularly reliant on the Dover—Calais crossing."[40] It was yet another testimony of the surprising ignorance of some cabinet ministers when dealing with EU-related issues.[41] A new proposal started to take shape, which now included the so-called backstop; a safety net, which ensured that regulatory standards in Northern Ireland would remain identical to those in the EU, and thus were in line with those in Ireland. It would also establish a single customs territory between the whole of the UK and the EU. The backstop, however, would only come into force should a trade deal between the two sides could not be agreed by the end of 2020. Once again, May had to handle a difficult and ultimately irreconcilable conundrum: the backstop avoided a hard border. It therefore was good for trade on the island of Ireland and met the objectives of the Good Friday Agreement. Yet, it also meant that regulatory standards across the UK could be different between mainland Britain and the Northern Irish province, thereby compromising national unity. This was a tricky endeavor for a prime minister who was also leader of the governing party whose official name is the "Conservative and Unionist Party." Even worse, terminating the backstop would have to be agreed jointly by the UK and the EU, which once more nourished Boris Johnson's interpretation of a country being treated as an EU colony. Dominic Raab, by now all too familiar with island entities, resigned in protest.

Table 4.4 The Withdrawal Agreement (November 2018)

Britain to leave the EU on March 29, 2019
Twenty-one-month transition period ending in December 2020
Divorce Bill of forty-two billion euros
Backstop for Northern Ireland
Residency rights for EU citizens who lived in the UK at the time of Brexit
Political declaration for a future EU-UK relationship

Apart from the backstop, the whopping 585-page document had three further key areas. There was a brief political declaration for a future EU-UK relationship, which ran to only twenty-eight pages and which in vague terms set out a future "ambitious and wide-ranging" partnership that integrated not just trade but also defense and security cooperation. The divorce bill of forty-two billion euros was confirmed, which included around twenty billion euros of financial contributions during the transition period. The rights of EU citizens in the UK and vice versa were also confirmed in line with the December 2017 agreement (which gave EU citizens who had lived in the UK prior to the country leaving the EU the right to claim residence). In line with Article 50, the agreement set out a leaving date of March 29, 2019, followed by a transition period of twenty-one months before the ultimate exit in December 2020 (see table 4.4), unless a mutual agreement extended the transition period until the end of 2022.

Just as with Chequers, May tried to perform a precarious balancing act. To please Brexiters, the Withdrawal Agreement respected the referendum result. Britain would leave the EU and the free movement of people would be terminated. The country would also no longer be part of contentious EU policies such as fisheries and agriculture. To please those worried about economic uncertainty, a long transition period of twenty-one months would allow businesses to adjust, while further negotiations on the precise nature of the future trade relationship could be agreed upon. Yet, during the transition period, the country would still be subject to EU rules, (and be under the jurisdiction of the ECJ). And national sovereignty and the ambition to "take back control" were seriously compromised by a backstop that could only be terminated with the consent of Brussels. The accusation of BINO—short for "Brexit in name only"—started to make the rounds at Westminster.

MAY'S DEPARTURE AND THE FAILURE TO RATIFY THE WITHDRAWAL AGREEMENT

May concluded negotiations with Brussels in November 2019 only to be met with a Conservative Party that was deeply divided over the Withdrawal

Agreement. Thus, began the series of humiliations. In December, the influential 1922 Committee of backbenchers[42] forced a vote of confidence. May won by a margin of 2:1, but a third of her parliamentary party colleagues and half of her backbenchers were against her. The most dreadful setback came in January 2019, when parliament rejected her deal by 230 votes. This was the worst defeat in modern times that a prime minister had to endure. In total, 118 members of the Conservative Party voted against the deal. May returned to Brussels to secure the mild concessions that the Withdrawal Agreement explicitly stated the temporary nature of the backstop. A largely unchanged deal was placed before parliament once more on March 12, 2019, only to be rejected; this time by 149 votes with seventy-five Conservative MPs rebelling against the prime minister. May's authority began to collapse. With the Brexit date of March 29 just around the corner, May threw the dice for a third time, in the vain hope that members of parliament would come to realize that a further rejection of her agreement would mean the UK remaining in the EU, as no other credible alternative was able to command a majority. On the presumed day of Brexit, parliament voted once more, and yet again the outcome was negative: A defeat by fifty-eight votes.

In the meantime, and just four days before the Article 50 deadline, parliament tried to wrestle control from the prime minister by holding a series of votes on other Brexit alternatives.[43] As seen in table 4.5, none of the options was able to garner enough support with the proposed continuation of the customs union with the EU coming closest by just missing out by three votes. It seemed that every parliamentarian knew precisely which option they did not support but parliament as a whole failed to manufacture a compromise agreement. Westminster was logjammed and the UK became the laughingstock of Europe.

Flabbergasted EU leaders regarded a cliff-edge scenario, where the UK would be leaving without a deal, as an ever more likely outcome. On March 21, the member states decided to give Theresa May some breathing space by granting an extension until April 12 in case the UK parliament failed to ratify the Withdrawal Agreement. The EU then expected May to come up with new proposals on how to solve the impasse. In case parliament did after all manage to pass the agreement, then an extension until May 22 was granted, allowing the government a couple of extra weeks to press through with the domestic ratification process. All these deadlines became obsolete on April 11, when EU governments offered a final so-called flextension: agree on a deal and leave by June 1 or stay in the EU until October 31, 2019, but in return participate in the elections to the EP on May 23. So, with no further developments in London, British political parties scrambled to get ready for the EU elections.

These elections represented yet another twist in a convoluted tale. A country cannot legally be a member of the EU without political representation of

Table 4.5 Indicative Votes in the Houses of Parliament, March 2019

	First-Round Indicative Votes		*Second-Round Indicative Votes*	
	Yes	*No*	*Yes*	*No*
Confirmative public vote (i.e., another referendum on any Brexit deal)	268	295	280	292
Customs Union (i.e., having the same external trade policy as the EU)	265	271	273	276
Labour's Alternative Plan (i.e., customs union with EU, close alignment with the Single Market, participation in EU agencies and funding programs as well as collaboration in security matters	237	307	–	–
Common Market 2.0 (i.e., membership of Single Market and customs union)	189	283	261	282
Revoke Article 50 to avoid no deal (i.e., revoke the March 29 deadline)	184	293	–	–
No deal (i.e., leave the EU without a deal)	160	400	–	–
Contingent preferential arrangements (i.e., specific trade arrangements with EU in case UK is unable to implement a withdrawal agreement)	139	422	–	–
EFTA and EEA (i.e., membership of Single Market but no customs union)	64	377	–	–
Parliamentary Supremacy (i.e., it is parliament that determines the type of Brexit)	–	–	191	292

its citizens in the EP. The newly elected EP was scheduled to convene for the first time in July, so an EU with Britain still on board logically required British parliamentarians in that institution. Of course, as soon as the UK exited the EU (which was still scheduled for October in five months' time), those parliamentarians would lose their mandate. Given the almost comical proceedings in the House of Commons in the preceding months, the British electorate punished the political party establishment of Conservative and Labour parties. Disgruntled voters elevated Nigel Farage's newly formed Brexit Party—which ran a campaign without even agreeing on a manifesto apart from leaving the EU—into first place with 30 percent of votes but also offered big gains to the pro-Remain Liberal Democrats (20 percent) and the Greens (12 percent). Labour came a distant third (14 percent) and Theresa May's Conservatives could only manage a devastatingly low 9 percent.

May had reached the ridiculous end of her utterly unsuccessful premiership. She set out to unify the country and to deliver Brexit. She failed miserably on both accounts: a prisoner of her own red negotiation lines, which she so prematurely announced in the Lancaster House speech, of her inability to communicate and reach a broader consensus and of her limited tunnel vision.

Triggering Article 50 and thereby imposing a needless time limit of two years, without actually having a concrete Brexit plan in place also proved to be spectacularly counterproductive. She left office on July 27, 2019, after three years in power, having overseen the resignation of thirty-two ministers.

But the blame for failing to reach a solution should not be placed solely on the shoulders of Theresa May. She assumed office in an impossible situation: a divided country split right down the middle, with two out of four UK nations wanting to stay in the EU; a predecessor as prime minister who had failed to make any contingency plans; her own governing party that had been at loggerheads over the European issue for the best part of thirty years. The attitudes of a majority of Brexiters also did not help. It was always their default position to blame the EU for every malaise that beset the UK, thereby conveniently masking their own inability to come up with concrete Brexit plans, while manifesting their irresponsible refusal to reach a compromise. Any Brexit—unless it was the hardest of departures—could never please the likes of Jacob Rees-Mogg, Bill Cash, Steve Baker, or John Redwood. Against this set of adversarial circumstances, reaching a deal—albeit one that was ultimately rejected by parliament—could also be regarded as an impressive achievement. But in the run-up to this deal, May could be accused of tactical naivete, when presenting the end product to a flabbergasted party, parliament and country. Building consensus before the negotiations started with Brussels, consulting with UK nations, with opposition parties, with her own party rank and file, and also with representatives of wider stakeholders in UK society might have laid the necessary groundwork for a deal to be accepted. She failed to do this for three long years, and in the process, "Leavers" and "Remainers" became ever more entrenched in their positions. It left parliament, but also the entire country bitterly divided and paralyzed.

BORIS JOHNSON: GETTING BREXIT DONE?

May's resignation triggered an electoral contest on her succession as leader of the ruling Conservative Party and thus on who would become the country's next prime minister. Tory members of parliament narrowed the field of candidates to two, with foreign secretary Jeremy Hunt and his predecessor Boris Johnson the final candidates being presented to the wider party membership for selection. It was hardly a contest with Johnson winning by a margin of 2 to 1. This meant that the UK prime minister, tasked with leading the country out of the EU, was voted into office by 96,000 Conservative Party members; a mere 0.2 percent of the UK's voting population with the majority being white, male, and of an older age and thus hardly representative of the country's electorate.[44] During his time as Mayor of London (2008—2016),

Johnson had been a hugely popular politician. His image took an unfavorable turn during the referendum campaign, notoriously encapsulated by Johnson's and the "Leave" campaign's controversial claim that the UK should fund the NHS instead of paying large sums to Brussels. For some, he had become the epitome of the career politician, who would do and say almost anything in order to reach the ultimate objective of coming to and staying in power. But there were also many voters, who believed that Johnson had the required chutzpah, skill, and energy to finally deliver on Brexit. It was to this gallery, which he started to play.

It is customary for the UK parliament to meet for a couple of weeks after the summer recess, followed by a party conference season in October, before parliament reconvenes at the end of that month. In September 2019, Johnson suspended parliament for five weeks, arguing that an extended period was required to prepare a new legislative agenda (which would subsequently be made public by the monarch's address to parliament). More conveniently, a parliamentary suspension would have cleared the way for Johnson to approach the Brexit deadline of October 31, 2019, without any parliamentary scrutiny. In a verdict, which did not mince its words, his action was termed illegal by the UK's Supreme Court.[45] Parliament quickly retaliated by passing the so-called Benn act,[46] which required the prime minister to seek an extension to Article 50 beyond October 31, in case members of parliament were not able to agree on an EU exit deal. Johnson promptly withdrew the whip from twenty-one Conservative parliamentarians who had supported the act. These politicians included Theresa May's former chancellor Philip Hammond, her justice secretary David Gauke, as well as Tory grandees, including Winston Churchill's grandson Nicholas Soames, and the longest-sitting MP Ken Clarke. Although he had voted against May's Withdrawal Agreement on three occasions, Johnson came down hard on any dissenters. It further augmented divisions within his own party ranks and his slender parliamentary majority vanished at a stroke. The prime minister's divisive actions were complemented by a bellicose rhetoric, which described the Benn legislation as the "surrender act," while notoriously stating that he would rather be "dead in a ditch" than ask for a Brexit extension.[47]

Amid the turbulence in the House of Commons, Johnson's team of negotiators had rekindled discussions with Brussels. Michel Barnier and other EU leaders had repeatedly stated that May's Withdrawal Agreement would not be reopened. Yet, on October 17, the UK government signed a new Brexit deal (see table 4.6). Many crucial issues of May's Withdrawal Agreement remained untouched. As such, Johnson confirmed the UK's divorce bill of forty-two billion euros. He also reiterated the rights of EU citizens residing in the UK. The transition period until December 2020 also remained unchanged. But adhering to EU standards on the environment and on workers' rights were now no longer legally binding. The biggest departure from May's deal, however, was Johnson's change to the status of Northern Ireland. Gone was the backstop, which called for the province to be in a regulatory alignment with the EU until the two sides have reached a trade agreement. Instead, Northern Ireland would now adhere to EU rules and be part of its customs territory, unless Northern Ireland's regional parliament voted against it in four years' time.

In effect, the deal created two borders: one regulatory border in the Irish Sea that separates Northern Ireland from the rest of the UK, and second, a physical border on the island of Ireland between an EU and a non-EU entity. Theresa May persistently refused to sacrifice national unity and coherence in such a fashion. Johnson had no such qualms. In the future, Northern Ireland might well move in a different regulatory direction than Britain, whether it be for product or environmental standards or for workers' rights. This could result in a competitive advantage for businesses in the province, yet it could also develop into an entity that feels somewhat different from the rest of the UK. The deal shed a further spotlight on the ambiguous nature of Northern Ireland. On the one hand, the province constitutes a part of the UK. Yet, because of the prevalence of a large minority of Catholic Irish citizens, it always had a dual identity, held together to a significant extent by the EU's free movements, which allowed for a seamless interaction between North and South. Leaving the EU jeopardized this double identity, and Johnson's deal recognized that Northern Ireland is not fully British and thus needed to be treated differently. In return, the deal offered Johnson the scope for a much harder Brexit than May's Agreement. The transition time frame remained intact. But if no new trade deal was agreed between the two sides, then the UK could easily revert to a no-deal scenario by the end of December 2020.

It came as little surprise that the DUP, which draws its support from sections of the Protestant British population in Northern Ireland, instantly withdrew the support of its ten members of parliament for the Johnson government. After kicking out twenty-one rebels from his Conservative parliamentary party, the prime minister could now count on only 296 members—far below

Table 4.6 Boris Johnson's Deal (October 2019)

1 Majority of Theresa May's Withdrawal Agreement stays intact, including Rights for EU citizens residing in the UK, and the financial settlement of the Divorce Bill.

2 "Level playing field" provisions (EU standards for workers' rights and the environment) moved from the legally binding section to the nonbinding political declaration.

3 Special arrangements for Northern Ireland:
- No more Irish Backstop
- Northern Ireland to remain aligned to the EU standards
- Northern Ireland to adhere to EU's custom code

the majority threshold of 326. Alas, on October 22, 2019, nine days before the latest deadline, he achieved what Theresa May had failed to deliver on three occasions: The UK parliament, with the backing of all 21 Conservative rebels plus a further 19 Labour MPs who defied their party line, voted 329 to 299 to approve his deal. Yet, in a second motion, parliament rejected Johnson's frantic timetable by a margin of 322 to 308, which had aimed to turn the Brexit legislation into law by October 31, fearing that the prime minister might simply fail to follow through with this step, and thus taking the UK out without any deal. Facing a deadlocked parliament once again, Johnson announced that the legislation will be "paused" and in return was granted a further extension by the EU until the end of January 2020.

Only a general election could solve this impasse. On December 12, 2019—and for the fourth time in a little over four years—citizens were asked to cast their votes in a nationwide poll. Johnson won by a landslide, which enabled him to govern with a comfortable majority of eighty seats and the UK at last left the EU in January 2020. Upon closer inspection, however, the election outcome reaffirmed the country's deep political division. The UK's majority voting system resulted in the Conservatives gaining 56 percent of seats. Yet, only 45 percent of voters cast their ballots in favor of the Conservatives. By adding up the percentages for the Green Party, the Liberal Democratic Party, the Scottish National Party, as well as Plaid Cymru, 18.6 percent of votes were given to parties who opposed Brexit. In Northern Ireland, every party with the exception of the DUP was opposed to Brexit and their vote share added a further 1.4 percent. Add to this the support for Labour (32.2 percent) who wanted a renegotiation with the EU and a subsequent second referendum, a total of 52.6 percent of voters cast their ballots for parties that were opposed to the Brexit deal as envisaged by Johnson. The country remained as split as ever.

It was not necessarily the Conservatives who had won the election, but instead the Labour Party who had lost it. The share of votes for the Tories had only increased by a marginal 1.2 percent. Yet, Labour's share dropped by 6 percent and droves of citizens, who never in their lives had voted for the Tories, now abandoned party leader Jeremy Corbyn, thereby echoing the demise of other center-left parties across the continent.[48] In particular, in northern England, in communities that had struggled to emerge from the decline of their former traditional industries, the Conservatives manage to break new electoral ground. The party had been in power for nearly a decade. Their austerity measures brought hardship to many with widespread cuts to welfare benefits and public spending. Yet, Johnson was regarded as the sole politician who could deliver Brexit, and consequently, many had cast their vote for a party that had never been their natural political ally. There is considerable doubt whether these new allegiances are sustainable once

Brexit starts to lose the overpowering immediacy of 2019. If the Johnson government fails to deliver on improving the lives of its first-time supporters, the political volatility of UK politics is set to continue once the next general election comes around.

For many, Labour's electoral meltdown and the breakup of its traditional voter base was the responsibility of the lackluster leadership of Jeremy Corbyn. In the immediate aftermath of the election, he complained that the Brexit impasse was all-consuming and had prevented him from convincing voters of his notion for a more equal and fair society. There is some truth to this, as his party manifesto—though ambitious at times—mirrored social democratic orthodoxies as practiced by many center-left governments in Northern Europe.[49] But Corbyn failed to lead the party on Brexit. He never campaigned on a clear "Remain" or "Leave" platform. Labour came up with ever more elaborate constructs on how to please both sides of their electoral college: the "Leave" supporting socially conservative, working-class voters that can be found predominantly in northern England, and the progressive, younger, and metropolitan types who argued for "Remain." Just days before the election, Corbyn maintained his dithering stance on the EU, stating that he would stay "neutral" in a potential second referendum. This was a failure of leadership, and the Labour Party paid the price with its worst electoral defeat since 1935.

Johnson also might never had made it across the finishing line, if it wasn't for Nigel Farage, whose Brexit Party did not contest those seats that the Conservatives had won in the 2017 elections. As a consequence, the "Leave" vote in these seats now firmly went to the Tories, while "Remain" votes were split between the anti-Brexit parties. Farage might not have liked the deal that Johnson had negotiated with the EU, but he was to some extent the kingmaker of the 2019 elections. Johnson's options at the start of the negotiations over the precise nature of the UK's relationship with the EU were now plentiful. He could just sit out the transition period until December 2020. The UK would then automatically revert to a "no deal scenario" with trade conducted on WTO terms. But his large parliamentary majority also meant that he no longer had to pander to every fraction of his party, including the hard-line Brexiters around Jacob Rees-Mogg. The 2019 results allowed him the freedom to pursue a Brexit deal shaped by his own personal convictions. Over the coming years, the UK public would find out about his true EU ambitions.

THE DILEMMA

Back in 2016, many commentators believed that Brexit might just spell the beginning of the end for the EU. One by one, other Eurosceptic-inclined countries like Poland, Hungary, France, or Italy would leave the bloc, bringing the European house crushing down to its foundations. Surprisingly, Brexit told an altogether different story.

In sharp contrast to the British political establishment, the EU managed to maintain a remarkably unified front. May's government tried to sow seeds of disharmony by approaching individual national governments in an attempt to bring some EU states closer to the British position. It failed spectacularly. Never in the history of European integration had the EU been so unified. The Commission with its chief negotiator Michel Barnier, the member states under the guidance of their chairperson Donald Tusk and even the EP all sang from the same hymn sheet. Protecting the Single Market, and, in particular, the integrity of all four freedoms associated with it, and supporting Ireland's objectives when it comes to finding a solution to the Northern Ireland conundrum were always judged to be of greater priority than any concessions given to a country, which was intend on leaving the bloc. For the UK, the entire negotiation process presented an often humiliating and thumping come-down that cast aside any hopes that a Brexit deal might indeed represent the outcome of negotiations between two equal partners.

It was clear from the start that the cards were stacked firmly in favor of the EU. Granted, countries, such as the Netherlands, Ireland, and Germany, would see a great slice of their export markets compromised if the UK left without a deal. But for many continental businesses, the notion of sacrificing European integration in order to hold on to previous export markets was, to the surprise of the UK government, never a viable option. In any case, the risk for the UK of being denied access to the lucrative European markets was much more significant. May's government realized this. Back in January 2017, she stated at Lancaster House that "no deal" was preferable to a "bad deal." But a host of analyses begged to differ. Leaving the Single Market in one swoop would have resulted in a "Brexodus" with firms establishing new headquarters on the continent, taking with them highly qualified personnel.[50] While some hard-line Brexiters continued to argue for a clean break from the EU followed by subsequent bilateral trade relations along WTO lines, the majority of commentators, parliamentarians, and indeed most members of the British government gradually began to regard a "no deal" scenario as the worst outcome of Brexit.

Instead of spelling disaster for the European union, the referendum result and the subsequent Brexit negotiations shed a highly negative spotlight on the UK and its political system. Although Theresa May made concessions to the DUP of Northern Ireland, her successor Boris Johnson rapidly dismissed Northern Irish objections, while throughout the process, Scottish or Welsh voices were completely ignored. The irony was clear for many to see: The integrity of a union was severely compromised; but it was not the European one, but the one governing parts of the British Isles. Ultimately, this was an English-dominated Brexit, and not one negotiated among all the nations of the UK.

We also witnessed many constitutional conflicts. Gina Miller had to take her case to the Supreme Court to argue that it was parliament as the representative of the people, which should have the final say over the Brexit deal. Without her, we would have had an undemocratic power grab by the executive. In a similar vein, Boris Johnson attempted to suspend parliament, just when this institution's scrutinizing power was most needed. But we also had a clear referendum outcome to leave the EU, which parliament and two successive governments struggled to deliver. That too can hardly be described as good democratic practice. Calls for widespread constitutional reform and indeed a written constitution, which would properly enshrine the interplay between the country's institutions, were widespread. Amid this tug of war between "Remainers" and "Leavers," between Westminster and the regional parties in Belfast, Edinburgh, and Cardiff, and between parliament and the government, the UK found itself in a tight political deadlock. Already in 2016, the country was not in the best of shapes. Years of austerity in the aftermath of the financial crash revealed a plethora of reform issues: A shortage of affordable homes, the shaky financing of the country's NHS, inadequate social care for the elderly, job insecurity, lack of social mobility, a growing prosperity divide between north and south, and tax evasion were just some of many challenges that were swallowed up by the utter dominance of the Brexit paralysis. Brexit ought to have cast the EU in an unfavorable light. Instead, it was the UK whose shortcomings were revealed in a brutal fashion.

What will a post-Brexit UK look like in ten years' time? Leaving the EU will impose severe pressures on Northern Ireland. Brexit in whatever shape or form simply does not work for the province: in case of a deal that offers a seamless interaction across the Irish border, different regulatory regimes between Northern Ireland and Britain will compromise the integrity of the UK. And in case of a border being erected across the island of Ireland, the dual identity of Northern Ireland and thus the peace process might be jeopardized. Political unrest over Brexit might then prompt a so-called border poll, where the people of Northern Ireland—a majority of whom after all voted "Remain"—will vote to join the Republic in the south. Let's also assume that across the UK, the divisive political rhetoric between Remainers and Brexiters continues, while the Brexit-related economic realignment results in factory closures, rising unemployment, and stagnating living standards. A domino scenario could then potentially unfold, where Scotland would press on with its demand for a referendum and this country too would leave the UK. Wales subsequently might then reevaluate its position given that its population of three million is dwarfed that of England, which has 55 million inhabitants. At the end of this doomsday process, we would have the reduction of a former four-nation kingdom to a one-nation England: A country, which would be politically divided, economically poorer, and geographically smaller. This is a highly unlikely scenario. It seems fanciful that Northern Ireland will leave one state in order to join another, while the economic cases for independence in Scotland and Wales and the mechanisms of a possible reentry into the EU have not been made in a convincing fashion. But Brexit will exert pressures on UK unionism, and the possibility of a breakup cannot just be wiped off the table.

In the December 2019 elections, Boris Johnson's campaign slogan was to "Get Brexit Done." But Brexit and thus a future relationship between the EU and the UK will never be "done." No bilateral relationship ever is "done," but instead represents a dynamic partnership that is subject to change whenever new political, economic, or social developments arise, or whenever new governments might have different objectives from their predecessors. Imagine a future incoming Labour government that seeks closer trade relations with the EU along the lines of the Norway model. For this to happen, the constitutional remit of the UK would merely require a simple vote in parliament. Or imagine the same government loosening visa rules to allow hospitality workers or healthcare professionals from the EU to settle in the UK. Or imagine a transnational cyberattack by a rogue state, or an environmental catastrophe that requires closer collaboration among European (EU and non-EU) states. International relations are never "done."

For the foreseeable future, the EU and the UK will be engaged in negotiations over a relationship that integrates trade issues but might also stretch to security collaboration to tackle such issues as cybercrime, terrorism, or drug and human trafficking. The EU's recent trade deal with Canada is often mentioned as a warning benchmark since it took seven years of negotiations for both sides to agree. Given that the UK seeks to cement a closer relationship than its erstwhile dominion (a so-called Canada plus), a short negotiation period seems fanciful and will most definitely not be "the easiest trade deal in human history" as anticipated by former trade minister Liam Fox.[51] On the plus side, as a recent member, the UK still has a very high regulatory alignment with the EU, which will certainly speed up the process. But out of a multitude of issues, Johnson's deal has only reached agreement on Northern Ireland, the divorce settlement and rights of EU citizens. As crucial as these are, they pale into insignificance when compared with, for instance, the regulation of the banking sector and other financial services. To reach at least a momentary end point will therefore take many years. Joining the bloc at the moment takes at least ten years. It is not inconceivable that leaving the EU and establishing a new bilateral relationship could take just as long.

During this process, the UK will be facing a persistent conundrum. On the one hand, the outcome of the referendum must be respected, and citizens need to be assured that the UK has indeed left the EU. On the other hand, however, a continuing close collaboration with the bloc could not only be a highly practical solution but could also represent the best option when it comes to saving taxpayers' money and securing jobs, in particular, in light of the fact that such economic circumstances hugely affect the popularity of any government and thus the outcome of elections. A telling example is offered by the Galileo satellite system. Launched in 2016 at a cost of ten billion euros (with funding also coming from the UK since at that stage, the country was still a EU member), Galileo provides an independent positioning system so that European countries do not have to rely on the GPS system offered by the United States or the Russian GLONASS, which could be disabled by their operators at any stage. What is the best option for the UK? Relying on the United States or Russia could have security implications and launching its own system would be prohibitively expensive. In most likely circumstances, the UK would want to participate in Galileo, which, of course, would come with a user fee. Galileo could therefore be a template for a future UK-EU relationship. Nominally, Brexit will happen, and the country will exit all EU institutions and programs. But gradually, over a process that will cover many years, the UK will rejoin or participate in EU programs, simply because these make economic and procedural sense. At first glance, the UK will be a former member. Look closer, and a picture might emerge that will see tight collaboration as if the UK had never left. Such interaction with the bloc will come at a price through, and EU negotiators will make sure that collaboration with the EU as an outsider will be more expensive than collaboration among EU members through regular budget contributions. We could indeed witness BINO—Brexit in name only—since a close bilateral relationship is in the best economic and financial interest of the UK. In such a scenario, the Brexiters' objectives of independence and sovereignty would be greatly compromised. Ultimately, a Brexit could emerge, where not much will have substantially changed. Instead of multilateral agreements between EU members (including the UK), we would then have multilateral agreements between EU members (without the UK), which lead the way to bilateral deals with the UK, with the additional costs for the institutional setup of such an arrangement paid by both sides: A cogent scenario, yet ultimately depressing for both "Remainers" and "Leavers."

Changing UK demographics will also make sure that a potential reintegration into the EU cannot be discounted and indeed has much capital for political parties to tap into. As mentioned previously, the outcome of the referendum revealed an explanatory variable, in which older voters tended to prefer "Leave" and younger ones opted for "Remain." Brexiters might argue that with age comes a "wiser" perspective and thus a more EU-skeptic attitude. Yet, older UK generations had their formative years during a time without mass tourism, without the ease of interacting with other cultures, which is now so prominent in our digital times. They were also educated under a school curriculum that until the 1970s still promoted notions of Britain's empire superiority. It is, therefore, safe to assume that not every young voter turning older will shift their current pro-EU stance. Hence, in the time of ten or fifteen years, there is the highly distinct possibility that the majority of UK citizens are "Remainers," and thus would be open to a reintegration into the EU, with some politicians (and ultimately governments) only too eager to please this objective. The Brexit case is far from settled (or "done" in Johnson's words). It will infiltrate the country's political discourse for many decades to come.

While negotiating with the EU, the UK will also embark on a series of bilateral trade deals. Freed from the shackles of the EU's CCP, it is in particular the United States that the government hopes will compensate (at least to a certain extent) for the projected loss in trade emanating from the Single Market. The problem is that US standards, whether for food, the environment, consumer protection, or financial services, are all substantially lower than those in the UK. The United States is already the country with which the UK trades the most, yet both sides are keen to expand on existing trade relations. The substantially different sizes of the economies (the United States is five times bigger) means a vastly inferior UK negotiation platform, and there is every reason to assume that a lowering of British standards is on the cards. We could well see the UK—having given up a say in establishing the rules of one of the most successful trading blocs ever established—finding itself as a junior partner in a potentially scrappy trade deal, which offers mutual market access, in return for the acceptance of US standards in a regulatory push to the bottom.

Beyond the Atlantic, the UK will also seek enhanced trade relations with the likes of China, Japan, and India. But in particular with regard to the latter, market access for British goods and services might only be secured if in return the UK eases visa restrictions for Indian citizens, thereby increasing migration pressures that the Brexit referendum ought to have rectified. We therefore might see a country, going it alone in the world of global trade, which because of its modest size, must on many occasions be forced to accept the role of rule taker. A Global Britain, a country reaching out beyond European shores is certainly an enticing prospect, and one that just might deliver on a post-Brexit future. But much careful navigation is still required before a final, prosperous destination will be reached.

But it is not only the UK whose very foundations have been shaken by Brexit. The EU too will greatly regret the loss of one of its key member states with the legitimacy of the European project greatly compromised. After all, Brexit was the manifestation of a perspective that sees a nation's interest being better served outside the bloc. Naturally, Europhiles point to the shoddy referendum campaign, the long running, inner-party quarrels of the Tories over Europe, the false information given in the run-up to the referendum, or the overblown and unfulfillable expectations of a Brexit future. But the fact remains that a country decided to leave. Whichever way you turn it, Brexit is one of the EU's darkest hours. For decades, multinational collaboration was seen as the panacea for how to meet Europe's challenges. Now, the UK has decided that going it alone is the better way forward.

The EU will take a considerable hit. Of all the exports by EU countries, 8 percent ended up in the UK.[52] The UK's financial contribution to the EU budget represented close to 12 percent.[53] This will undoubtedly have significant ramifications once the spending plans for the Common Agricultural Policy and the Cohesion policy have been finalized. The burden on financing EU integration will therefore fall even more on the shoulders of net contributors, including Sweden, the Netherlands, Germany, and Denmark. The bloc will also greatly miss the UK's expertise when it comes to surveillance, security, and counterterrorism. And with regard to foreign policy, apart from the UK, there might arguably only be France, who accepts that the world is a dangerous place and requires proactive foreign policy intervention. Many smaller states, but for historical reasons also Germany and Italy, are still uncomfortable operating on the international stage. With the departure of the UK, Europe will lose the member state that often acted as the bloc's natural leader. In the end, suffering from a massive legitimacy blow, the EU will be smaller and poorer with its voice reverberating less distinctly on the international stage.

Maybe the UK would have been wise to resist joining the EU in 1973 in the first place. But forty years ago, Britain was regarded as the "sick man of Europe"—the economy was in dire straits, inflation rampant, productivity low, and industrial relations confrontational. The EU on the other hand propelled many countries to enviable levels of prosperity and Britain felt that maybe they too could catch some of that economic vibe. The UK benefited tremendously from European integration. The high output in the car industry and the phenomenal financial position of the City of London would be unthinkable without the developments surrounding the Single Market project, which transformed the UK from one of the poorest EU member states in the 1970s to the second richest country (after Luxembourg) just before the financial crash of 2008. But Britain's political culture was always at odds with the European project: In favor of economic integration, but firmly against political integration or indeed an "Ever Closer Union" as stated in the Maastricht Treaty of 1992.

But the biggest regret comes in the shape of David Cameron's decision to hold a referendum. It seems shameful to gamble with the future of a country by attempting to silence Eurosceptic voices within his own party. The UK's fundamental relationship with its neighbors should not have offered the stage for inner-party quarrels, which subsequently roped in an entire country based on occasionally misleading and false information on highly technical and bureaucratic matters that were often beyond the comprehension of even the most informed citizens. A referendum should never be a game show, although at least the host resigned from a job delivered in such careless and contemptuous fashion.

In the post-Brexit world, "Leave" supporters might also arrive at the realization that many aspirations of the referendum campaign will not materialize. Improving the state of democracy in the UK will not be achieved by merely leaving the EU. It requires widespread domestic reforms, which a government, embroiled for many years by Brexit negotiations, will find hard to deliver. One might also question the degree of national sovereignty, which will be gained once the country operates outside the EU. It seems ambitious to believe that a country with a market of 65 million people can negotiate trade deals on an equal footing with the likes of China (a market of 1.4 billion people) or the United States (330 million people). Migration will also most certainly continue in order to keep productivity, tax revenues, and thus prosperity at acceptable levels, and no government would seriously be contemplating shooting itself in the (economic) foot by pulling up the draw bridge. Any notion of "taking back control," of a rejuvenated Global Britain that affirms its new-found place in the world might just be too fanciful. And how will all that pent-up anger, which had propelled Brexit, the desire for jobs, for decent wages, for social justice, for social mobility express itself then?

But it is not all doom and gloom for Britain and for the EU. The UK is engulfed in a culture war, where citizens—largely influenced by age, education, and socioeconomic status—are either passionately against or in favor of Europe. But both the EU and Britain must rescue much of their intricate economic and political relationship, which had served both sides so well in the past decades. Still, the British people have spoken, and it is now time to define a new relationship that respects British notions of national sovereignty and democracy. The UK never caught the European bug. Its experience of World War II was not one of loss, of invasion, of occupation, of political repression. As such, an existentialist urge to cement a strong Europe was never part of its political psychology. The EU ought to respect this, and ought to find ways to ensure that the undeniable assets of Britain continue to form an integral part of the European story. Failing to do so will almost certainly result in a lose-lose situation. And here is the dilemma. The UK and the EU are separating. The former intends to find a Brexit future that is very likely to fall short of the benefits it had enjoyed while being part of the bloc. And the latter has to defend the integrity of the European project, so that no member will be tempted to follow the British example. But a tight collaboration is in the interest of both. The divorcees have signed the papers annulling their previous relationship. Yet, for the sake of their citizens, they ought to live together as closely and harmoniously as possible. Donald Tusk, chairperson of the European Council, summed it up succinctly: "We already miss you."[54]

NOTES

1. As a member of the German parliament in the 1950s, Helmut Schmidt, Chancellor of West Germany between 1976 and 1982, voted against the ratification of the Treaty of Rome (1957) arguing that a Europe without Britain would stand no chance of succeeding.

2. The EU budget is an odd creature given that it does not accumulate debt (i.e., all allocated money must be spent by a previously agreed date) and is ratified in seven-year periods (the so-called financial perspective). Every member state contributes around 1 percent of its GDP. Still today, the EU spends most of its money supporting agriculture. But when Britain joined in the 1970s, the share of the budget allocated to the Common Agricultural Policy reached some 70 percent. This was great news for big agribusinesses in France, but disappointing for the UK since the farming sector only accounted for a fraction of its economic output. This meant that the UK at a stroke became the biggest EU net contributor (either in absolute terms or per capita).

3. Stephen George. *An Awkward Partner: Britain in the European Community* (Oxford: Oxford University Press, 1998).

4. With the "Big Bang" Enlargement of 2004, the EU at one stroke increased in size from fifteen to twenty-five members, integrating Estonia, Latvia, Lithuania, Poland, Hungary, the Czech Republic, Slovakia, Slovenia, Cyprus, and Malta. Nearly all of the old EU-15 member states imposed restrictions on the free movement of people lasting for seven years; the only exceptions being Sweden, the UK, and Ireland. It therefore came as little surprise that in particular young EU citizens from central and eastern Europe sought to improve their material standard of living by moving to those counties where wages were as much as eight times higher. By 2007 and with the integration of Bulgaria and Romania, all EU-15 states imposed the seven-year restrictions rule, although with the accession of Croatia, a country of only four million people, restrictions were much less severe and were only applied by some member states (such as the UK, but not Germany for instance).

5. In December 2015, the unemployment rate across the EU was 8.9 percent. In Germany, it was 4.6 percent, and in the UK, 5.3 percent, which was in marked contrast to figures in France (10.4 percent) and Italy (11.9 percent). Source: Eurostat.

6. Simon Hix, Sara Hageman and Doru Frantescu. *Would Brexit Matter? The UK's Voting Record in the Council and the European Parliament.* Vote Watch Report, 2016.

http://60811b39eee4e42e277a-72b421883bb5b133f34e068afdd7cb11.r29. cf3 .rackcdn.com/2016/04/VoteWatch-Report-2016_digital.pdf.

7. In a BBC television interview after the referendum, Nigel Farage claimed that it was terribly easy to win over working-class voters, as Labour activists were nowhere to be found.

8. A picture of the poster and a summary of the controversies it caused can be accessed on: http://www.dailymail.co.uk/news/article-3644716/Nigel-Farage-racism -storm-Brexit-poster-showing-thousands-male-refugees-warning-country-breaking-point.html.

9. UKIP was at a great disadvantage because of the "First-Past-the-Post" electoral system that is applied in the UK. The country is subdivided into 650 electoral districts, and whoever wins that constituency becomes a member of parliament. As such, 12.6 percent of voters cast their ballots in favor of UKIP candidates at the general election of 2015. However, the party only managed to secure one seat; a drastic misrepresentation of the public will.

10. See chapter 1.

11. www.standard.co.uk/news/politics/zac-goldsmith-ive-not-got-a-racist-bone-in -my-body-sadiq-khans-team-outplayed-us-a3381156.html.

12. In February 2019, Tom Enders, the German CEO of the airplane manufacturer Airbus warned of the potentially negative impact of Brexit. The Conservative MP Mark Francois denounced Enders, accusing him of Teutonic arrogance while stating "My father, Reginald Francois, was a D-Day veteran. He never submitted to bullying by any German. Neither will his son."

https://www.independent.co.uk/voices/brexit-mark-francois-history-jacob-ree s-mogg-suez-second-world-war-a8758806.html.

13. See: *Sunday Times*: "£1bn of livestock but no vets at Rotterdam bottleneck." December 16, 2018, p. 21.

14. A news clip on Leadsom's faux pas can be watched at: https://www.youtube. com/watch?v=Bxu624RpEJE.

15. Leadsom wasn't done yet. As Leader of the House of Commons in May's cabinet, she frequently accused opposition MPs or journalists of being "unpatriotic," or "unhelpful" when criticizing the government's Brexit strategy, thus in effect questioning the scrutinizing function of other parties and the media as vital corner stones of a viable democracy. A good example of her mindset is revealed in an interview with the BBC news broadcast "Newsnight." The journalist Emily Maitlis interviewing Andrea Leadsom on Brexit can be watched on https://www.youtube.com/watch? v=zEMlSSSOErk.

16. Parts of Faisal's interview with Gove can be viewed on: https://www.youtube. com/watch?v=GGgiGtJk7MA.

17. Pro-Remain commentators on the Brexit vote should be very careful when labeling those who voted to leave as "ignorant" or "stupid." As mentioned in chapter 1 on populism, a university education is often enriched by foreign cultural and personal exchanges resulting in a mindset that tends to integrate "Europe" as a part of one's psychological environment. But someone is not ignorant, just because the privilege of experiencing such a broadening of horizon is compromised by the desire or the need to seek employment without academic qualifications.

18. As recently as 2014, the government awarded the status of "nation" to Cornwall, thus bringing the count to five, although regional representation, such as an own parliament or recognition of the Cornish language in school curriculums are still outstanding.

19. During rainy weather, for instance, voter turnout particularly among older voters tends to be lower.

20. In 2016, 5.3 million of the 63.7 million people living in the UK were born abroad. According to the Office for National Statistics, the largest group with 853,000 was from Poland, followed by Ireland (331,000) and Portugal and Romania (both 175,000).

21. Ever since 2005, net migration—the difference between the number of people settling in and leaving the UK hovered around a mark of 200,000 per year. By 2014, the figures had jumped to 300,000 and in June 2016 was 336,000. A year on, and net migration had dropped significantly to 230,000. See: Office for National Statistics. Migration Statistics Quarterly Report, November 2017.

22. The BBC journalist Nick Robinson produced a documentary entitled "The Truth about Immigration" (January 2014) in which he interviewed Alistair Brooks, a strawberry farmer from Kent who had just advertised jobs for the backbreaking work of fruit picker. Only five Brits applied, two of them showed up on the first day, but none returned for the second day, forcing the farmer to fill vacancies with workers from eastern Europe.

23. According to the Office for National Statistics, in 2016, employment rate for UK residents from central and eastern Europe was 83 percent. The figures for the old EU of fifteen-member states were 76 percent; for UK citizens, 74 percent; and for non-EU residents, 61 percent.

24. This opinion was voiced by Nigel Farage in: Nick Robinson, The Truth about Immigration," BBC, January 2014.

25. See chapter 2.

26. Monique Ebell is a research fellow at the National Institute for Economic and Social Research and has published extensively on the effects of Brexit on trade. One of her articles can be accessed at: https://www.niesr.ac.uk/blog/will-new-trade-deals-soften-blow-hard-brexit.

27. Car manufacturers are facing a multitude of challenges. In addition to a potentially detrimental trading environment caused by Brexit, the industry must also respond to a gradual switch toward electric vehicles, public outrage over false emission standards, a regulatory crack down on diesel vehicles and slowing demand in China. In February 2019, Honda announced that it will be shutting down its plant in Swindon in southeast England in 2021. Nissan also declared that further investment in the UK might not be forthcoming with the new generation of its popular X-trail SUV being moved from Sunderland back to Japan. Jaguar Land Rover also confirmed the cutting of thousands of jobs, while in June 2019, Ford announced the closure of its plant in Bridgend in Wales. See: www.theguardian.com/business/2019/jun/05/ford-planning-to-close-bridgend-plant-more-than-1500-jobs-at-risk.

28. See chapter 1.

29. See: https://www.theguardian.com/uk-news/2016/mar/24/europol-chief-rob-wainwright-brexit-mistake-uk-security-richard-dearlove.

30. Davis was interviewed by Andrew Marr, one of the UK's most prominent political journalists in the immediate aftermath of the conclusion of the first round of negotiations.

See: http://www.telegraph.co.uk/news/2017/12/10/britain-should-sign-canada-style-trade-deal-european-union-brext/.

31. Gina Miller, an investment manager and philanthropist, paid a heavy price for standing up to the government. Branded a traitor by many tabloid publications, she now required personal security and encountered death threats on a frequent basis. The Supreme Court judges did not fare too well either, as witnessed by a front page in the Daily Mail, which included pictures of every judge under the headline "enemies of the people."

See: http://www.dailymail.co.uk/news/article-3903436/Enemies-people-Fury-touch-judges-defied-17-4m-Brexit-voters-trigger-constitutional-crisis.html.

32. The support of the DUP did not come cheap. In return for supporting the government's agenda, May had to fork out an additional one billion pounds of public spending in Northern Ireland. Other struggling UK regions, such as Wales and Scotland, were suitably outraged at this perceived preferential treatment.

33. Nine months after triggering Article 50, the government still had no clear picture how Brexit in whatever shape or form might affect the UK and its economic sectors. Alarm bells were ringing on December 6, 2017, when Davis appeared for one of his frequent briefings to the parliament's Brexit Committee. Hilary Benn, chair of the Committee and a leading Labour politician frequently had to catch his breath in amazement that the government so far had not commissioned any impact studies on the consequences of Brexit for the automotive, aerospace, or financial services sector. Davis simply replied. "*The answer is going to be no to all of them*," further stating that the use of economic models is questionable, as they all have been proven wrong in the past. See: *The Guardian*: "*Davis admits impact forecasts don't exist but escapes censure*," December 7, 2017, p. 14.

34. See: *The Guardian*: "*No deal outcome scenario is the worst imaginable, say peers*." December 7, 2017, p. 15.

35. Any EU citizen living in the UK who so far has not been granted (or has not applied for) permanent residency will also have his or her rights protected under a new procedure that will grant those citizens eventual "settled status." The deal also includes the reunification of relatives who might join their family members at a later stage, and extends to unborn and adopted children, but not to future spouses or civil partners.

36. The December 2017 agreement postponed any decisions on the rights of expat Brits to move to another EU country post-Brexit, or indeed the rights of Brits to work cross-border in more than one EU state. Those issues were deferred to the second round of negotiations.

37. As a member of the European Parliament, Nigel Farage is also entitled to an EU pension, which in his case will total around 73,000 pounds per year, payable upon his sixty-third birthday. When confronted with claims of hypocrisy, Farage insisted that he will take up this pension, arguing that with Brexit, he had in fact voted for the abolition of his job. "I am the turkey that voted for Christmas," he stated.

38. See *Financial Times*: www.ft.com/content/3a8059ca-8435-11e8-a29d-73e3d454535d.

39. The Instagram feed of Donald Tusk, chairman of the European Council, which represents the national EU governments, caused a social media storm. It depicted a photo of him offering Theresa May a piece of cake with the tagline "a piece of cake perhaps? Sorry, no cherries."

40. A video of Raab's speech can be accessed at: ww.facebook.com/BBCPolitics/videos/raab-i-hadnt-quite-understood-reliance-on-dover-calais-trade/168044794149520/.

41. A look at a map would have helped Raab in reaching this rather obvious conclusion, as would the website of the port of Dover, which states that the cargo terminal alone handles over 300,000 tons annually with over 9,000 container movements. In total, some fifty ferries leave the port every day filled with passengers, goods, cars, trucks, motorcycles, and buses.

See: http://www.doverport.co.uk.

42. The term "backbenchers in British politics" is reserved for those parliamentarians who do not act as ministers in government departments. In total, around 100 members of parliament have an extra job of running the government. The remaining ones can concentrate exclusively on representing their constituents.

43. See: www.theguardian.com/politics/2019/mar/27/alternative-brexit-options-what-will-john-bercow-select-for-indicative-votes.

44. With an overall membership of around 160,000, 97 percent of the Conservative Party's members are white, compared to 86 percent of the UK population. Most are above 55, and nearly 40 percent are above sixty-six years of age. Seven in ten are men.

See: https://qz.com/1644202/who-are-the-160000-conservatives-picking-the-next-uk-prime-minister/.

45. Lady Hale, president of the Supreme Court stated that "the court is bound to conclude, therefore, that the decision to advise Her Majesty to prorogue parliament was unlawful because it had the effect of frustrating or preventing the ability of parliament to carry out its constitutional functions without reasonable justification." See: https://www.theguardian.com/law/2019/sep/24/boris-johnsons-suspension-of-parliament-unlawful-supreme-court-rules-prorogue.

46. Hilary Benn was a senior Labour politician who represented the constituency of Leeds central. His father Tony—an outspoken Eurosceptic during the first EU referendum of 1974—was a cabinet minister in the Labour governments of Harold Wilson and James Callaghan.

47. A clip of Johnson's speech, which includes the "dead in a ditch" reference can be accessed on: https://www.youtube.com/watch?v=__Kn-AOCd3I.

48. See chapter 1.

49. The Labour Party campaigned for the renationalization of railways. In Germany and France, this sector had not been privatized. Corbyn also argued for the creation of workers' councils in bigger businesses; something that is very common in Germany. Under his proposal, corporation tax would have increased to 26 percent (it is over 30 percent in France and Germany). But Labour also offered free broadband

to every household, and also intended to bring utilities under public ownership, which would have gone beyond the agenda of many European social democracies.

50. Jonathan Portes the former chief economist to the Treasury in Gordon Brown's government who moved to the National Institute for Economic and Social Research claimed in November 2016 that a no-deal Brexit would result in lower tax revenues of 1 percent of GDP.

51. See: https://www.bbc.co.uk/news/av/uk-40667879/eu-trade-deal-easiest-in-human-history.

52. See: https://fullfact.org/europe/uk-eu-trade/.

53. See: https://www.statista.com/statistics/316691/european-union-eu-budget-share-of-contributions/.

54. Donald Tusk's press conference after he had just received the UK government's letter, which triggered Article 50, can be viewed at: https://www.youtube.com/watch?v=c6RR7hoQutc.

Chapter 5

Enlargement

Britain is not the only country that has reservations about the European project. The microstates of Liechtenstein, Andorra, the Vatican, San Marino, and Monaco never had any intentions of joining the EU. In 1972 and 1994, the people of Norway rejected referendums called by their governments to join the bloc and given the high levels of prosperity and quality of life, a change in the country's attitude is not on the horizon. In 2015, Iceland withdrew its application out of concern over the ongoing sovereign debt crises in the Eurozone. Belarus under President Alexander Lukashenko is Europe's last dictatorship and as such automatically ineligible for closer economic or political ties. But apart from these cases, all other European countries outside the EU have applied, or at least have expressed their intention to apply for membership. At a summit in 2003 in Thessaloniki, EU leaders drew up a list of potential candidates, which omitted Russia, but included the former Soviet republics of Ukraine, Moldova, and Georgia.[1] European integration as practiced by the EU is therefore far from over and could conceivably reach thirty-five members (see table 5.1).

Joining the EU is a time-consuming process that requires an applicant to change its political system, its economy, and its administrative structures to EU standards. The key requirement is the EU's insistence on accepting the so-called EU acquis. Formerly known as the acquis communautaire, it consists of all EU laws, regulations, and treaty provisions ever since European integration started with the signing of the European Coal and Steel Community in 1950. This means that candidates are not granted any opt-outs from EU policies (such as the single currency, for instance), thus making them more integrated than some existing members.[2] The acquis currently totals some 170,000 pages and continues to grow by about 10,000 pages every year.[3] This means that an accession process to the EU could easily last ten years, but

Table 5.1 Status of EU Affiliation by Country

Status	*Year of Status*	*Country*	*Membership Count*
Member	1957	France, Italy, West Germany, Netherlands, Luxembourg, Belgium	6
	1973	Denmark, Ireland, UK	9
	1981	Greece	10
	1986	Portugal, Spain	12
	1990	Unification of West and East Germany	n/a
	1995	Austria, Finland, Sweden	15
	2004	Malta, Cyprus, Poland, Hungary, Slovakia, Czech Republic, Slovenia, Estonia, Latvia, Lithuania	25
	2007	Bulgaria, Romania	27
	2013	Croatia	28
Former Member	2020	UK	27
Candidate	2005	North Macedonia, Turkey	29
	2010	Montenegro	30
	2012	Serbia	31
	2014	Albania	32
Former Candidate	2015	Iceland	n/a
Association Agreement	2014	Ukraine	33
	2016	Bosnia and Herzegovina, Kosovo	35

could be significantly longer if a candidate struggles to establish a pluralist democratic system, finds it difficult to have a functioning market economy, or cannot make sufficient inroads in the fight against corruption and nepotism that might undermine its administrative sector.

The term "enlargement negotiation" is misleading. It is not the EU, which negotiates with the candidate on how integration might best be achieved. Instead, it is foremost the member states that negotiate among themselves on the specific reforms that a prospective member ought to undertake. Within this process, the European Commission screens the candidate along thirty-five thematic lines (the so-called chapters) in such areas as the environment, human rights, transport, or the Single Market (see table 5.2). The Commission then suggests two sets of reforms per chapter (referred to as opening and closing benchmarks) to which all member states must agree to. Once a candidate has implemented what is in effect a "to-do list," all member states must agree that the reforms were completed in a satisfactory manner. Hence, on seventy occasions—thirty-five chapters, each with opening and closing benchmarks—all member states must give their explicit consent that

Table 5.2 The Thirty-Five Chapters of Enlargement Negotiations

	Title		*Title*
1	Free movement of goods	19	Social policy and employment
2	Free movement of workers	20	Enterprise and industrial policy
3	Right of establishment and freedom to provide services	21	Trans-European networks
4	Free movement of capital	22	Regional policy and coordination of structural instruments
5	Public procurement	23	Judiciary and fundamental rights
6	Company law	24	Justice, freedom, and security
7	Intellectual property law	25	Science and research
8	Competition policy	26	Education and culture
9	Financial services	27	Environment
10	Information society and media	28	Consumer and health protection
11	Agriculture and rural development	29	Customs union
12	Food safety, veterinary, and phytosanitary policy	30	External relations
13	Fisheries	31	Foreign, security, and defense policy
14	Transport policy	32	Financial control
15	Energy	33	Financial and budgetary provisions
16	Taxation	34	Institutions
17	Economic and monetary policy	35	Other issues
18	Statistics		

the candidate has made enough progress. The eventual admission into the EU is granted in a final accession treaty, which must once again be approved by all member states, but on this occasion also by the European Parliament. And if, during this long process a candidate's democratic development suffers a setback, the EU can at any moment suspend negotiations; this time not by unanimous consent, but by qualified majority, that is, by at least 55 percent of member states (which after the UK's departure equates to 15 countries) representing at least 65 percent of the EU population. Short of war or revolution, it could arguably be stated that EU integration represents the most radical transformation, which a county could be subjected to.

Studies have demonstrated that joining the European Union has by and large highly positive effects on new members.[4] Often lengthy transition processes usher in a reform of a candidate's political system, its laws and policies, but also its norms and standards, with a process of "Europeanization" prevalent, in particular, among younger citizens. The concept of the EU as an anchor of legitimacy[5] works in several ways. In order to join, candidates must conform to a set of rules as manifested in the EU acquis. More importantly though, integration into the EU most often results in better democracy, a more efficient and transparent administration, and also higher living standards. In simple terms, being a member of the bloc usually improves the quality of life for many new EU citizens. The EU has a long and proud history of integrating countries that subsequently made a successful transition from fascist or communist dictatorships. Even before the "Big Bang" enlargement of 2004 to the countries of central and eastern Europe, West Germany and Italy sought to anchor their young, postwar democracies within a community of like-minded states. In the 1980s, Greece, Spain, and Portugal embarked on a similar journey. From an economic perspective, poorer members such as Belgium and Ireland managed to raise their standards of living to hitherto inconceivable levels. And fifteen years after joining the EU, many new states in central and eastern Europe, in particular, Malta, the Czech Republic, Cyprus, and Slovenia had made impressive inroads to close the cohesion gap to their counterparts in the West.

But there is also much counterevidence to these positive developments. As seen in chapter 3, Poland and Hungary are careering off their democratic paths and it would be doubtful whether the state of democracy in these countries would qualify them for EU membership now. When Greece joined the EU in 1981, the country's prosperity was comparable to that of Ireland at around 60 percent of the EU average. Forty years later, Ireland has soared to be the second wealthiest EU country, while Greece even before the financial crisis struggled to make any incursions. Bulgaria and Romania too, thirteen years after joining the bloc, continue to be firmly rooted to the bottom of the EU prosperity table,[6] with corruption and an inefficient public sector as persistent worries.

What will the EU look like once the next wave of candidates is integrated? Will the concept of the legitimacy anchor receive further vindication? Or will new members follow in the economically more challenging footsteps of Greece? Will public sector reforms be comprehensive and abide to standards of efficiency and transparency? And will democratic norms and practices be firmly rooted in the political cultures of the new members? Further enlargement also poses intricate challenges for the EU. To what extent will the decision-making process be altered, when in particular a sizeable country such as Turkey aims to make its mark in the corridors of Brussels? And will existing redistributive policies like agriculture or cohesion be able to cope with the integration of by and large economically backward candidates? In short, will the candidates be ready to join the EU and conversely, will the EU be ready to integrate new members?

THE STABILIZATION AND ASSOCIATION PROCESS

All applicants, whether current candidates that are undergoing the thirty-five-chapter negotiation process, or future candidates that have not yet reached a sufficient level of economic and political stability, are part of the Stabilization and Association Process (SAP). These not only include the current candidates of Albania, North Macedonia, Montenegro, Serbia, and Turkey but also future potential members including Bosnia and Herzegovina, Kosovo, as well as Ukraine. The SAP consists of four key elements. On the one hand, the EU unilaterally opens its markets and removes trade barriers, thus granting applicant economies free access to 500 million consumers with the aim of boosting economic growth in the region. Regional cooperation is a further focus designed to establish free trade relations among the applicant countries. For those countries subjected to the violent disintegration of Yugoslavia, collaboration with the International Criminal Tribunal for the Former Yugoslavia (ICTY) in The Hague was also a prerequisite before the court ceased operations in December 2017.

The basis for the SAP, however, is individual Stabilization and Association Agreements (SAAs), which address country-specific development challenges. As such, every SAA focuses on the areas of public and administrative reform, rule of law, sustainable economy (including energy, transport, environment, and climate change), agriculture and rural development, as well as people (including gender equality, inclusion, education, or skills). In order to fund these programs, the EU established the so-called Instrument for Pre-Accession (IPA) and between 2007 and 2013, a total of 11.5 billion euros was spent in the region. For the next financial perspective (2014–2020), the funds were marginally increased to 11.7 billion euros.[7] Hence, prior to the start of the thirty-five-chapter negotiations, the EU imposes a wide-ranging reform package on every applicant, which is backed up by a significant amount of money. While the proper and far-reaching transformation does not start until official candidate status is granted, the SAP's aim is to achieve economic, political, and institutional stability, without which the accession negotiations would not stand much chance of success.

THE CURRENT CANDIDATES

Albania

As seen in table 5.3, Albania is by some margin the poorest of the current candidate states. Burdened by a long history of brutal Stalinism, the integration of the country into the family of European market democracies represents a formidable challenge. Until the demise of the communist dictator Enver Hoxha in 1990, Albania existed virtually in isolation and was very much cut off from its neighbors. The 1992 elections finally marked the end of forty-seven years of oppression culminating in the country's integration into NATO in 2009. The Socialist Party of Prime Minister Edi Rama, who came to power in 2013, started to implement much-needed reforms with its

Table 5.3 GDP Per Capita in the EU and Candidate States, 2017

EU 15	*EU 13 (Joined after 2004)*	*EU Candidates*
258 Luxembourg	96 Malta	64 Turkey
183 Ireland	88 Czech Republic	45 Montenegro
128 Austria, Netherlands	83 Cyprus	37 North Macedonia
124 Denmark	83 Slovenia	37 Serbia
123 Germany, Sweden	77 Slovakia	29 Albania
118 Belgium	75 Estonia	
109 Finland	75 Lithuania	
107 UK	68 Poland	
104 France	67 Hungary	
97 Italy	65 Latvia	
92 Spain	60 Croatia	
77 Portugal	58 Romania	
68 Greece	49 Bulgaria	

Purchasing Power; EU 28 is at index 100.
Source: Eurostat, December 2017.

fight against corruption and organized crime whose widespread prevalence saw the electorate turn against his predecessor, the conservative Sali Berisha.

But the path to democracy is long and winding. In its annual report of November 2016,[8] the Commission criticized a lack of judicial independence, while also highlighting the continued existence of money laundering and organized crime based on a far-reaching "informal" (i.e., black market) economy. The Commission urged the government to achieve fiscal consolidation, and to raise professional standards, which would ultimately improve the country's administrative capacity. The gloomy assessment by the EU authorities was mirrored in a report by Washington-based Freedom House.[9] Assessing Albania's state of democracy, the think tank argued that the democratic progress had worsened between 2007 (when the score was 3.82, with 1 representing the highest level and 7 the lowest) and 2017 (with the score at 4.14). The report paid specific reference to the reemergence of vote buying, and the application of pressure on voters in two regional by-elections in 2016.

The government's reforms started to have an impact. The local elections of 2015 were largely free from the customary violence and aggression. A judicial reform in 2015 finally banned previously convicted criminals from holding public office. A further reform package was passed the following year, aimed at curbing corruption, organized crime and the meddling of politicians in the judicial process. The efforts were acknowledged by the European Commission in its 2019 report. The political system continued to suffer from "strong polarization," while more efforts were needed to combat money laundering. However, EU officials highlighted positive developments in the fight against corruption (in particular the dismissal of eighty-eight corrupt magistrates) and noted steady progress toward a more transparent and efficient public service.[10]

Signing off reforms is one thing. Making sure those measures are implemented on the ground is another matter altogether. The spread of marijuana plantations serves as a telling example. In an impoverished society that is blighted by widespread youth unemployment, ruthless operators continue to take advantage of poor farmers and a corrupt police bureaucracy, thereby turning this "industry" into a questionable pillar of the Albanian economy. What is required for Albania to take the final and ambitious steps toward a European-style democracy is a fundamental change in its political culture. For decades, the state was regarded as either an oppressor or as a vehicle ready to be exploited for personal gains and to fortify privileges. But a state cannot thrive if it is abused as a potentially lucrative means in a society where notions of a common good are only weakly developed. It is for these reasons that negotiations with the EU on individual chapters have not started, as these depend on tangible progress in the country's effort to establish a law-abiding state structure buttressed by an independent judiciary.

For the EU, integrating Albania, a predominantly Muslim country with a truly horrific postwar history, scarred by poverty, corruption, and organized crime would certainly represent a notable achievement, which could lend considerable moral clout to an organization that after all, aims to spread stability and prosperity across the continent. The Commission's proposal in May 2019 to start the thirty-five-chapter negotiations are a step in this direction, although at this stage, the member states have not given their consent. But with Albania, the EU has taken on a mighty challenge, and it is by no means assured that even with outside guidance and considerable financial support, the country would be able to make such a far and wide-reaching transition.

North Macedonia

One of the more absurd quarrels in Europe finally came to an end in June 2018. For years, relations between this small, landlocked Balkan country and the EU were dominated by a disagreement over the country's name. The EU member state Greece persistently challenged the official name of "Republic of Macedonia" because of its semantic proximity to a province in northern Greece, also called Macedonia. As such, the EU for a long time referred to the country as FYROM—the Former Yugoslav Republic of Macedonia—which in the history of diplomacy must go down as one of the more ridiculous names. At one stage, Greece even proposed a sillier solution: Skopia in reference to the country's capital Skopje. This did not go down too well, as citizens might then have been referred to as "Skopians," which is rather close to a description more accurately used in the animal kingdom. Further blushes were finally spared when the Greek parliament narrowly approved the name compromise of North Macedonia, which the country in question duly accepted. The path was therefore clear for a more constructive interaction between the two sides.

Apart from the controversy over the name, North Macedonia got off to a very promising start in its attempt to join the EU. After gaining independence from Yugoslavia in 1991, the country signed a SAA with the EU in 2001. Together with Croatia and Turkey, candidate status was granted in 2005. But progress came to a shuddering halt, in large part caused by the premiership of Nikola Gruevski who governed the country from 2006 to 2016. During his time in office, his ruling VMRO-DPMNE—"short" for Internal Macedonian Revolutionary Organization, Democratic Party—oversaw a gradual transition from a tender, but improving democracy to an autocratic and deeply corrupt regime. In 2009, the Commission recommended the start of negotiations, but reservations, mainly from Bulgaria and Greece, mean that no chapters have been opened so far (see table 5.4).

Internal stability was severely tested in the spring of 2015 when a wiretapping scandal caught senior politicians discussing the cover-up of killings and the rigging of elections. Further investigations revealed widespread government manipulation of electoral lists, the media and the judiciary. Despite public protests, Gruevski was able to hold on to power, although his interior and transport ministers, as well as the head of security were forced to resign. In July 2015, the EU and the United States tried to mediate in the conflict with the signing of the Pržino agreement, which foresaw the involvement of opposition parties in government, an early resignation of Gruevski by

Table 5.4 State of EU Enlargement Negotiations by Candidate, June 2019

Country	*Candidate Status since*	*Chapters*
Albania	2014	None opened None closed
North Macedonia	2005	None opened None closed
Montenegro	2010	Thirty opened Two closed: thirty (external relations), twelve (science and research)
Serbia	2012	Fourteen opened Two closed: twenty-six (education and culture), twelve (science and research)
Turkey	2005	Fifteen opened One closed • EU decision in 2016 not to open any new chapters because of "prevailing circumstances" • Eight chapters will not be opened unless Turkey recognizes Republic of Cyprus

January 2016, the appointment of a special prosecutor to investigate government activities, as well as a care-taker government that should lead the country to new elections by June 2016. These elections finally took place after a six-month delay, when to the consternation of the international community, Gruevski's party secured the highest number of votes, though not enough seats in parliament to form a government. Under such circumstances, the Macedonian constitution hands such a right to the main opposition party, which President Gjorge Ivanov hesitated to do. In April 2017, an angry nationalist mob descended onto parliament injuring the opposition leader Zoran Zaev. An outraged Ivanov called elections for June 2017, which Zaev promptly won, resulting in the formation of a new government for the first time in eleven years.

In its annual progress report of 2016,[11] the Commission's assessment of North Macedonia provided grim reading. It refers to "clientilistic" politics of which all parties, whether those in government or in opposition were being guilty of. This is a deeply divided and polarized country whose political discourse is increasingly organized along antagonistic ethnic lines between Macedonians on one side, and Albanians, Turks, and Roma on the other. The EU's demand for urgent democratic reforms was left unanswered. Freedom of expression was in steady decline with ruling economic and political elites unwilling to relinquish any influence. Prime Minister Zaev and his ruling center-left Social Democrats were facing an epic challenge. Democracy and the rule of law were constantly undermined. Economic progress was painfully slow, with the country being one of the poorest in Europe (see table 5.4).[12]

But Zaev deserves some credit in turning around North Macedonia's fortunes. Three years after assuming power, the Commission's assessment of May 2019[13] praised the government for a hitherto unimagined reform push. The EU bureaucrats referred to a political atmosphere that now was "inclusive" and "open." Zaev's administration achieved tangible results in the reform of the judiciary and the intelligence services, as well as in the fight against organized crime and corruption. The interethnic situation was described as "calm" with a better climate for civil society organizations. It came as little surprise that the Commission once again proposed the start of the thirty-five-chapter negotiations, which would bring fifteen years of zero progress to a much-needed end. It therefore seems imminent once the EU national governments have given their consent that North Macedonia will soon join Montenegro and Serbia in going through the chapter motions.

Montenegro

Unlike North Macedonia, the tiny Mediterranean country of Montenegro made rapid strides toward EU integration. After leaving the union with Serbia in 2006, the country quickly applied for EU membership and negotiations commenced in 2012. By 2019, steady progress had been made with two chapters being closed and a further thirty chapters being opened. This makes Montenegro the most advanced of all the candidate countries; a development recognized by the Commission who mentioned an accession target of 2025.

But the thorny issue of NATO membership exposed severe rifts in Montenegro's political landscape. NATO welcomed its twenty-ninth member in June 2017, thus closing the last gap in an alliance-controlled coastline, which now stretches from Gibraltar to Syria. But NATO membership came merely eighteen years after 500 Montenegrins perished in the bombing campaign against Milosević's Yugoslavia. The country was therefore evenly divided over the merit of joining the alliance.[14] Montenegro enjoys strong cultural, religious, and economic connections with Russia and many people argued that NATO membership might severely compromise those ties. What follows was straight out of an old-fashioned spy thriller. Parliamentary elections, and therefore the last chance to stop integration into the alliance were scheduled for October 2016. One day before polling, the country's chief prosecutor alleged that a group of twelve Serbian nationalists supported by two Russian intelligence officers had plotted a coup to seize control of parliament and to kill the leader of Montenegro's most popular party Duško Marković. However, the Russian spies were sent back to Russia before a trial could commence, and the opposition claimed that this was a fake coup planned by Marković to increase his electoral chances. Russia's head of security later apologized for the incident, stating that it was a rogue operation not sanctioned by the Kremlin. What precisely happened continues to be a mystery.

But the episode revealed the key role of Moscow in Montenegrin politics. Russia is by far the biggest foreign investor[15] and the financial ties become only too apparent when visiting the country's coastal resorts, which are full of Russian tourists and Russian-owned real estate. Montenegro under Russian influence would also give Moscow a highly strategic access point to the Mediterranean Sea, while the country's NATO integration represented a severe blow to Russia's strategic ambitions. Relations were further soured in March 2014, when Montenegro joined western sanctions; one day after a referendum brought the Crimea under Moscow's control. In retaliation, Russia has warned its citizens not to travel to Montenegro, thereby greatly diminishing revenues in the tourist sector, while also banning the import of Montenegrin wine; one of the country's major trade assets.

The coup—fake or real—also shed light on the tender state of democracy. The Commission in a report in 2016 highlighted a judicial and administrative capacity that was "moderate";[16] EU speak for the prevalence of corruption. The country is led by Marković and his Democratic Party of Socialists backed by several smaller parties representing ethnic minorities. But the government only had a very narrow margin of support and when Marković was about to be voted into power in parliament, opposition parties boycotted the procedure on grounds of electoral irregularities. Opposition politicians had only started to return to parliament when the country was engulfed by the "envelope affair" of January 2019. Duško Knežević, a fugitive Montenegrin businessman now residing in London, had claimed that he had secretly been feeding cash to the ruling Democratic Party for thirty years. Later, a video made in 2016 emerged, which showed Knežević handing over an envelope to the mayor of the country's capital Podgorica. Knežević claimed that this envelope contained 200,000 US dollars. No wonder that the Commission report on the state of Montenegro's political development provided grim reading.[17] The EU bureaucrats wrote about a "fragmented and polarized political scene . . . marked by a lack of genuine political dialogue." The Montenegrin public too seemed to have had enough and street protests were widely common in early 2019.

Montenegro's path toward European integration is therefore far from assured. At this stage, a coherent political alternative has not been forthcoming, and it seems that EU integration continues to depend on Marković and his party, which could turn out to be a rather shaky bet. On current evidence, the Commission's envisaged entry date of 2025 can therefore be classified as wildly optimistic.

Serbia

For a long time, Serbia, the biggest constituent republic of the former Yugoslavia, was regarded as Europe's pariah state. The country's former leader Slobodan Milosević contributed much to this questionable reputation. In the violent civil war in Bosnia and Herzegovina between 1991 and 1995, Serbia gave very significant military assistance to Bosnian Serbs under their political leader Radovan Karadzić and his military commander General Ratko Mladić. In Kosovo, in 1999, Milosević's brutal response to an uprising by Kosovo Albanians triggered a military response by NATO. Once Milosević was ousted in 2000, the persistent refusal to hand Mladić and Karadzić to the ICTY prevented closer relations with the EU. Serbia at the time was also not necessarily in favor of European integration, which had its reason in the prevalence of a strong nationalist political culture, which regards itself as the supreme power in the region and is supported by a prominent ally in Russia that shares the same Christian-orthodox faith. But the situation dramatically changed once Boris Tadić became president in 2004. Karadzić had continued to live in Serbia but was eventually captured in 2008. Mladić, who for a long time was sheltered by loyal nationalist followers and family members, followed in 2011.The EU quickly granted the country candidate status in 2012.

Progress in the accession negotiations has been slow. Under Prime Minister Aleksandar Vučić, crucial chapters had been opened, most notably judiciary and fundamental rights (chapter 23) justice, freedom, and security (chapter 24), as well as relations with its former province and now independent neighbor Kosovo (chapter 35). But internal democratic reforms on a noteworthy scale failed to materialize. In fact, Freedom House noted[18] that Serbia's democratic score in 2016 was the lowest since 2005, and observers of the Balkan region cited the by-now-all-too-familiar systemic deficiencies, such as corruption, election irregularities, media intrusion, and lack of judicial independence. One incident illustrated the state of democracy in Serbia in a remarkable fashion. Referred to as the *Savamala* case, in April 2014, masked men closed off a street in the center of the Serbian capital Belgrade and proceeded to bulldoze homes to make way for a private real estate development called the "Belgrade Waterfront," which was championed and backed by the government. Investigations later revealed that the police failed to respond to calls for help by affected homeowners, pointing to a collusion of police officials with the highest levels of government. Rule of law works differently.

On a positive note, the public is now much more critical and willing to express any dissatisfaction with the political authorities, whether through media channels or through demonstrations. The example of Ana Brnabić also stands out. In June 2017, Vučić won the presidential elections and appointed the US- and UK-educated novice politician as his new prime minister, which in the Serbian constitution is regarded as the most powerful office in the country. Brnabić is not only the first female head of any government in the Balkans, she is also openly gay, which in a country known for its often-rampant homophobia[19] represented an extraordinary development. Her appointment did much to improve the LGBTQ agenda, and in the process, might also improve notions of tolerance and respect in what is still a very traditional, conservative, and male-dominated country. Then again, Brnabić is an independent politician without a power base, while Vučić stills remains as the head of the ruling Serbian Progressive Party, which over the years exercised a powerful grip on state institutions and the media. Accusations of window dressing were therefore widespread. Still, credit where credit is due. Democratic progress might be slow, but with seven million people, Serbia is by far the most populous candidate in the region, and the economic potential, should the political, financial, and cultural elites be able to unleash it, is promising.

Turkey

As seen in table 5.3, Turkey is no longer an economic backwater. Its prosperity levels are the highest of the current candidates and are in line with some EU member states, including Greece, Latvia, Hungary, or Poland. In fact, the country recently enjoyed one of the highest GDP growth rates in the world with an average 5.4 percent annual increase between 2003 and 2013.[20] The country also has a very young population[21] with an average age of just thirty—a strong bonus for any market economy where consumer spending is very much driven by people under the age of forty-five. Add to this the size of the economy (Turkey has a population of eighty million citizens, which is expected to rise to ninety million within one generation), and the economic advantages of the country joining the EU's Single Market become a no-brainer. In fact, Turkey could even represent the panacea for an economically stricken Eurozone, offering a growth boost of huge potential, which reforms to the EU's single currency so far have struggled to deliver. In addition, from an economic perspective, Turkey is already well integrated since it shares a custom union with the EU, giving both sides access to each other's markets.[22] The country is a very significant trade partner, ranking fourth for EU exports (behind the United States, China, and Switzerland) and fifth for EU imports (behind China, the United States, Switzerland, and Russia).[23] Wages are low, and the government has set up multiple free trade zones that offer international manufacturers the chance to produce at greatly reduced tax rates. Add to this the much closer geographical proximity to European markets than, for instance, China or India, and it is little wonder that Turkey has started to turn into Europe's manufacturing sweat shop.

But such an economic prize must be balanced against several challenges in the political domain. Under former prime minister and now president Recep Tayyip Erdogan, the country implemented large-scale democratic reforms (most notably the abolition of the death penalty), which encouraged the EU to grant candidate status in 2005. But as of 2019, only fifteen chapters have been opened, and only one closed: the rather short chapter on science and research. Erdogan's style of government over the past years has also been increasingly autocratic. Backed by large support among socially conservative and low-income earners most notably outside the main cities, human rights violations and media intrusions became ever more prevalent.

The image of Erdogan as a strong man was encapsulated by the Taksim Square riots in July 2013. A small group of mainly young people was demonstrating against the development of the inner-city Gezi Park to make way for apartments. Encouraged by Erdogan, the Istanbul mayor Kadir Topbaş, sent in the riot police, including unemployed people hired on one-day contracts to squash what had been a mild and harmless demonstration and thus showing an excessive force of strength that left demonstrators shocked and running for their lives. EU institutions and member state governments were alarmed and disconcerted. Erdogan went even further in his no-nonsense approach in the summer of 2015 when a group of opposition politicians, backed by senior figures in the military, the media and academia orchestrated a failed coup. Erdogan ordered widespread purges and over 50,000 people were either fired or suspended from their positions. It remains doubtful whether so many people were involved in, or even supported the coup, and many commenters concluded that Erdogan had used this opportunity to incapacitate dissenting voices, often without the application of appropriate judicial means. For the EU member state governments, this was one democratic derogation too many and in December 2016, they decided to keep any remaining chapters unopened as long as "the prevailing circumstances" remain unchanged. Not that this had the slightest effect on Erdogan, when a referendum in April 2017 on constitutional changes massively increased his status. As such, Turkey's parliamentary democracy was replaced by a presidential system, which gave Erdogan significant powers in the appointment of judges and prosecutors. It cemented the government's strong position against the opposition during a potentially highly unstable time, but it was also a major democratic setback and an autocratic power grab.

The contentious issue of Cyprus—currently the longest running conflict in international relations—also greatly undermines the country's relationship with the EU. In 1974, Turkish military forces invaded the former British colony as a response to persistent harassment of Turkish Cypriots by nationalist-minded Greek Cypriots. The invasion divided the island into a Greek-Cypriot southern part, and a Turkish-Cypriot north. Turkey claimed that the intervention came to the rescue of an embattled people, but nonetheless, the military operation was a breach of international law. Subsequently, Turkey encouraged the establishment of a government in the self-styled Turkish Republic of Northern Cyrus (TRNC); a state that is only recognized by Ankara. In return, Turkey refuses to recognize the Republic of Cyprus in the South, and once more, it is the only government in the world to do so. Numerous attempts, often brokered by the UN, failed to reunify the island, most notably in 2004 when a referendum was approved in the north, but failed to win enough support in the south. Without solving the reunification issue, the Republic was allowed to join the EU just weeks after the referendum was held. It would have been more conducive to both Turkey and the EU, if the accession of Cyprus had been conditional on the Cyprus problem being solved. A breakthrough in negotiations was on the horizon in 2016, but a deal fell apart at the last moment, when agreement over the presence of approximately 25,000 Turkish soldiers could not be reached. The EU and the Republic argued that Erdogan ought to remove the troops before a settlement can be reached, but Turkey insisted on a transition period.[24] The stalemate continues. Turkey does not recognize one of the members of an international organization, which it intends to join, while in return recognizing a state, which the EU claims to be on the territory of one of its member states: A formidable mess indeed. For the enlargement process, this means that eight chapters, which would directly affect the Cyprus division (including fundamental rights, energy, as well as education and culture), cannot be opened until the island's recognition and unification issues are resolved.

Beyond Cyprus, Turkey's geopolitical location also represents grounds for concern. The country shares land borders with Iran, Iraq, and Syria, and many commentators fear that such a vast area would be practically impossible to police and thus the EU would find itself prone to terrorist and Muslim-fundamentalist attacks. While such concerns cannot easily be disregarded, and a policing of the Turkish border would require a great degree of EU financial support, one also has to recognize that Turkey—at least until Erdogan's autocratic tendencies started to become apparent in the aftermath of the Taksim Square riots—functioned as a role model in a region, which ever since the 2011 Arab spring continues to struggle to unify cultural forces that are drifting ever further apart. A successful integration of Turkey could therefore undoubtedly increase the EU's diplomatic influence in one of the most volatile regions in the world.

If Turkey, led by Erdogan or by a successor, manages to overcome the Cyprus problem, and pursues widespread reforms to meet the requirements of the thirty-five chapters, it is by no means guaranteed that EU integration would be forthcoming. Public opinion across Europe is deeply divided on the issue,[25] and calls for a referendum on Turkish membership have been voiced in France and Austria, while German chancellor Angela Merkel continues to argue that Ankara should have a special relationship with the EU, which would fall just short of full membership. Such a development could be catastrophic to EU-Turkey relations. Imagine a candidate that is undergoing what would most certainly be an often-painstaking process of meeting EU norms, only to be told after a decades-long reform process, that there still is no place for it in the EU. Such an outcome would be truly ridiculous.

But it could also be argued that the EU is not ready for Turkey. By the time of accession, the country might have a population of close to ninety million, thus making it by far the biggest member state. According to current voting rules in the Council of Ministers, 55 percent of states representing 65 percent of the EU population would be required to pass legislative acts. An EU by then might have mastered Brexit but could also have integrated Serbia and Montenegro thus bringing the number of EU citizens to approximately 540 million. The share of Turkish citizens would be around 16 percent of the overall EU population, which would give the country very significant voting powers. In fact, Turkey plus one other larger member state (such as France and Germany), plus two more mid-sized states (such as the Netherlands and Belgium) could potentially block EU legislation. As such, four states could scupper the legislative intentions of twenty-six fellow members. No wonder analysts refer to a potential institutional deadlock.

Policies too, might have to be revamped to a considerable extent. The Turkish agricultural sector is substantial, and while it continues to shrink, just under 30 percent of its labor force still works on the land. If unchanged, the budget for the Common Agricultural Policy would not be able to cope with the integration of such large numbers. The same scenario also applies to the cohesion policy. As it stands now, Turkish regions would be eligible to apply for 85 percent of the cohesion budget earmarked for poorer regions having less than 90 percent of the EU's average GDP.[26] Based on current population figures, around 175 million people are living in these regions. With Turkey's accession, the EU average GDP could be reduced by as much as 10 percent, which would subsequently exclude the likes of Malta, the Czech Republic, Slovenia, and Slovakia, but also potentially Spain and regions in southern Italy from these funds as their average GDP would be above 90 percent. This would bring the number of people to around 110 million EU citizens who then must share the funds with Turkish regions housing 80 million people. Even if these figures are just a rough projection, they nonetheless highlight that cohesion, just like agriculture, would need to be subject to considerable reforms. Consequently, a potential institutional deadlock could very conceivably be complemented by a policy breakdown. To conclude, Turkey, after many decades of reform might find itself knocking on the door of an EU that is not only unwilling but also unfit to integrate such a large candidate. It is for these reasons that an integration of Turkey under the current circumstances has next to no chance of succeeding.

FUTURE CANDIDATES

Beyond the current five candidates, there are a further three countries with whom the EU has established firm bilateral relations with a view to eventual accession. These include Bosnia and Herzegovina, Kosovo, as well as Ukraine.

Bosnia and Herzegovina

One of the constituent republics of the former Yugoslavia, Bosnia, and Herzegovina was heralded as a shining light of multiculturalism with three distinctively different ethnicities, all following different faiths, living alongside one another: Bosniaks (who follow the Muslim faith), Bosnian Croats (who are Roman Catholics), and Bosnian Serbs (who are Orthodox Christians). But with the demise of communism, which forbade and thus held in check any cultural or political expressions of nationalism, old ethnic tensions resurfaced in the most ugly and disastrous fashion. The country's leadership under Bosniak Alija Izetbegović declared independence from Yugoslavia in April 1992. Fearing a Muslim dominance in a newly independent state, Radovan Karadzić, leader of the minority Bosnian Serbs, had warned from the outset that such a move would not be acceptable to his people. During the subsequent civil war between 1992 and 1995, an estimated 100,000 were killed,[27] 80 percent of whom Bosniaks. Backed by military support from neighboring Serbia, Karadzić embarked on a military strategy of ethnic cleansing, the most notorious example happened in Srebrenica in July 1995 where Bosnian Serb forces under the command of Ratko Mladić massacred 8,000 Bosniak men and boys; the largest massacre in Europe since the Holocaust. Throughout this conflict, the EU stood helplessly on the side-lines, imposing a half-hearted weapons embargo on the country, which only helped to establish Karadzić's military supremacy as he continued to receive support from Serbia. In the end, US intervention under President Bill Clinton brought the bloodshed to a halt with the Dayton Peace Agreement of 1995. It split the country into three distinct areas: the center of the country is now governed by the so-called Federation of Bosnia and Herzegovina, largely occupied by Bosnian Croats and Bosniaks and split further into ten cantons along ethnic lines. The north and east of the country are controlled by the Republika Srpska,[28] consisting overwhelmingly of Bosnian Serbs. In addition, the Brčko district—little more than a small town—is wedged between the northern and the eastern parts of the Republika Srpska, designed to avoid a geographical coherence of that entity. Hence, what used to be a lively example of multiculturalism with ethnically mixed towns and villages is now by and large a country with ethnically homogenous administrative units. Overall, according to the 2013 national census, Bosniaks represent 50 percent of the country's population.[29] Bosnian Serbs make up 30 percent,[30] and Bosnian Croats 15 percent.

Dayton brought peace, but it also gave the country a highly complex constitution, which failed to establish a political settlement required for an integration into the EU. Although a SAA entered into force in June 2015, politics at the state level continues to be undermined by Bosnian Serb separatist notions. Its president Milorad Dodik has argued persistently that he would much rather have political independence for his statelet than pursue a path of collaboration with his Bosniak and Bosnian-Croat counterparts. There was also the acrimonious legal case of Seidić-Finci. Both parties took the government of Bosnia and Herzegovina to the European Court of Human Rights (ECHR) at the Council of Europe, claiming that Dayton violated their human rights as it requires voters to declare themselves as Serb, Bosniak, or Croat in order to participate in presidential or parliamentary elections. Finci (of Jewish faith) and Seidić (a Roma) successfully convinced the court. Alas, the ruling so far has not resulted in constitutional changes.

Economic, political, and bureaucratic structures also have not reached sufficient levels for negotiations to start. The Commission stated in 2016[31] that Bosnia and Herzegovina is still at an early stage in the development toward a functioning market economy. As far as democratic standards are concerned, there are threats to the judiciary from the political establishment. Corruption is prevalent, journalists are frequently intimidated, and collaboration with civil society is lacking. As for the EU acquis, a great range of issues require deep reforms, with the Commission highlighting justice, freedom and security, competition, agriculture, the environment, as well as energy. As it stands now, Bosnia and Herzegovina is at the bottom end of the EU's candidates list, and it remains highly doubtful whether the country has the ability to make any strides unless a fundamental constitutional reform and a departure from Dayton can be agreed upon. Only then would it be possible to tackle the widespread shortcomings that the Commission criticized in such a vocal manner. However, without outside help, these monumental changes have little chance of succeeding. Much depends on the position of Serbia, which has the capacity to take the wind out of Dodik's nationalistic agenda. The ground is still not fertile for a democratic, economic, and bureaucratic transformation. Yet, the EU is demanding that seeds of change ought to be sown first, before proper chapter negotiations can begin.

Ukraine

EU relations with the former Soviet republic rest on three pillars. Since 2004, Ukraine has been part of the European Neighborhood Policy (ENP), which extends to sixteen non-EU entities and focuses on democratic institutional development in return for financial aid.[32] In addition, an association agreement was signed in November 2014, which covered standard areas that are also instrumental in the accession process of western Balkan countries, including human rights, corruption, financial services, or agriculture supported by a financial package of 12.8 billion euros.[33] The agreement entered into force in September 2017. In the same month, the Deep and Comprehensive Free Trade Area (DCFTA) also started, which gave Ukrainian producers preferential access to EU markets, while also commencing with the long process of harmonizing product standards and regulations. One month later, in October 2017, additional trade measures increased the number and volume of agricultural products that could enter the EU without tariffs or other trade barriers. The measures had an instant effect as trade between the two partners increased by 23 percent during the first half of 2017.[34]

But trade and other bilateral relations cannot even begin to paint a coherent picture. Including Ukraine in the 2003 list of potential EU candidates took many observers by surprise as it potentially represents a deep eastern expansion of the EU right to the border with Russia. Ukraine is a vast country with forty-five million people, geographically the largest of all countries whose boundaries are solely within Europe. Only Turkey, with most of the country located in the Middle East is a bigger EU applicant. But despite its Soviet past, parts of Ukraine have a strong central European tradition and at some stage belonged to Poland or to the Austro-Hungarian empire. After two brief spells of independence after World Wars I and II, political sovereignty was achieved with the dissolution of the Soviet Union in December 1991. The ethnic division of the country, however, continues to be a large source of instability. During Soviet rule, Moscow had moved sizeable numbers of ethnic Russians to the eastern part of Ukraine to accelerate industrialization and still today, most people in the eastern area surrounding the cities of Donetsk and Lugansk are of Russian origin and speak Russian instead of Ukrainian. In April 2014, an armed conflict between Ukrainian troops and a Russian-backed separatist movement resulted in the de facto annexation of this area by anti-government forces. Movement of troops and military equipment between Russia and the region was widely reported throughout 2014, prompting widespread international condemnation.

Equally explosive was the political escalation in the Crimea. The peninsula had been a part of Russia ever since the end of the eighteenth century. In 1954, Soviet leader Nikita Khrushchev placed the region under the domain of the Soviet Republic of Ukraine, where it remained until independence in 1991. However, Vladimir Putin annexed the Crimea in March 2014, arguing that the area had for centuries been a part of Russia and was inhabited by a large majority of Russians. The international community once again condemned this act of aggression.

Not surprisingly, domestic politics suffered from the Ukrainian-Russian antagonism. The 2004 presidential elections provided an illustrative example. The election was won by incumbent Prime Minister and Moscow-leaning Victor Yanukovych. His opponent Victor Yushchenko had campaigned for a western integration with EU accession as the eventual benchmark. Yanukovych won by a small margin, but Yushchenko claimed that election rigging, and voter intimidation had cost him the victory. Widespread street protests followed, and the Supreme Court declared the elections void. Yushchenko won the rerun and became president and appointed his ally in the so-called Orange revolution Yulia Tymoshenko as his prime minister. However, by the next presidential elections in 2010, the two had become bitter enemies. Tymoshenko decided to run for office, thereby turning the elections into a three-horse race between her, Yushchenko and the reemerging Yanukovych. The latter won the second round of the contest against Tymoshenko and imprisoned her over corruption charges a year later. In 2013, Yanukovych refused to sign the EU Association Agreement, which once again brought pro-western Ukrainians out onto the streets of major cities in the second Ukrainian revolution in ten years. Yanukovych saw his fate sealed when the parliament removed him from office in February 2014 and replaced him with the Tymoshenko ally Oleksandr Turchynov. In June 2014, presidential elections were held once again, with the wealthy oligarch Petro Poroshenko assuming office.

For the first part of his presidency, Poroshenko was popular, in particular among pro-western Ukrainians who can be found predominantly in the western part of the country, although the government's legitimacy continued to be challenged in the more pro-Russian, eastern area of the country. But just like some of his predecessors, Poroshenko was accused of corruption and the embezzlement of public funds. In a remarkable development that could not have been dreamed up in a more vivid fashion by a Hollywood script writer, the actor Volodymyr Zelensky—who incidentally played the Ukrainian president in a TV soap opera—ousted Poroshenko with a staggering vote share of 73 percent in the presidential elections of March 2019. Ukrainians therefore placed their faith into the hands of a completely inexperienced political novice. This fact alone tells the desperate story of a country that is deeply disillusioned with its political establishment. It remains to be seen whether Zelensky can take inspiration from his progressive and engaging TV character amid a stark political reality, which is shaped by a powerful financial tribe of oligarchs, and an ungovernable eastern part where Vladimir Putin is intent on causing further disruption. The challenge remains the same for Zelensky as for his predecessors: overcoming deep divisions in a country ravaged by a phenomenal income disparity and conflicting visons over a pro-European or pro-Russian identity. Ukraine is very far from being settled and stable, which does not bode well for the massive reform processes that precede any potential EU membership.

Kosovo

With a population of just under two million, the small landlocked country of Kosovo is the second poorest in Europe after Moldova. Around one-third of its population is without a job, and youth unemployment is staggeringly high at 66 percent.[35] Most of its population lives in rural areas hampered by an inefficient agricultural sector based on small-plot farming and limited mechanization. Corruption, unreliable contract and law enforcement, and patchy energy supply continue to undermine the economy. Financial contributions from the international community, as well as from the Kosovar diaspora mainly in Germany, Switzerland, and Scandinavian countries account for 10 percent of GDP. Here is a country that desperately needs European integration.

But many serious obstacles remain in the way. Kosovo is populated by a large majority of Muslim ethnic Albanians complemented by a minority of ethnic Serbs. As a part of Yugoslavia, it was not a constituent republic like Croatia or Slovenia but organized as a semi-autonomous province within Serbia. During the 1960s and 1970s, the Yugoslav government granted significant powers, which eased the previous dominance of Serbs in the regional government, the police, the army and the state-run economy. An Albanian-speaking university was established in the capital Priština, and the province was given a self-governing assembly, administration, and judiciary. However, resentment against the "host" republic Serbia persisted, partially caused by the high levels of poverty, low degree of public investment, and a general lack of economic opportunities. Peaceful calls for more independence and for giving Kosovo the status of a republic gradually descended into an armed conflict with the arrival of the Kosovo Liberation Army (KLA) in 1996. Under the presidency of Slobodan Milosević, Yugoslavia—by now merely consisting of Serbia and Montenegro—launched a military campaign against Kosovo in 1998, which forced over one million Kosovo Albanians to escape across the border into Albania. It resulted in a NATO intervention and the bombing of Yugoslav cities between March and June 1999. Milosević eventually gave in and withdrew his armed forces from Kosovar territory. Subsequently over half of Kosovo Serbs were expelled. An estimated 13,000 people died, around 12,000 of them ethnic Albanians with 1,700 people still reported missing twenty years after the conflict. Kosovo's ethnic configuration is now 90 percent Kosovo Albanian and 8 percent Serb who mostly live in a handful of enclaves scattered around the country, the biggest of which in the northern part of the town of Mitrovica right on the border with Serbia. For a successful EU integration, interethnic relations, which on occasion are still combustible, need to be more harmonious, and a productive collaboration with its northern neighbor Serbia is paramount to quell any ethnic tensions. Many Serbs, however, continue to regard Kosovo as a cultural part of Serbia and the issue of recognition is controversial, to say the least.

Kosovo declared independence from Serbia in 2008. However, Belgrade never recognized Kosovo's new-found status, and neither did five EU countries—Spain, Cyprus, Greece, Slovakia, and Romania—that felt that a *lex Kosovo* could set a dangerous legal precedent for the independence movements of their own ethnic minorities in, for instance, Catalonia or Northern Cyrus. For the EU, this makes a bilateral relationship with Kosovo a diplomatically awkward undertaking. The EU has been actively engaged in the country since 2008 with the establishment of the scary-sounding EU Rule of Law Mission (EULEX), which succeeded a UN sponsored mission. EULEX focuses mainly on administrative support, which is designed to improve administrative capacity in such areas as the police, customs, or the judiciary.

In addition, a SAA entered into force in 2016, concentrating on areas, which are typical of the bilateral relationships that the EU had established with other western Balkan countries, such as justice, economic matters, anti-corruption, and agriculture.[36] In return, trade barriers to EU markets—but not visa restrictions—were lifted. Ever since the end of the war in 1999, the EU had invested around 2.3 billion euros in the country with a further 1 billion euros coming from other international donors. While the initial focus was on relief action and reconstruction, efforts are now channeled toward institution building and a much-needed sustainable economic development. Still, in its 2016 report,[37] the Commission described the fight against corruption and organized crime as being "at an early stage," while the economy continues to be in a desperate state. Matters improved only marginally for the 2019 Commission report.[38] The same description of "early stage" was still used for the judiciary, as well as the fights against corruption and organized crime. The size of the government was branded as "excessive" with a worrying rise in the number of deputy ministers. Such nepotism also pervaded public administration with political influence being cast during the appointment of senior civil servants. The parliament was also judged to operate in a "highly polarized political context."

The biggest challenges, however, continue to be the ethnic tensions with the Serbian minority and in particular the attempt to come to terms with the atrocities committed during the war. Any former Yugoslav country intending to join the EU had to collaborate with international courts over alleged war crimes. The EU was instrumental in the establishment of the ICTY in The Hague. The court dealt with war crimes committed in Croatia, Serbia, Bosnia, and Herzegovina, Montenegro, and North Macedonia, and ceased to operate in December 2017. For Kosovo, however, a new court was set up, referred to as the Kosovo Relocated Specialist Judicial Institution (KRSJI), once again located in The Hague. A gruesome case came to light in 2010, where senior members of the KLA were alleged to have been involved in the harvesting and selling of organs of Serbian prisoners of war. In December 2017, newly elected prime minister Ramush Haradinaj threatened to walk away from KRSJI proceedings arguing that any Serbian-committed atrocities were not handled by the court (as this fell under the jurisdiction of the ICTY) and thus, only Kosovar Albanians would be indicted. A further reason might be the prime minister's brother Daut Haradinaj, who as a former KLA commander might be in line to appear before the court. Given that collaboration with an international court is a prerequisite for advancing EU relations, the warnings given not only by EU leaders but also by the United States were unequivocal, reminding the country that such a move would severely jeopardize relations with Europe and with NATO. By February 2018, the government had backed down, assuring the full cooperation of the country with this new EU

Court. In a further twist, Ramush Haradinaj resigned in July 2019, arguing that he could not be a prime minister at the same time as being a war crime's suspect.[39]

Kosovo represents a special case. Its poverty levels are more extreme than those of its Balkan neighbors. Its economy sees little sign of improvement and its status as an independent, sovereign state is questioned by some EU states, but also by other countries, which means that the UN have so far refused to grant membership. The Commission is attempting to revitalize the enlargement process of the Western Balkan states—the so-called WB6 of Albania, Kosovo, North Macedonia, Montenegro, Serbia, as well as Bosnia and Herzegovina—by calling for more bilateral efforts, starting with a summit in Bulgaria in May 2018. Alas, the diplomatically sensitive nature of relations with Kosovo was exemplified by the Spanish government in January 2018, which called for the country to be excluded from the WB6 process. Kosovo's only chance for closer EU ties might rest with Serbia, which was promised a potential accession by 2025, but only on the condition that neighborly relations with Kosovo stabilize. Serbia might therefore find itself in an acrimonious conundrum where its EU ambitions are tied to that of Kosovo.

THE FORMER CANDIDATE: ICELAND

Together with the UK, the Scandinavian island in the middle of the North Atlantic has recently turned its back on European integration. Iceland is a signatory state to the EU's Schengen agreement, which provides for passport-free travel. For years, the country, together with Norway and Liechtenstein, was quite content at being a member of the EEA. This meant that it accepted any rules emanating from the regulation of the EU's Single Market without having a say in the making of those rules. In return, the country enjoyed unfettered access to 500 million EU consumers, albeit for a fee. Although it did not benefit from the EU's redistributive policies for regions, fisheries or farmers, Icelandic territorial waters, and thus a lucrative fishing industry remained under national control without any interference from Brussels. The country was also able to negotiate trade deals with other countries, as it stayed outside the EU's custom union.

All this changed with the US subprime mortgage crisis and the subsequent collapse of Lehman Brothers in 2008. Previously, Iceland's heavily deregulated banking sector accumulated almost laughable balance sheets without much collateral capital, and the global financial crisis brought the country to the verge of bankruptcy with its banking industry collapsing like a house of cards. With the currency in free fall and the economy contracting, the country submitted a desperate application to join the EU in July 2009. Both sides viewed integration as a straightforward and speedy affair, supported by the fact that the Single Market and thus large sways of the *EU acquis* were already part of Icelandic law. What was to follow, however, was a farce worthy of a slapstick movie. Before the credit crunch, *Landsbanki*, one of the country's biggest banks had offered savings accounts but also bonds to European customers, predominantly from the UK and the Netherlands. Severely affected by the subprime crisis, the bank went under in 2008. The UK and Dutch governments stepped in, to secure outstanding debts of 3.7 billion euros, and demanded that the Icelandic government ought to foot the bill. Alas, two referendums in Iceland in 2010 and 2011 rejected legislation intended to comply with an EU-imposed financial settlement. Eventually, less harsh terms were negotiated between Iceland, the Netherlands, and the UK, and the country fulfilled its debt obligations with the last tranche reaching British and Dutch accounts in January 2016. In the meantime, however, and boosted by export revenues and a tourist boom, the Icelandic economy made an impressive recovery, just as the EU struggled for growth caused by the sovereign debt crises in the Eurozone. The acrimonious nature of negotiations over debt repayment and a subsequent anti-EU public discourse prompted a government rethink and Iceland suspended its application in May 2013, with twenty-seven chapters opened and eleven closed. The application was formerly withdrawn in March 2015. With the economy booming and the financial sector now firmly regulated, the country sees no reason to depart from the EEA deal, which had served it so well until 2008. It would require another massive crisis for this attitude to change and thus further EU integration is currently not regarded by Iceland as a necessity.

THE DILEMMA

When analyzing democratic, economic, and governance standards among potential EU states, it becomes quite apparent that the EU is negotiating with a vastly different set of candidate and accession countries. The geopolitical status of Ukraine is far from being settled. Kosovo has not been unilaterally recognized by the EU. Bosnia and Herzegovina's constitution does not offer a coherent working basis for the country to advance. Turkey's economy continues to expand at impressive speed; a progress that the WB6 countries have little hope of achieving any time soon. Serbia and Montenegro are going through the motions of the thirty-five-chapter negotiation process and are tentatively judged by the EU to be in line for accession by 2025. Yet, as of 2019, Albania and North Macedonia still have to start this process. Discussions with Turkey are suspended, and candidate status has not even been granted to Bosnia and Herzegovina, Ukraine, or Kosovo. Such different development stages mean that another "Big Bang" enlargement along the lines of the EU's extension into central and eastern Europe in 2004 is highly unlikely. Instead, a tailor-made approach, which alludes to country-specific developments, might be more helpful.

In all countries of the WB6, progress has been undermined by a political culture, which is markedly different from those in western European states and falls short of the standards expected from Brussels. Political interference in the judiciary, corruption, nepotism, and a general sense that the powers emanating from state authority are there for the taking for one's personal benefits continue to cast a depressing shadow. But it is the EU's duty to act as the promoter of democracy; a process that it delivered successfully to former fascist states, including Portugal, Spain, Greece, Italy, and West Germany, as well as to the former communist states in central and eastern Europe. Not only is it the EU's moral duty, but in return, much legitimacy will be bestowed on the European project. Alas, who else but the EU could fulfill this role?

The thirty-five-chapter process has proven to be a highly suitable vehicle. If completed successfully, it represents an in-depth transformation toward a stable and functioning market democracy with the chapters acting as manuals on how to achieve this target. It is also noteworthy that from the start negotiations with the WB6 emphasized the two key chapters—chapters 23 (judiciary and fundamental rights) and 24 (justice, freedom, and security)—which serve as the crucial passage for the establishment of more democratic societies that respect the rule of law and human rights. For this, the EU deserves credit as no other organization, or indeed no process other than enlargement could achieve such an outcome.

But there are several categories of countries within the WB6. Notwithstanding further reform, Montenegro and Serbia are currently top of the pile and are well ahead of their neighbors. In most likely circumstances, these countries will represent member state number twenty-eight and twenty-nine in a post-Brexit EU. But it is too early to set a target for the other four countries. In Albania and North Macedonia, all the key areas of reform—democracy, economy, governance—show significant shortcomings. This is also the case in Kosovo and in Bosnia and Herzegovina. However, their progress is further complicated by constitutional and diplomatic issues that require considerable efforts to be settled before any chapter negotiations can even begin. The often-disappointing lack of progress in those countries does not undermine the logic of the enlargement process. But it does cast serious doubts on the intensity of the EU effort. In recent years, the Eurozone meltdown in the aftermath of Lehman, the migration crisis, and Brexit have consumed much time and energy in Brussels and in the capitals of the member states. Yet, an integration of the WB6 cannot be successful if the onus on meeting reform targets is placed on the candidates alone. More effort, money and proactive political dialogue is required, and established member states such as Spain, Italy, and Germany would be well advised to look at their recent history to remind themselves of the powerfully stabilizing effect, which European integration can have on a young democracy: a boost and a legitimacy anchor that the WB6 countries have every moral right to benefit from as well.

The relationship with Turkey is of a different nature altogether. Currently, the country's accession is not supported by all member states or indeed their electorates. Turkey's integration would naturally necessitate that outstanding chapters would be completed, but also that the EU would embark on widespread institutional and policy reforms. There is a considerable uncertainty over both processes. Hence, an entirely different relationship seems highly feasible. Stronger economic ties (such as a further integration into the EU's Single Market) would be very beneficial to both sides. Collaborations in the fields of security, antiterrorism, migration, environmental protection, as well as climate change are also desirable. But unless EU attitudes toward Turkey change, and unless the EU revises its redistributive policies (agriculture, cohesion, and fisheries), and reorganizes its institutions, a comprehensive integration remains a pipe dream. Just as with Brexit, Turkey offers a scenario where the EU's one-size-fits-all approach to European integration cannot provide coherent answers. The UK might be open to European integration but not as exercised by the EU. Turkey too wants European integration but this time several EU members do not want to extend the EU's understanding of European integration to that country. Consequently, both the UK and Turkey give ample nourishment to the idea of variable geometry: A European project, which functions along different levels of integration in line with the political culture and aspirations of a country (in this case the UK) or in line with prevailing attitudes of member states (as is the case with Turkish accession). But such a new geometry requires fundamental treaty changes, which necessitate far-reaching discussions on the future of European integration. What are the objectives of the EU in twenty-first-century Europe, and how can it best achieve these targets? At the moment, Turkey is far from ready to join the bloc. But neither is the EU equipped to master a successful integration of its biggest enlargement conundrum.

NOTES

1. In 1987, Morocco applied to join the EU, but was told that the Union does not extend to African countries. This geographic prerogative was later formalized at a summit meeting in Denmark in 1993 under the so-called Copenhagen criteria.

2. Every country that joins the EU is automatically obliged to adopt the single currency, although the EU used to grant new members a transition of around five

years to align their economic and monetary policies with those of the Eurozone. As such, countries such as the Czech Republic, Hungary, or Poland, which joined the EU in 2004, ought to have issued the euro in or around 2009. Alas, considering the financial downturn in the aftermath of the US subprime mortgage crisis of 2008, the Commission decided to cast aside any road maps and to leave the timing and completion of the process to the respective member states.

3. See: http://www.aalep.eu/just-how-big-acquis-communautaire.

4. See: Heather Grabbe. 2014. “Six Lessons on Enlargement Ten Years on: The EU’s Transformative Power in Retrospect and Prospect.” *Journal of Common Market Studies*. Volume 52, pp. 40–56.

5. See: Gergana Noutcheva. 2012. *European Foreign Policy and the Challenges of Balkan Accession: Conditionality, Legitimacy and Compliance* (London: Routledge).

6. In 2018, Ireland’s GDP per capita was 187 percent of the EU average, making it the second-richest EU country after Luxembourg (253 percent). The figures for the other member states mentioned in this section were Malta: 98 percent, Czech Republic: 90 percent, Slovenia and Cyprus: 90 percent, Greece: 68 percent, Romania: 64 percent, Bulgaria: 50 percent. See: Eurostat June 2019.

7. IPA focuses of five key areas: transition assistance and institution building, cross-border cooperation with non-EU neighbors, regional development, human resource development, as well as rural development.

8. See: https://ec.europa.eu/neighbourhood-enlargement/sites/near/files/pdf/key_documents/2016/20161109_report_albania.pdf.

9. https://freedomhouse.org/report/nations-transit/2017/albania.

10. See: europeanwesternbalkans.com/2019/05/29/key-findings-2019-european-commission-report-albania/.

11. See: https://ec.europa.eu/neighbourhood-enlargement/sites/near/files/pdf/key_documents/2016/20161109_report_the_former_yugoslav_republic_of_macedonia.pdf.

12. In 2014, GDP per capita was an estimated 4,100 euros, which is a fraction of the EU average of 27,600 euros. Among EU candidates, only Albania has a lower figure with 3,500 euros.

Source: Eurostat, January 2018.

13. See: ec.europa.eu/neighbourhood-enlargement/sites/near/files/20190529-north-macedonia-report.pdf.

14. In a poll in December 2016, 39.5 percent of respondents were in favor of NATO integration, but 39.7 percent were against it. See: https://www.theguardian.com/world/2017/may/25/montenegro-tensions-russia-joins-nato-member.

15. *The Guardian* claimed that around one-third of foreign investment in Montenegro originated in Russia. See: https://www.theguardian.com/world/2017/may/25/montenegro-tensions-russia-joins-nato-member.

16. See: https://ec.europa.eu/neighbourhood-enlargement/sites/near/files/pdf/key_documents/2016/20161109_report_montenegro.pdf.

17. See: ec.europa.eu/neighbourhood-enlargement/sites/near/files/20190529-montenegro-report.pdf.

18. https://freedomhouse.org/report/nations-transit/2017/serbia.

19. In a poll in Serbia, 65 percent of respondents believed that homosexuality was an illness.

See: www.theguardian.com/world/2017/jun/15/serbia-gains-its-first-female-and-gay-prime-minister-ana-brnabic.

20. See oxfordbusinessgroup.com/overview/turkey-records-strong-economic-growth-last-decade.

21. See www.indexmundi.com/turkey/demographics_profile.html.

22. Agriculture (but not processed agricultural products), services, and public procurement are excluded from the customs union.

23. In 2016, the EU exported goods worth seventy-eight billion euros to Turkey. In return, sixty-six billion euros worth of Turkish goods entered the EU.

See: Eurostat, February 2017.

24. If this logic had been applied during the unification process of Germany, the eastern part might not have been able to integrate so smoothly into the EU. Unification was in October 1990, but the last Russian troops only left Germany in August 1994.

25. In a YouGov poll in July 2016, respondents across Europe were asked about the support for Turkish integration into the EU. The figures were staggeringly negative: people in Germany (81 percent), Finland (78 percent), Denmark (76 percent), as well as Sweden and France (66 percent) were overwhelmingly against accession.

See: https://yougov.co.uk/news/2016/08/03/turkey-less-popular-choice-join-eu-even-russia/.

26. For the financial perspective 2014–2020, 51 percent of funds are earmarked for regions that have less than 75 percent of the average EU GDP. This money is distributed through the European Regional Development Fund (which mainly supports infrastructure) and the Social Fund (which supports HR development). As part of the Cohesion Fund, which specifically targets transport and the environment, a further 21 percent is given to regions with less than 90 percent of EU average GDP.

27. See: www.ushmm.org/confront-genocide/cases/bosnia-herzegovina.

28. Translated into English, the term "Republika Srpska" simply means Serbian republic. In order to avoid confusion with the state of Serbia, the term is used in international relations to refer to the Bosnian Serb entity of Bosnia and Herzegovina.

29. The census was carried out by the Agency for Statistics of Bosnia and Herzegovina. The Republika Srpska did not acknowledge its outcome although the EU's official statistics agency Eurostat confirmed that the census followed international guidelines.

30. A total of 2.7 percent of respondents did not belong to any of the three ethnicities, while the remainder choose not to declare their ethnicity altogether.

31. See: https://ec.europa.eu/neighbourhood-enlargement/sites/near/files/pdf/key_documents/2016/20161109_report_bosnia_and_herzegovina.pdf.

32. In addition to Ukraine, entities include Armenia, Azerbaijan, Belarus, Egypt, Georgia, Israel, Jordan, Lebanon, Moldova, Morocco, Palestine, and Tunisia. Because of the questionable state of democracy, agreements with Belarus, Libya, and Syria are currently suspended in those countries.

33. The issues covered in the agreement are human rights, rule of law, political dialogue and reforms, movement of persons, as well as cooperation in energy, the environment, climate actions, transport, financial services, public finances, anti-fraud measures, agriculture and rural developments, consumer protection, and civil society.

34. See: eeas.europa.eu/delegations/ukraine/1937/ukraine-and-eu_en.

35. See: www.cia.gov/library/publications/resources/the-world-factbook/geos/kv.html.

36. The specific areas are justice, freedom, and security; innovation, information society, and social policy; agriculture, fisheries, forestry, and food safety; internal market, competition and consumer/health protection; trade, industry, customs, and taxation; transport, energy, environment, and regional development; economic and fiscal matters.

37. See: ec.europa.eu/neighbourhood-enlargement/sites/near/files/pdf/key_documents/2016/20161109_report_kosovo.pdf.

38. See: ec.europa.eu/neighbourhood-enlargement/sites/near/files/20190529-kosovo-report.pdf.

39. See: https://balkaninsight.com/2019/07/22/guerrilla-politician-suspect-the-legal-battles-of-kosovos-haradinaj/.

Conclusion

If unaddressed, the five dilemmas have the potential to challenge the very existence of European integration. First, the EU formed a vital part of the economic and political consensus of the past decades. Yet, this consensus saw the emergence of ever-rising levels of inequality, of a disjointed political party landscape where many voters felt unrepresented, and of significant cultural changes brought by migration. They provided the fertile ground for populist movements, which emerged across the continent. Second, the sovereign debt crisis in several Eurozone countries resulted in the structural reorganization of EMU, but it also brought hardship to many people caused by the draconian austerity measures imposed on debt-ridden countries. Instead of bringing prosperity, the EU was regarded by many as an agent of superimposed destitution. The crisis also exposed an antagonistic union, which was still divided on the precise course on how to "deepen" European integration. Third, the issue of migration was handled by the EU and its member state governments in a precarious fashion. Migration forms the bedrock of a prosperous economic future, while taking care of refugees fleeing from war zones represents a moral imperative that Europe, because of its recent history, should not find difficult to relate to. Furthermore, the challenge of migration will continue since conditions in Africa and the Middle East remain in place, which prompts people to leave their homes and head for European shores. Yet, a coherent discourse on how to integrate migrants (whether at national or EU level, or whether in practical or cultural terms) had been found wanting. Fourth, Brexit represented the ultimate existentialist challenge to the European project because a member decided that a country's interests were better served outside the bloc. Although the EU represented a remarkably unified front, it also became clear that the current model of European integration does not suit every member state. Yet, there is also compelling evidence that the EU and the UK ought to establish a future relationship, which maintains very close economic and financial ties, which might mitigate the effects of a lose-lose scenario. Fifth, throughout the history of postwar integration, enlarging the EU brought undeniable benefits to new member states and their developing democracies and economies, Increasing the number of members became one of the most powerful legitimacy anchors for the European project. But the next rounds, which include Turkey and the countries of the Western Balkans, represent endeavors that will bring an altogether different set of challenges. Without significant changes to the EU's modus operandi, the union might encounter an institutional deadlock and a policy breakdown. The different political cultures of those new countries might also threaten the coherence and efficacy of European politics.

Beyond the five dilemmas, the EU has its work cut out. The much-maligned Common Agriculture Policy continues to account for the biggest slice of the EU's budget with a vast financial discrepancy between small family farms and large agribusinesses, and an environmental and biodiversity record that needs significant improvement. The Single Market continues to offer morally dubious loopholes for tax avoidance. The bloc represents one of the most powerful actors in the global economy, yet it continues to be a political dwarf in foreign policy and security matters. Reforms to close the democratic deficit between appointed institutions (such as the Commission) and elected ones (such as the European Parliament) have been decisive yet remain incomplete. Making the union more transparent and thus improving the political discourse between European authorities, national governments and EU citizens is still an ongoing process. Yet, any reforms in these areas, though vital, might not address the true challenge to European integration, as these would focus on alterations to the existing model, and the prevalent mechanisms that organize the interaction between member states and EU institutions. What the five dilemmas demand, however, could be a new form of European integration.

But there are competing visions over the direction of European integration.[1] On one side is the German-dominated approach supported by the Netherlands and Finland, which anchors the EU on a strong Single Market and fiscal discipline as evidenced by the handling of the Greek and Cypriot debt crises. Although further political integration is not necessarily discounted, this is essentially an economics-based, neoliberal understanding of European integration. In contrast, French president Emmanuel Macron argues for a Europe that protects (*l'Europe qui protège*) and calls for deeper integration in the wake of terrorist threats and migration pressures. In practice, this means a deeper policy integration accompanied by budget increases and more fiscal redistribution. This is a center-left understanding of the future of the EU. But then we also have the populist governments in Poland and Hungary, as well as politicians such as Marine le Pen, Nigel Farage, and Matteo Salvini who propagate an ethno-centrist Europe based on nation states, which protects "Christian" values and emphasizes cultural and ethnic homogeneity. The first two options are well-trodden visions of how Europe ought to be organized. But the populist third version runs directly opposite to the former two, by despising their central tenant: cross-border collaboration and in particular the free movement of people. This fundamental schism has the potential to break the union apart. One might want to look at Italy as a case in point: a dysfunctional national microcosm, where all three visions have garnered strong support among sections of Italian society, but which also paralyze one another resulting in an almost permanent political deadlock.

Europe therefore could face the implosion of a bloc, which is lurching from crisis to crisis without ever coming up with cogent solutions. But addressing crises is one of the key purposes of the EU. If a crisis cannot be addressed through national action or bilateral cooperation, it is the union that often provides an indispensable and coherent framework. Yet, any notion of a supranational United States of Europe seems fanciful at the moment, as it is the nation-state that represents the focus of people's loyalties. "Europe" in this respect often merely constitutes a bureaucratic apparatus of norms and procedures. In the absence of a European "demos," it is governments, parties, and politicians at national level that are the key reference points. While this reality might have been less accentuated at the end of the twentieth century, such a vital structural element of European integration has always been present. The "Ever Closer Union" as manifested by the Maastricht Treaty did not mean that the nation-state was about to disintegrate. It simply allowed for nation states to engage in closer cooperation. Granted, populism, economic hardship, and migration issues resulted in the revitalization of a national agenda, which is often opposed to European integration. But it is also fair to regard multilateral collaboration as practiced by the EU as a highly attractive vehicle because it offers a regular and institutionalized form of political interaction between states. It is certainly not an idealistic notion of a united European family, but in fact a highly practical method for transnational interaction. The recent crises might have challenged this assumption, but it is certainly preferable to a national-based approach, which seeks to find solutions to an ever more complex world in a unilateral fashion.

VARIABLE GEOMETRY

Propelled into action by a decade of crises, the member states issued the so-called Rome Declaration in March 2017, at the sixtieth anniversary celebration of the signing of the Treaty of Rome. It states that "we will act together at different paces and intensity where necessary, while moving in the same direction, as we have done in the past, in line with the treaties and keeping the door open to those who want to join later." In the same month, Commission president Jean Claude Juncker added further weight to the debate by offering five scenarios around which the future of European integration could be organized.[2] The options included the following: first, an exclusive focus of EU's activities on the Single Market; second, a flexible option, which allowed those countries "who want more, to do more"; third, an alternative that advocated "doing less, more efficiently"; fourth, the ambition to "do more together"; and fifth, the continuation along existing parameters. Option two in particular harked back to a version of European integration, which has also been referred to as variable geometry, or a multispeed Europe.

Discussions on a more flexible approach to European integration are not new and first came to public attention more than twenty years ago, when Wolfgang Schäuble (then interior minister of Germany) and the disgraced former IMF director Dominique Strauss-Kahn (then economics minister of France) placed their considerable political weight behind it. With Brexit, the EU had learned the painful lesson that it had failed to accommodate different national objectives of what European integration ought to deliver (and the policy areas it ought to refrain from). Hence, a variable geometry might be the solution, where every member state would commit to a set of core EU policies, including the Single Market, external trade, the environment, as well as foreign policy. Those seeking more integration could then sign up to the Schengen zone of passport free travel, the single currency, defense, or policing.[3] But this approach has drawn criticism from ardent EU federalists who fear a weakening of the bloc's institutional set up. Eurosceptics too were less than enthusiastic, arguing that variable geometry might lead to a highly integrated Eurozone, which in turn would side-line outsiders and treat them as second-class members.

But ever since the EU granted the Euro opt-out to Denmark, Sweden, and the UK, European integration was always forced to adopt a flexible approach (see table II.1). The three recent treaties of Maastricht (1992), Amsterdam (1997), and Lisbon (2007) would not have been ratified without granting opt-outs to some members that could not sign up to the full package of the treaties' proposals. In addition to the Euro opt-outs at Maastricht, there was an opt-out for the UK on the social charter.[4] Amsterdam established the Schengen zone, which, however, does not include Ireland, the UK, Croatia, Bulgaria, Cyprus, and Romania, although it integrates the non-EU states of Switzerland, Liechtenstein, Iceland, and Norway. Amsterdam also introduced the "Area of Freedom, Security and Justice" (formerly referred to as Justice and Home Affairs). The UK once more, but also Ireland and Denmark have opt-outs. Lisbon's proudest achievement was the Charter of Fundamental Rights. However, it does not apply in Poland and in the UK. Lisbon also

Table II.1 Variable Geometry in the EU

Opt-outs	Economic and Monetary Union (EMU)	UK, Denmark, Sweden
	Area of Freedom, Security, and Justice	UK, Ireland, Denmark
	Schengen	UK, Ireland*
	Charter of Fundamental Rights	UK, Poland
Enhanced Cooperation	Patent Law Divorce Law Property rights for international couples	At least nine member states must participate
Inter se Agreements	Euro Plus Pact	Not signed by the UK and the Czech Republic
Permanent Structured Cooperation	New military and security structures	Never applied so far
Constructive Abstention	Common Foreign and Security Policy	At least one-third of members with at least one-third of EU citizens
European Economic Area (EEA)	Acceptance of the Single Market by non-EU states	Norway, Iceland, Liechtenstein

*The Schengen area includes the non-EU countries, that is, Switzerland, Norway, Iceland, and Liechtenstein. Bulgaria, Croatia, Cyprus, and Romania have not been permitted to join so far.

focused on police cooperation, which was now agreed upon through qualified majority voting, yet the UK reserved the right to pull out from any future developments, thereby maintaining a national veto.

In addition to opt-outs, the EU has what it refers to as "enhanced cooperation." This method was introduced in the Amsterdam Treaty and allows a minimum of nine countries to pursue more cooperation as long as these actions adhere to the existing EU structures (i.e., the involvement of the European Commission as well as the continued jurisdiction of the European Court of Justice). The collaboration also must not harm the Single Market and has to remain open for other members to join at a later stage. So far, we have seen three areas where enhanced cooperation was applied: The European Patent Law of 2012 (with sixteen signatory members), the Divorce Law of 2013 (with twenty-five member states), and Property Rights for International Couples in 2019 (eighteen member states).[5] There is also PESCO (permanent structured cooperation), which allows for new military and security structures among a group of member states. However, PESCO so far has never been used. Adding to the mix of flexible options are "inter se agreements," which refer to a group of member states signing a bilateral agreement outside the existing EU structures. This method was used during the ratification of the Euro Plus Pact, which imposed further checks on the financial industry, but to which the Czech Republic and the UK did not sign up to. The EU's Common Foreign and Security Policy (CFSP) allows for a so-called constructive abstention, whereas a third of member states (who must represent at least a third of the EU population) can refrain from participating in foreign policy measures that had been agreed upon unanimously by the other members. Beyond the EU, we also have the EEA, which grants the non-EU states of Iceland, Norway, and Liechtenstein participation in the Single Market. Switzerland too has its own deal with the EU, which is similar to the EEA. Faced with these multitude of options, the question arises how much more flexible can European integration be?

Amid these multitude of options, a school of thought emerged that called for the dismantling of the entire EU structure.[6] The key tenet of this line of argumentation is the current impasse over the future of European integration. Ever since the start of the European project, a succession of treaties built a European structure that was enhanced and expanded upon, whenever political, economic, or social pressures called for solutions that could otherwise not be found at the national level. At the moment, Emmanuel Macron intends to continue with this strategy, calling for an ambitious new treaty, but to which some countries including Hungary and Poland would never agree to. The EU therefore finds itself trapped between ambition and reticence. To get out of this deadlock, the EU needs to disintegrate before a process of reintegration can start. Taking inspiration from Schäuble and Strauss-Kahn, European integration would then focus on the Single Market (although without the free movement of people) and a customs union to which all European countries must adhere to. Those countries seeking further integration could subsequently sign up to the free movement of people, membership of the Eurozone, Schengen, foreign, and security policies, as well as police and judicial cooperation. As a convenient side effect, such an approach would allow for the seamless reintegration of the UK. In this scenario, the country would have left the EU (since it no longer exists) and could rejoin European integration in line with its prerogatives.

But which countries would sign up to a flexible Europe? According to a report by the European Council on Foreign Relations, which interviewed government officials, as well as experts from think tanks and universities, three different camps might emerge.[7] At the moment, Hungary and Poland would represent the "rebel" faction, which regards a flexible Europe as a chance to increase national sovereignty. Their participation in European programs might therefore be greatly compromised. A total of eight countries—France, Germany, Italy, Spain, Finland, Sweden, the Netherlands, and Belgium—would welcome variable geometry. But this leaves seventeen so-called "swing" countries, which are concerned about a potential hollowing out of EU institutions and the increasing power of bigger states that such a reorganization might provide. From the start, variable geometry might therefore never get off the ground. There are also practical concerns over finance, and in particular the

EU's redistributive policies of agriculture and cohesion on which poorer countries depend on. Hence, instead of ironing out the messy landscape of different vehicles to participate in European integration, variable geometry might make the situation even worse. The challenge of offering a more coherent form of European integration to the Western Balkans and to Turkey would also be completely unaddressed. Where would these countries fit in?

A COMPROMISE? THE CONTINENTAL PARTNERSHIP

Let us return to Brexit once more, which in whatever shape will most certainly be highly challenging for the UK. But it will also constitute a major setback to the EU, to its economic vitality and its standing in the world. Maybe both sides ought to agree on a set of concessions, and should reach a compromise, which would safeguard a close economic and financial collaboration, which for over four decades had resulted in concrete benefits for all sides concerned. European leaders ought to remind themselves that the EU is not Europe, and Europe is not the EU. Instead, the EU is an organizational vehicle that unifies European countries economically and politically. But viewed from this perspective, it is not and never has been the sole vehicle. After World War II, communism under the leadership of the Soviet Union inadvertently organized central and eastern Europe. Some countries chose neutrality (Sweden, Finland, and Austria), while others were ostracized because of their fascist regimes (Portugal, Spain, and more recently Belarus). At one stage, EFTA, which was founded in 1960 by Norway, Sweden, Denmark, Austria, Switzerland, the UK, and Portugal, had more members than the EU.[8] It is true, that European integration in the form of the EU is now by far the most popular model on the continent, but that does not mean it was or will remain the only one.

How could a continental partnership work? In essence, access to the EU's big prize, the Single Market, would be granted, although the free movement of people could be compromised in order to meet one of the UK's red lines, but also to calm fears over mass migration from south-eastern to western Europe (see table II.2). Such a free movement could still be implemented, however, not for all citizens, but merely for EU citizens with secure job offers. This already could bring immigration numbers down, thus safeguarding one of the key concerns that underlined Brexit. In return for this concession, the UK, however, would need to make contributions to the EU budget without having access to the EU's "money policies" of agriculture, fisheries, and cohesion. The UK could also continue to be involved in the making of Single Market rules through a new bilateral organization. The same applies to Single Market jurisdiction, which could be handled by a new institution

Table II.2 Brexit Options

	Norway	*Turkey*	*Continental Partnership*	*Canada*	*World Trade Organization*
Single Market Access	Yes	No	Yes	No	No
Labor Mobility	Yes	No	Limited to job offers	No	No
Single Market rulemaking	No	No	Partial	No	No
Bound by ECJ decisions on Single Market	Yes	No	Jointly with UK courts	No	No
Duty Free Access for Goods	Yes	Yes	Yes	Yes	No
Duty Free Access for Services	Yes	Yes	Yes	Partial	No
Part of EU External Trade Policy	No	Yes	Potentially	No	No
Part of EU "money" policies	No	No	No	No	No
EU Budget contributions	Yes	No	Yes	No	No

integrating ECJ and UK judges. Judicial cooperation, which extends to catching criminals but is also prevalent in civil matters such as divorce or alimony payments, could also be handled in a new bilateral fashion. The same could also apply to other EU targets, such as security and defense. The "Continental Partnership" model would result in the establishment of new governmental and bureaucratic layers and as a consequence would increase the cost of politics. But it would also undoubtedly be a boost to democracy since different national political cultures might no longer be compromised by the prevailing notion of an "Ever Closer Union" as outlined in the Maastricht Treaty of 1992. It would also offer lagging EU candidates the chance to benefit from European integration much sooner and in a manner that the standard EU enlargement process currently does not allow.

OUTLOOK

Can variable geometry solve the five dilemmas? The "Continental Partnership" has significant potential in safeguarding a close economic relationship between the UK and the EU, underlining the referendums' demands for greater national sovereignty and less migration. The model could also function as a highly useful blueprint for candidate countries as an alternative vehicle for European integration, which the current enlargement process of the EU struggles to offer.

The picture becomes more complicated, however, when looking at populism. After all, Brussels is regarded by populist politicians and their supporters as one of the key agents of the political and financial establishment that brought about such widespread dissatisfaction. Out of the three causes of populism—turbocharged capitalism and an unfair distribution of wealth, a distant and unrepresentative political process, as well as a perceived threat to cultural coherence caused my migration—the responsibility for the first two lies firmly in the hands of national governments. Implementing a fairer tax system, raising welfare standards, and improving job security fall predominantly under the domain of national and not EU politics. Granted, the democratic deficit in the EU needs to be tackled further, but the state of democracy at national level—as evidenced by Brexit or France's *gilet jaunes*—has much to account for. But it is the third underlying current of populism, the fear of an erosion of cultural norms, where the EU could make a substantial contribution aimed at taking the wind out of the sails of populist movements and tackling directly one of the key fears of voters. The free movement of people is one of the tenets of European integration. But instead of being an asset, it has emerged as the weakest link of EU integration with continued migration threatening to undermine the foundations of the European project. Instead of seeing it as a right and as an asset that enriches one's life, citizens have increasingly turned against what in the immediate postwar era was a phenomenal achievement. It is no longer about maximizing the interaction between formerly antagonistic peoples. As vital as this development was, it is regarded by many as a threat to employment opportunities, to cultural integrity, and to the coherence of the welfare state, to public services like schools, hospitals, or housing. Without question, the default position of any EU member state should still be free and open borders. But member states ought to discuss whether on tightly specified occasions, a country could be given the right to apply temporary emergency brakes to the free movement of people, in case immigration is starting to impose a heavy burden on communities. Otherwise, the EU will continue to offer a marvelous gift to populist, nationalist, and right-wing movements. Restricting the free movement of people, however, is not necessarily a question of variable geometry: it is about amending the rules of the Single Market—the sacrosanct totem of European integration, which would be a very difficult concession for many EU federalists. But the populist phenomenon might just require such drastic action.

Establishing the Eurozone constitutes arguably the biggest manifestation of variable geometry with opt-outs given to the UK, Denmark, and Sweden, and with Poland, Hungary, and the Czech Republic showing no intentions of joining EMU any time soon. But for Greece, Cyprus, Italy, Ireland, Spain, and Portugal, participation in the single currency resulted in a painful and often involuntary restructuring of their economy along imposed austerity lines. It represented a significant loss of national sovereignty. This was variable geometry out of financial and economic necessity, not out of design. EU leaders continue to keep their fingers crossed, that the governments of crisis-affected countries persist with these structural reforms without being blown off course by potentially disillusioned electorates. The Eurozone crisis has European integration hanging by a precarious thread, and no treaty restructuring, and no variable geometry of any sorts can alleviate the situation.

Addressing the refugee crisis also offers much scope for EU activity. The summer of 2015, when thousands fled from the atrocities of the Syrian civil war, was characterized by a unilateral response from Germany, which opened its doors to refugees without much consultation with its European partners. What followed was an embarrassing scramble at EU level, and to this day, we still do not have a coherent EU asylum policy worthy of this title. Given the reticence, prevailing in many central and eastern European variable geometry might offer a cogent way out of this impasse. The treaty structure of the EU already allows for "enhanced cooperation" as long as nine member states agree to pursue a certain policy path. From a legal perspective, support from other EU partners is not required. The severity of the refugee crisis, the extent of human suffering, coupled with the fact that this challenge will not disappear any time soon, ought to prompt a structural rethink. Countries including Germany, the Netherlands, France, Belgium, Luxembourg, Finland, and Sweden, as well as the disproportionally affected Italy and Greece, could very well establish new, shared asylum policy. It would place a virtuous onus on some central and eastern European countries, yet failure to address this precarious situation means falling short of a moral imperative: helping people in distress.

It seems futile to speculate on the precise direction that European integration might take in the decades to come. There are simply too many variables involved that are difficult to assess in an accurate fashion. Timothy Garton Ash made a succinct point. "The question is not whether to have more or less Europe. It is: More of what and less of what?"[9] A more flexible Europe has the potential to address some of the dilemmas, namely Brexit, migration, and enlargement. But variable geometry might also result in a convoluted menu of membership options, which from a practical point of view might be very difficult to operate. And agreeing to it will either require a treaty to which all EU countries have to give their consent, or it necessitates a total dismantling of the union—once again with the consent of all members—before a new structure can be created. More variable geometry is possible, yet ambitious to get off the ground and potentially cumbersome to operate. Given these constraints many hurdles need to be cleared before a new European treaty landscape might see the light of day. But as the five dilemmas have shown, continuing to operate in the same vein is also not an option. One thing remains certain: Europe without European integration is inconceivable. The world in the twenty-first century is an interconnected, inter-dependent place, and any multilateral collaboration makes countries and citizens safer and more prosperous. However, whether it is the EU in its present shape and form that continues to be the vehicle for European integration remains an open question.

NOTES

1. See: www.theguardian.com/commentisfree/2018/jul/01/three-competing-visions-of-europe-threatening-to-tear-union-apart.
2. See: https://ec.europa.eu/commission/sites/beta-political/files/white_paper_on_the_future_of_europe_en.pdf.
3. See: Charles Grant. "Fast forward to two-speed Europe: Macron's calls for a more flexible bloc will make it more attractive to new members." https://www.politico.eu/article/fast-forward-to-two-speed-europe/.
4. The UK belatedly signed up to the Social Charter in 1997.
5. As of December 2019, the Financial Transaction Law has been agreed in principle, yet its implementation is still pending.
6. See, for example, Wolfgang Muenchau: https://www.ft.com/content/f01f1266-058e-11e7-ace0-1ce02ef0def9.
7. See: Almut Möeller and Dina Paradijs. *How the EU can bend without breaking. European Council on Foreign Relations.* https://www.ecs://fr.eu/specials/scorecard/the_future_shape_of_europe.
8. In contrast to the EU, EFTA only practiced the free movement of goods, but not of services, capital, and labor. Its political integration was also limited, as it had no supranational institutions such as a parliament.
9. See: www.theguardian.com/commentisfree/2014/may/26/europe-unhappy-european-union.

Postscript
COVID-19

The manuscript of this book was first completed in early January 2020, when the general election in the UK in December 2019 and the country's subsequent EU departure finally provided an endpoint, which allowed me to finish the chapter on Brexit. Soon after, the coronavirus pandemic arrived on European shores. By August, 3.3 million infections had been reported in European countries, including Russia and other non-EU states. The official death toll was over 200,000 with the UK (41,000), Italy (35,000), France (30,000), and Spain (29,000) as the most-affected countries.[1] In May 2020, the European Commission published a forecast, which estimated the EU's economy to shrink by 7.4 percent by the end of the year.[2] It is, however, much too soon to judge the full human, economic, and financial impact of COVID-19. Undoubtedly, the pandemic will put European solidarity to the test and might serve as a powerful accelerator to some of the five dilemmas.

With regard to Brexit, social distancing rules have prevented face-to-face interactions between the two sides' negotiation teams. Discussions are deadlocked at the moment: the EU wants the UK to follow the bloc's rules on state aid, labor laws, and the environment in order to establish a "level playing field." And the UK in return regards any such measures as an infringement on its national sovereignty, which after all was one of the driving forces that triggered Brexit.

As to enlargement, the Croatian EU Presidency during the first half of 2020 intended to boost the membership prospects of its nearby neighbors in the Balkans. While the candidacies of North Macedonia and Albania were reviewed in the spring of this year, it seems fair to assume that a swift accession will be undermined by the member states' focus on managing Brexit and handling the pandemic.

In a similar vein, the establishment of a more proactive migration policy—whether applicable across the EU or only by a group of at least nine members through enhanced cooperation in the field of justice and home affairs—might be the last thing on the minds of many governments. Migrants from outside the EU and refugees will find even more hostile ground, with politicians eager to seal off borders, citing threats to public health. The harshened rhetoric was exemplified by a vicious spat between Turkey and Greece. In February 2020, Turkish authorities ferried hundreds of mainly Syrian refugees to the Greek border in a move, which threatened to overwhelm border and security forces. This was an aggressive attempt by President Erdogan to shore up EU support for his intervention in northern Syria, but also to force a rethink over the financial contribution given by the EU to Turkey to house refugees. After two weeks, Erdogan backed down, but the tensions that rose to the surface at the Greek-Turkish border might be a further manifestation of the reality that migrants and refugees will be barred access at any cost.

But in two areas—populism and the governance of the Eurozone—we witnessed even more dramatic developments within a noticeably short space of time. Coming to terms with COVID-19 and analyzing the causes of the pandemic gave the populist rhetoric of de-globalization, de-growth, protectionism, and a national (or at least European) autonomy of supply chains a significant boost. The virus also represented an opportunity for increased antidemocratic behavior masked as essential public health measures. In March 2020, Victor Orbán extended his authoritarian grip on power when his ruling Fidesz party declared an open-ended state of emergency, giving the Hungarian prime minister the power to rule by decree.[3] A further bill was introduced at the same time, which imposed jail terms of up to five years for anyone spreading "mis-information" that might hinder a government response to the pandemic; a measure, which could be used in a blatant manner to silence the country's opposition or human rights activists. After much international outrage, Orbán announced in May 2020 that rule by decree and the law governing the state of emergency would be revoked. But this was mere window dressing, since the Hungarian parliament was quick to pass another bill, allowing the government to suspend any laws or measures that it deemed to be counterproductive in the fight against a public health crisis. Once again, a time limit was not imposed on this law, while also granting the government the power to impose a so-called state of medical emergency on the advice of a chief medical officer; a post that is under government control. This new law gave Orbán the power to restrict human rights (such as the right to assemble, free speech, and free movement) for six months with a chance to extend the emergency indefinitely. The bill was the latest chapter in the tragic demise of Hungarian democracy, where judicial and parliamentary scrutiny of government action has become ever more undermined. EU institutions and member state governments voiced their outraged concerns, yet concrete action against Orbán, for instance, the expulsion of Fidesz from the European People's Party grouping in the European Parliament, was not forthcoming.

Public health pandemics do not fall under the domain of EU politics. It is instead the member states, each with their own health systems, medical supply chains, their own fiscal policies, and above all the national supervision of borders that are implementing any responses. With member states eager to preserve their national sovereignty, the European Commission under the new leadership of Ursula von der Leyen struggled to establish any coordinated, trans-European measures. There was some much-needed bilateral collaboration when, for instance, Germany took care of some hospital patients from France and Italy. The EU also launched four tender calls for medical equipment and supplies valued at a total of 1.5 billion euros. But by and large concerned citizens expected their national leaders to rise to the organizational, financial, and medical challenges of the pandemic. This, however, was not the case for the handling of ballooning public debt. Here, yet another reorganization of Eurozone governance was quickly under discussion.

The ECB was swiftly off the mark. Already in March 2020, the bank's new president Christine Lagarde announced a massive bond buying scheme, referred to as the Pandemic Emergency Purchase Program (PEPP), which was designed to buy up government and corporate bonds. Initially set at 750 billion euros and forecast to operate until the end of 2020, by June, the program was increased to a staggering 1.35 trillion euros, lasting at least until the summer of 2021. Lagarde therefore repeated the strategy used by her predecessor Jean-Claude Trichet, who in 2012 and at the height of the sovereign debt crises stated that he would do "whatever it takes" to save the single currency.

In a parallel development, in March 2020, Eurozone finance ministers approved the suspension of budgetary rules, which obliged member states to keep an annual deficit of below 3 percent of their GDP. In addition, the governments of France, Spain, Italy, and Portugal called for increased EU actions and financial support, which according to Spanish prime minister Pedro Sanchez necessitated a new Marshall Plan to help member states weather the worst storm since World War II. Some southern countries, most notably Italy and Spain were disproportionally affected by the pandemic. Not only were they among the countries with the highest infection and death rates in Europe, their economies also rely to a significant extent on tourist revenues; an industry which was brutally affected throughout the 2020 summer season. In an unexpected development, in April 2020, Chancellor Angela Merkel dropped her long-time resistance against the mutualization of debt, and called for the establishment of EU bonds to finance the bloc's economic recovery. Her bold announcement was met with fierce criticism from the so-called frugal four of Austria, Denmark, the Netherlands, and Sweden, who demanded that any financial assistance, in particular if handed out as grants rather than loans, ought to come with significant conditions that would pave the way to a return to sustainable public finances. The intervention of the "frugal four" was designed to avoid a repeat of the precarious public spending patterns that had triggered the sovereign debt crisis a decade earlier.

The timing for deliberations on how to assist member states in their economic and financial recovery came at an opportune moment, since the EU was in the middle of agreeing on a new budget covering the years from 2021 to 2027. In July, an agreement was reached on an increased financial ceiling of 1.0743 trillion euro for these seven years, with the conditionality that at least 25 percent of the budget ought to be earmarked for climate policies. The member states also established a so-called Next Generation EU recovery fund of 750 billion euros, 312.5 billion euros of which ought to be handed out as grants. As with the bailout programs of the Eurozone crisis, and to pay reference to the concerns of the frugal four, any financial support would be conditional: catch phrases such as sound economic finances, structural reforms to aid European recovery, digital transformation, and green agenda were mentioned by the Commission in this context. But von der Leyen also announced what could turn out to be a significant game changer in the way the EU offers financial support to member states in distress. In a potentially groundbreaking departure from previous practices, the member states agreed to the Commission's proposal that from now on, the union will have the capacity to borrow on international money markets with repayments financed either through higher member state contributions or through the establishment of new EU taxes (von der Leyen mentioned corporation tax, tariffs, and a surcharge on the use of plastics). Issuing Eurobonds, raising taxes, and borrowing on international markets are measures that would represent a spectacular departure from previous practices and allow the EU to act more independently in international financial markets. This would indeed be "more Europe" with the tender establishment of a European economic government that complements the European monetary setup of having a single currency and a ECB.

Cometh the hour, cometh the EU? For seven decades, by and large the bloc raised its game whenever solutions to grave political, economic, and financial challenges could not be obtained at the national level. The coming years will shed light on whether the coronavirus pandemic indeed reignited the European spirit. Jean Monnet's assumption that Europe is forged in crisis is a much-used quote these days. If crises sow the seeds from which political change arises, one cannot imagine a bigger opportunity. It is down to Europe's leaders to make their marks on history—as weaklings who pay mere lip service to notions of solidarity, democracy, humanity, and sustainability or as architects of a much-needed new Europe.

Andreas Staab
London, August 2020

NOTES

1. As of August 20, 2020, over 22 million infections have been reported globally with a death toll approaching 800,000. See: https://www.ecdc.europa.eu/en/geographical-distribution-2019-ncov-cases.
2. See: https://www.euractiv.com/section/economy-jobs/news/eu-recovery-funds-with-strings-attached/.
3. See: Charles Grant: "*How Coronavirus Is Reshaping Europe in Dangerous Ways*." *The Guardian*, May 14, 2020. https://www.theguardian.com/world/2020/may/14/how-coronavirus-is-reshaping-europe-in-dangerous-ways.

Bibliography

Badinger, Harald, and Volker Nitsch. 2015. *Routledge Handbook of the Economics of the European Union*. London: Routledge.

Batsaikhan, Uurriintuva, Zsolt Darvas, and Inès Goncalves Raposo. 2015. *People on the Move: Migration and Mobility in the European Union.* Brussels: Bruegel.

Breulli, John (ed). 2013. *The Oxford Handbook of the History of Nationalism.* Oxford: Oxford University Press.

Buonanno, Laurie, and Neill Nugent. 2013. *Policies and Policy Processes of the EU.* London: Palgrave.

Chalmers, Damian, Gareth Davies, and Giorgio Monti. 2014. *European Union Law.* Cambridge: Cambridge University Press.

Chang, Michele. 2016. *Economic and Monetary Union*. London: Palgrave.

Clarke, Harold D., Paul Whiteley, and Matthew Goodwin. 2017. *Brexit: Why Britain Voted to Leave the European Union.* Cambridge: Cambridge University Press.

De Grauwe, Paul. 2012. *Economics of Monetary Union*. Oxford: Oxford University Press.

Dinan, Desmond. 2010. *Ever Closer Union: An Introduction to European Integration.* London: Palgrave.

Eatwell, Roger, and Matthew Goodwin. 2018. *National Populism. The Revolt Against Liberal Democracy*. London: Pelican Books.

Ebell, Monique. 2017. *Will New Trade Deals Soften the Blow of a Hard Brexit?* National Institute for Economic and Social Research. https://www.niesr.ac.uk/blog/will-new-trade-deals-soften-blow-hard-brexit.

El-Agraa, Ali. 2015. *The European Union Illuminated.* London: Palgrave.

Evans, Geoff, and Anand Menon. 2017. *Brexit and British Politics*. Cambridge: Polity Press.

Fukuyama, Francis. 1992. *The End of History and the Last Man*. New York: Free Press.

Gateva, Eli. 2016. *European Union Enlargement Conditionality*. London: Palgrave.

Geddes, Andrew, and Peter Scholten. 2016. *The Politics of Migration and Immigration in Europe*. London: Sage.

George, Stephen. 1998. *An Awkward Partner. Britain in the European Community*. Oxford: Oxford University Press.

Goodhart, David. 2017. *The Road to Somewhere: The Populist Revolt and the Future of Politics*. London: C. Hurst & Co.

Gözde Yildiz, Ayselin. 2016. *The European Union Immigration Policy: Managing Migration in Turkey and Morocco*. London: Palgrave.

Grabbe, Heather. 2014. 'Six Lessons on Enlargement Ten Years On: The EU's Transformative Power in Retrospect and Prospect.' *Journal of Common Market Studies*. Volume 52, pp. 40–56.

Hix, Simon. 2009. *What's Wrong with the European Union and How to Fix It*. Cambridge: Polity Press.

Hix, Simon, and Bjørn Hoyland. 2011. *The Political System of the EU*. London: Palgrave.

Hix, Simon, Sara Hageman, and Doru Frantescu. 2016. *Would Brexit Matter? The UK's Voting Record in the Council and the European Parliament*. http://60811b39eee4e42e277a-72b421883bb5b133f34e068afdd7cb11.r29.cf3.rackcdn.com/ 2016/04/VoteWatch-Report-2016_digital.pdf.

Hobsbawn, Eric. 2012. *Nations and Nationalism since 1789: Program, Myth, Reality*. Cambridge: Cambridge University Press.

Huntington, Samuel. 1997. *The Clash of Civilizations and the Remaking of World Order*. New York: Simon & Schusters.

James, Harold. 2012. *Making the European Monetary Union*. Cambridge: Harvard University Press.

Kant, Immanuel. 2003. *Perpetual Peace*. Indianapolis: Hackett.

Kenealy, Daniel, John Peterson, and Richard Gorbett (eds.). 2015. *The EU: How Does It Work?* Oxford: Oxford University Press.

Keynes, John Maynard. 2007. *The General Theory of Employment, Interest and Money*. London: Palgrave.

Mair, Peter, and Jan Zielonka (eds.). 2012. *The Enlarged European Union: Diversity and Adaptation*. London: Frank Cass.

Mehlhausen, Thomas. 2015. *European Union Enlargement: Material Interest, Community Norms and Anomie*. London: Routledge.

Moffitt, Benjamin. 2016. *The Global Rise of Populism: Performance, Political Style and Representation*. Stanford: Stanford University Press.

Müller, Jan Werner. 2016. *What Is Populism?* Philadelphia: University of Pennsylvania Press.

Noutcheva, Gergana. 2012. *European Foreign Policy and the Challenges of Balkan Accession: Conditionality, Legitimacy and Compliance*. London: Routledge.

Nugent, Neill. 2017. *The Government and Politics of the European Union*. London: Macmillan.

Pissany-Ferry, Jean, Norbert Roettgen, André Sapir, Paul Tucker, and Guntram Wolff. 2016. *Europe after Brexit; A Proposal for a Continental Partnership*.' Bruegel. http://bruegel.org/2016/08/europe-after-brexit-a-proposal-for-a-continental-partnership./.

Prpic, Martina. 2015. *Towards a New European Agenda on Security'*. http://www.europarl.europa.eu/thinktank/en/document.html?reference=EPRS_ATA(2015)545727.

Sajdik, Martin, and Michael Schwarzinger. 2017. *European Union Enlargement: Background, Developments, Facts*. London: Routledge.

Sanchis i Marco, Manuel. 2013. *The Economics of the Monetary Union and the Eurozone Crisis*. Heidelberg: Springer.

Schelkle, Waltraud. 2017. *The Political Economy of Monetary Solidarity*. Oxford: Oxford University Press.

Smith, Anthony. 1991. *National Identity*. Reno: University of Nevada.

———. 2013. *Nationalism*. London: Polity Press.

Smith, Karen. 2013. *European Union Foreign Policy in a Changing World*. London: Polity.

Staab, Andreas. 2013. *The European Union Explained*. Bloomington: Indiana University Press.

———. 1997. *Separation after Unification? The Crisis of National Identity in Eastern Germany*. Westport: Greenwood.

Stiglitz, Joseph. 2016. *The Euro and Its Threat to the Future of Europe*. London: Allen Lane.

van Wolleghem, Pierre Georges. 2018. *The EU's Policy on the Integration of Migrants*. London: Palgrave.

Wallace, Helen (ed). 2014. *Policy Making in the EU*. Oxford: Oxford University Press.

Weinar, Agnieszka, Saskia Bonjour, and Lyubov Zhyznomirska (eds.). 2018. *The Routledge Handbook of the Politics of Migration in Europe*. London: Routledge.

Whyman, Philip. 2018. *Rethinking Economic and Monetary Union in Europe*. London: Routledge.

Wunsch, Natasha. 2018. *EU Enlargement and Civil Society in the Western Balkans*. London: Palgrave.

Index

About the Author

Andreas Staab is the founder and director of the European Policy Information Centre (EPIC), a UK-based consultancy on the European Union. A former lecturer in European Integration at the London School of Economics, he has worked in numerous EU candidate and accession countries and continues to teach for the London program of Washington University in St. Louis. He is the author of *The European Union Explained: Institutions, Actors, Global Impact*, as well as *Separation after Unification: The Crisis of National Identity in Eastern Germany*.